THE SECRET OF
ATLANTIS

THE SECRET OF
ATLANTIS

OTTO MUCK
TRANSLATED BY FRED BRADLEY

NYT
Times
BOOKS

Library of Congress Cataloging in Publication Data

Muck, Otto Heinrich.
  The secret of Atlantis.

  Translation of Alles über Atlantis.
  Includes index.
  1. Atlantis. I. Title.
GN751.M813 1977 398'.42 77-79035
ISBN 0-8129-0713-2

Contents

(Illustrations follow page 84)

Introduction

MORE BOOKS are said to have been written about Atlantis than about any subject short of the Bible, some twenty thousand. I have not seen that many, or anything like it, though I have had the subject on my mind for almost as long as I can remember, and have had access to some rare collections, public and private, over the years. Up until now none of the works on Atlantis that have come my way has done much more than rehash or revamp what can be found in the nineteenth century classic reconstruction of the story by the congressman from Minnesota, Ignatius Donnelly. Even such a lovely example of bookmanship as Stacey B. Judd's *Atlantis, Mother of Empires* (1939), merely illustrates the tale with sensitive links to Mesoamerica. Of the more recent books on Atlantis, the most thoroughly professional is that of the Soviet engineer N.F. Zhirov, *Atlantis* (1970), with its massive catalog of scientific evidence; yet its geological data is already attacked as dated.

Geniuses or mavericks of all sorts have placed Atlantis and its empire in every corner of the globe from pole to pole, with full-length treatises adorned with abundant illustrations. Almost all have the merit of a conscientious mind at work, and the anomaly of ancient Atlantis being so scattered may someday be reconciled when it is realized that civilized man was far more widely rooted on this planet in prehistoric, or pre-cataclysmic, times than has yet to be admitted.

But one thing must be made clear in any discussion of Plato's Atlantis: the recent discoveries made by archaeologists and oceanographers in and around the Aegean island of Thera or Santorini are of a later epoch than the one specifically described by Plato, and though Thera may have been located on the fringes of an Atlantean empire, it was not and could not be the great island spoken of by Plato which he placed beyond his pillars of Hercules, our straits of Gibraltar, on the way to the great continent of America. The same applies to the ancient remains being discovered in Bahamian and Caribbean waters which are more likely relics of outer islands of an Atlantean empire, than of the capital island of Poseidonis whose discovery in the late 1960s was clairvoyantly prophesied by Edgar Cayce.

From all these works one thing is missing: a single cause which could account for the disappearance of Plato's Atlantis and for the multitude of myths and legends which so persistently survived it.

In this book that lacuna is filled with a lucid exposition of relevant facts as scientifically evaluated as is possible for modern man with his fractured disciplines, and his lack, when called upon to evaluate conflicting "scientific" data, of an Olympian viewpoint.

Here you have the greatest case of genocide that ever hit the planet, one that exterminated all your forefathers—with the exception of such as Noah, Deucalion, Ut-napishtin, and Tespi—and you are asked to be a juror at the trial.

The first denunciation, given in a thin voice by the Athenian who changed his name from Aristocles to Plato, and got his facts from his maternal uncle, who in turn got them from some priest in Egypt, was vague, but piquing.

The charges, as preferred in the text before you, are more specific: that at 8 P. M. on June 5, 8498 B. C., the accused, named Asteroid A, did wildly go off its course, break into pieces, plunge into the Atlantic's Bermuda Triangle, and engender a holocaust worse than 30,000 hydrogen bombs, dragging with it, like some Lucifer, an entire island civilization and the better part of mankind on the planet.

In favor of the accused is the argument that being one of some two thousand wildly orbiting miniplanets with such lovely names as Ceres, Amor, and Adonis, all orphans of a defunct and unknown father, the accused was driven wilder by the incestuous conjunction of Selene and Aphrodite with Helios, the grandfather of them all.

Who is the prosecutor? A German scientist responsible with his inventions for the development of two of the deadlier instruments of World War II, the schnorkel and the guided missile rocket, the late Otto Muck.

Who defends the accused? None but a prejudiced society, hypnotized for millennia by the doggerel propaganda of self-emasculate transvestites, nurtured on a mythology so fanciful as to make science fiction plausible, who claim that nothing catastrophic ever happens to the divinely orchestrated roundelay of planets.

It can be tiresome to be yanked from life to do one's duty as a juror. But once the evidence is marshaled, it must be judged. The Atlantis tale may be your own.

According to the evidence, a cataclysmic event brought about the end of the last geological era and ushered in the present. In one terrible day and night, so goes the charge, a rift was opened in the Atlantic bottom, from Puerto Rico to Iceland, into which the island of Atlantis, 400,000 square miles of mountains, fertile plains, and tropical fruitland, as Elysian as Hawaii, was dropped three thousand meters to be submerged in boiling magma.

Great tidal waves, asphyxiating gases, and a blanket of lava are said to have extinguished all life, leaving nothing but a mysterious widening of the mid-Atlantic Ridge, with nine small islands, the tips of mountains that had once risen higher than Mont Blanc, our present Azores.

It put an end to Eden.

The great blue snake of the Gulf Stream, no longer impeded by Atlantis, could lap the shores of Europe.

Female eels, to become sexually matured, could no longer wriggle from their seaweed jungle womb in the Sargasso Sea up the freshwater rivers of Atlantis. Instead they had to swim an exhausting and dangerous two thousand miles to the rivers of Western Europe, and then back to the safety of Sargasso, to mate and spawn and start again their cycle.

Of the human survivors who could tell the tale, to the West were the proto-American contemporaries of the event, Red Indians and proto-Mayans. To the east the Cro-Magnons who arrived in Europe by ship, tall, big-boned, muscular, and strikingly similar to the redskins of America.

Their myths and legends tell of post cataclysmic eons when the radiance of the sun was dimmed. In the cold *daemmerung* of the north, pale-skinned Hyperboreans grew up in mist and moss. In caves, dwarfs hammered for the sons of Poseidon, the cyclopean giants who girdled the earth with megaliths.

Is it not strange that some stepped pyramids should simultaneously appear in both Middle America and the Middle East, along with the same astronomy, the same calendars, the same feet, fathoms, cubits, stadia? That in Iberia as in Yucatan the ballgames be the same? That the language of the Basques be familiar from Peten to Japan?

Sensitive notions of these extraordinary facts were indeed developed between the sixteenth and the nineteenth centuries by original researchers such as Diego de Landa, Sigüenza y Gongora, Brasseur de Bourbourg, Augustus le Plongeon: but all were mocked by their contemporaries as our contemporaries mock Barraclough Fell for filling in three thousand years of ignored American history, showing that the Algonquin and Hopi used Egyptian hieroglyphs before the birth of Plato.

The Chilam Balam, the Popul Vuh, the Völuspa, and many another tale of the knowledge and wisdom of primeval man, do testify to a horrendous cataclysm when a great flaming snake fell from the skies to the sea, submerging the land.

These myths, whose truths shift less than the "facts" of science, could explain the shifting of the axis of the earth, the rearrangement of the poles, the destruction and recreation of glaciers, the asphyxiation and freezing of several hundred thousand mammoths, the raising of dead mastodons from the swamps of Cartagena to the hills of Bogota, as the northeast corner of South America tilted suddenly down into the Atlantic, the northwest corner rose above the Pacific, hoisting the great temple of Tiahuanaco from the hot tropical sealevel, to the chill, rarified air of the present Andes, 12,000 feet above the sea.

From this cataclysmic moment, signed by a triple conjunction of the Sun, the Moon, and Venus, the Maya are said to count their time.

That is the evidence.

The trickiest professional witnesses will be, of course, the vulcanologist, the paleomineralogist, the paleoclimatologist, and the staid geologist, who, like the modern psychiatrist, in a field where only they can interpret the "facts," can sway the jury as they please.

Already circumstantial evidence has been adduced by such eminent geologists as Dr. Cesare Emiliani of the University of Miami, whose borings in the Gulf of Mexico confirm that a great flood of water from the melting icecaps of Wisconsin came down the Mississippi Valley to flood the Atlantic seaboard and its islands, drowning civilized communities, at just the time when Plato says Atlantis foundered.

Oceanographers have discovered great holes in the Bermuda Triangle, apparently made by some force gigantic beyond belief.

But the most surprising witness may be an academy of Soviets whose ships and submarines have taken a new interest in the Atlantic, and whose professors, less hidebound by nineteenth century eccelesiastical prejudice against Atlantis, have adduced all kinds of supporting evidence, meticulously marshaled by N.F. Zhirov in his *Atlantis*.

These Soviets are perfectly prepared to admit that a large landmass dropped out of the bottom of the Atlantic in the area of the mid-

Atlantic Ridge in recent geological times; and Zhirov's dates are consonant with Muck's.

To be a juror when the evidence conflicts, and the litigants are inclined to shout each other down as knaves or liars, is not easy; but in the end it is you who must decide, true or false, guilty or innocent. No one will be there to help you but the promptings of your conscience. And some of you, if Edgar Cayce saw it clear, may have had lifetimes and perhaps some heavy karma associated with Atlantis.

If it did happen once, it could happen again. In 1937 it almost did. Throughout history, as we know it, stargazers, from Mesopotamia to Mesoamerica, have scrutinized the heavenly bodies, learning to track them with an almost superhuman accuracy, so as to emulate their Noahs, in time.

No god could indulge idly in the sport of genocide. So it must be up to earthlings to decide what's to be done, by individual and society, to establish what may have happened to Atlantis, and avoid a repetition.

To avoid the Scylla of superficiality and the Charybdis of tautology, the American editors of this book have lightly pruned the original text which the more sanguine reader can recover from the German or the French edition. But the substance is all here.

It is up to you.

PETER TOMPKINS

PART ONE

MYTH OR REALITY?

Plato's Story of
Atlantis

WHAT WE KNOW about Atlantis is contained in the two famous dialogues by Plato[1] named after the Pythagorean Timaeus[2] and Plato's maternal uncle, Critias the Younger.[3] They are a direct continuation of Plato's ten political volumes, *The Republic*. Atlantis is described as an historical fact, as a state that really existed and was clearly defined in time and place, a perfect example of the postulates laid down by Plato's teacher Socrates[4] for the ideal state. Discussions on the subject had taken place among Socrates, Glaucus, Adimantus, and others during a festival celebrated at Piraeus in honor of the Thracian goddess Bendis.[5] They had continued on the following day among Socrates, Critias the Younger, Timaeus, Hermocrates,[6] and an unnamed fourth person, presumably Plato himself.

In the course of these conversations, Critias told "a story, strange but perfectly true" as the wise Solon,[7] who had brought it from Egypt to Greece, had claimed. It was the story of an ancient, glorious state on the peninsula of Greece, which the Greeks of Plato's time had long forgotten. But an aged priest of Sais, a large city in the Nile delta, had strange tales to relate of it. He began by saying that the Greeks were all like children, for they had no ancient knowledge based on many years of tradition or any lore hallowed by time. This was his story: "The cause is as follows: much destruction has befallen mankind, in varying ways, and it will continue in the future—the greatest disasters by fire and water, and the lesser by a thousand other causes. The tradition you share with others, according to which Phaëthon, the son of Helios[8], having put the horses to his father's chariot but unable to keep in his father's track, scorched everything on Earth and was himself struck dead by lightning, is passed on as something that sounds like a fable; but the truth it contains is the deviation from their courses of the stars in the heavens that revolve round the Earth, and

Plate 1. Aristocles, Plato (427–347 B.C.).

after long periods of time the destruction by much fire of everything on Earth. Naturally the inhabitants of mountains and dry uplands perish in greater numbers than those living on the banks of rivers and by the sea. To us, however, the Nile is the savior, as it is in all other things, for it bursts its banks and thus saves us from this disaster. But when the gods, cleansing the Earth with water, send a flood, those living on the mountains, the cowherds and shepherds, will be saved: but you town dwellers will be carried away to the sea by the rivers. In our country, however, neither in this case nor that is the water sent to the fields from above; on the contrary, nature has decreed that every-thing comes from below. This is why the tradition preserved among us is considered the most ancient: in truth, however, the numbers of mankind increase, greatly or not so greatly, wherever there is no excessive heat or cold to prevent it. But all the beautiful, great, or significant events that take place among you, or us, or anywhere else will be recorded wholly and fully in our temples as we receive word of them and will thus be preserved for posterity.[9] But with you and the others everything has only recently been newly established again through written documents and through everything that the state requires. And after the usual number of years the heavens open up on mankind again and like an epidemic sweep away all but the ignorant and the uneducated; and you will be as it were made young again as at the beginning of time, for you will know nothing of what happened here nor what happened to your ancestors in ancient times. At least what you, O Solon, have just said about the generations in your country, sounds almost like a fairy tale; first, you remember only one deluge on Earth, although many occurred before; nor do you know, because a long time ago only a small tribe survived, that the best and most beautiful race of men lived in your country, the race from which you and your nation sprang; all this has remained hidden from you, because for many generations the survivors have lived without leaving any written records behind.

"Once upon a time, O Solon, before it was utterly destroyed by water,[10] the state now inhabited by the Athenians boasted the most excellent laws for its army as well as for every other institution. It was also said to have performed the most valiant deeds and enjoyed the wisest constitution of all that have come to our knowledge.

"You therefore lived under the protection of such laws as well as of an excellent administration, and surpassed all other nations in every skill, as befits the children and wards of the gods. Many of your great deeds that have been recorded here are admired. One, however, stands out from all the others through its greatness and excellence. For the records mention the great power that your state once vanquished, a power that came from the Atlantic Ocean beyond and that invaded in its arrogance the whole of Europe and Asia. For the sea there was navigable at the time. There was, beyond the strait you call the 'Pillars of Hercules' [11] an island, larger than Asia and Libya together, from where it was still possible then to sail to the other islands[12] and thence to the whole continent[13] on the other side, which encloses the sea[14] truly named after it. For everything that is situated on this side of the strait of which we are talking appears like a bay with a narrow entrance; that sea may properly be called an ocean and the land enclosing it as properly a continent. On this island of Atlantis there existed a great and admirable kingdom, which had taken possession of the entire island as well as of the other islands and of parts of that continent; in addition of the lands situated this side of the strait it ruled over Libya as far as the borders of Egypt and over Europe as far as Tyrrhenia.

"This mighty power once tried to subdue both your country and ours and everything situated within the strait in a single attack. At that time, O Solon, the power of your state became clear to all, shining in valor and achievement. For the Greeks were the leaders of all the countries and surpassed them all in courage and fighting skill; and when the others defected, they were thrown back on themselves alone and were exposed to the greatest danger. But they beat the enemy and celebrated a victory; and they also saved those not yet subdued from defeat, and generously restored the freedom of all the others that lived within the Pillars of Hercules. But later when there came violent earthquakes and floods the entire valiant generation of your people was swallowed up by the earth, and the island of Atlantis was similarly swallowed by the sea and vanished in a single dreadful day and in a single dreadful night. This is why the sea is no longer navigable there and cannot be crossed in ships because this is prevented by the very deep mud, the remains of the island when it sank."

In the further course of this dialogue, which lasted several days, Critias painted a vivid picture of the island of Atlantis; its incomparably lush vegetation, its inhabitants and glorious cities, especially the capital with the royal castle, and gave all the details from the accounts handed down by the Egyptians through Solon and Critias the Elder.

"A plain extended from the sea toward the center of the island; of all the plains it was said to be the most beautiful and excellent. A mountain rose, gently sloping in all directions, near this plain, but also toward the center, at a distance of fifty stades. One of the men that grew there from the earth at the beginning, by the name of Euenor, lived on top of it with his wife, Leucippe; they had an only daughter called Cleito. Her father and mother died when she grew up. But Poseidon was attracted to her and they became lovers. He fortified the mountain on which she lived by cutting it off from the island surrounding it, making alternate circles of sea and land, first small circles, then larger and larger, two of land, three of sea, around the center of the island and everywhere equidistant from each other so that the mountain they encircled was inaccessible to man;[15] for there were no ships and navigation yet. It was easy for him as a god to improve the island in the center by raising two springs, one of cold, the other of hot water, from a hole in the ground and also by making varied and abundant produce grow from the soil. Five times he begat twin sons, and brought them up. After dividing the whole island of Atlantis into ten parts he allotted the maternal home and the surrounding portion of land—which was the best and largest—to the elder of the first pair of twins and made him king over all the others; and the other sons he made governors and gave each of them dominion over many people and much land.

"He also gave names to all of them, calling the eldest, the king, by a name that was given to the entire island and the ocean, the Atlantic, because the name of the firstborn, who was king at the time, was Atlas. The younger of the first pair of twins, who received as his portion the extreme regions of the island facing the Pillars of Hercules up to what is now called the country of Gadira, which derived its name from this part, he called Eumelus in Greek, which was Gadirus in the language of the country; his name may also have been given to this region.[16] Of the second pair of twins he named one Ampheres and the other Euaemon; the elder of the third pair he called Mneseas, and the younger Autochthon; of the fourth pair the elder, Elasippas, the younger Mestor; of the fifth and last, the elder was Azaes, the younger Diaprepes. These as well as their offspring dwelled there for many generations, ruling over many islands in the sea as well as over those, already mentioned, living within the Pillars of Hercules up to the borders of Egypt and Tyrrhenia.

"Atlas, then, was the ancestor of a numerous, distinguished royal line and because it was always the eldest that passed the rule of the country on to the eldest of the sons, it was maintained through many generations, possessing such riches as had never been amassed before in any kingdom nor will easily be found again; for all their needs in city and countryside were provided for. Much of what they received was in the form of tributes from the subject dominions abroad[17] but most of their necessities of life were met by the island itself: first and foremost all the metals mined from the ground, whether solid or metals for melting, among them that kind of metal of which only the name has remained today, but was more than a name then, that is orichalc[18] mined in many places on the island and after gold most highly prized by the inhabitants; moreover, the island was a rich source of timber for building and it sustained large numbers of

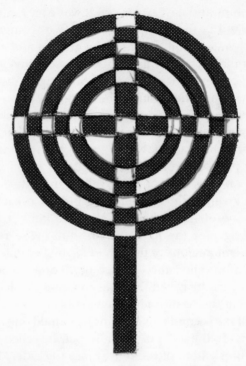

Fig. 1. The cross of Atlantis, a very ancient symbol recurring in prehistoric stone circles and on sacrificial altars. It contains the three circular
walls surrounding the island city and the canals traversing them. The
shaft of the cross is the large entrance canal.

animals domestic and wild, many elephants[19] among them. For there
was abundant grazing not only for all the animals that live in
swamps, ponds, lakes, as well as on the mountains and the plains,
but also for this largest and most voracious of all beasts. The island
also grew and amply provided all the aromatic substances, roots,
herbs, trees, various gums exuded by flowers and fruit that the soil
produces today. There were the mild fruit[20] and dried fruit[21] that
provide our staple diet, pulse (to give it its generic term) also needed
to sustain us. There were fruit-bearing trees that yield drink, food,
and oil,[22] but are perishable; they are grown for our delectation and
pleasure after meals as a welcome stimulant to the sated palate. All
this the island, which was bathed in the light of Helios, divine, beautiful, and a wonder to behold, produced in superb quality and im-

measurable abundance. And as they had everything provided by the land, they erected temples and royal palaces and harbors and wharves and organized the rest of the country, proceeding as follows:

"Their first task was to build bridges across the rings of water surrounding the old metropolis to construct a road to and from the royal castle. They built the royal castle at the very beginning in the abode of the goddess,[23] and their ancestors, the kings, received it from their fathers, adding as much as they could to its beauty, trying to outdo their predecessors until they had made the residence amazing to behold because of its size and beauty. For they had a canal dug three plethra[24] wide, a hundred feet[25] deep, and fifty stades[26] long from the sea to the outermost ring; they dug an entrance large enough to admit the largest ships; they also cut through the rings of land between the rings of water toward the bridges wide enough for a trireme to pass from one to the other. They roofed over the cuts so that the ships could pass underneath; for the rims of the rings were sufficiently high for this. But the largest ring of water that gave access to the sea had a width of three stades;[27] the next ring inside it was of the same width; of the two following rings the water ring was two stades[28] wide, and the ring it surrounded was just as wide. The ring of water surrounding the island's center had a width of one stade[29], but the island on which the royal castle stood had a diameter of five stades.[30] They surrounded this as well as the rings of water and the bridge of one plethron[31] width with a stone wall, with towers and gates on the bridges everywhere along the passages to the sea. They also quarried the stone under the island in the center of the ring and under the rings outside and inside it; it was white, red, or black, and within the quarries they excavated pairs of shipyards, roofed over with rocks. And some of the buildings they constructed were in one color and others in many colors, and they arranged the stone artistically to bring out its natural beauty. The whole circumference of the wall surrounding the outer ring of water was covered with bronze after it had been melted like oil; that of the inner wall was covered with tin, and the wall round the castle itself with orichalc gleaming with a fiery luster.

"The royal castle was constructed within the acropolis as follows: in the center of it stood a temple sacred to Cleito and Poseidon to which entry was forbidden; it was ringed with a golden fence, within which the ten royal princes had been conceived and born. Every year offerings to each of the parents were made there, from all the ten provinces. The temple of Poseidon measured one stade in length, three hundred feet in width and was of corresponding height; the image of the god had a somewhat outlandish[32] appearance. They covered the entire temple with silver except the pinnacles, which were covered with gold. Inside, the entire ivory ceiling was seen to be decorated with gold, silver, and orichalc and all the walls, columns, and floors were overlaid with orichalc. It also contained gold statues of the god driving a chariot with six winged horses, his head touching the ceiling, surrounded by a hundred Nereids sitting astride dolphins; for this was their number according to popular belief at the time.[33] There were many other statues, votive offerings of the citizens. The temple was ringed by gold statues of all the kings, their queens, and all the offspring of the ten kings, and by many other large votive offerings by the kings as well as by private citizens, some from the city itself, others from one of the dominions. The size and design of the altar was worthy of the entire building and the royal castle and similarly expressed the greatness of the realm and the splendor of the temple.

"And they made use of the cold as well as of the hot springs, which were plentiful; providing a supply of water eminently suitable for their purposes because of its wholesomeness and excellence; they surrounded the springs with suitable buildings and with well watered plantations of trees; the water was channeled into basins, some in the open air, others for hot baths indoors during the winter; there were separate basins for royalty, for the commoners, for women, and others for the horses and for other beasts of burden, each fitted for the use of those they were built for. The outflow was led to the grove of Poseidon, which contained a great variety of trees of magic beauty and size because of the excellence of the soil in which they grew, and on through channels to the outer rings of water by the bridges. Many shrines to many gods as well as gardens and gymnasia had been built there, some for men and some for horses, on each of the two islandlike rings; they also had an excellent race course in the center of the larger island, which was one stade[34] wide, and whose length was an entire circuit of the island, which was set aside for horse racing. The rings were surrounded on either side by the barracks of the lancers, varying with their numbers. The more trustworthy ones had the task of guarding the inner ring closer to the castle; but those whose loyalty surpassed that of all the others had been assigned quarters within the precincts of the castle to guard the king's person.

The wharves were full of triremes and all the appliances required for them. This is how the residence of the kings was arranged: once the three outer rings of water had been crossed, a wall was reached that began at the edge of the sea, running in a circle at a distance of 50 stades[35] from the largest ring enclosing the mouth of the canal into the sea. The whole was surrounded by many densely populated houses, and the roadstead and the largest harbor were crowded with ships and merchants arriving from all directions and creating a babel of voices, bustle and noise by day and by night.

"I have now told you everything about the city and everything connected with this ancient settlement as it had been described to me at the time; I must now try to recall also the natural condition of the rest of the country and its organization. To begin with, the whole region was said to be very high above and steeply rising from the sea; but the whole plain surrounding the city was in turn completely enclosed by mountains which came down to the sea; the plain was uniformly flat, oblong, measuring in length three thousand,[36] and in width, rising from the sea, two thousand stades.[37] This part of the island was open to the south and sheltered from the north wind. The mountains surrounding it were highly praised at the time, because their number, height, and beauty far surpassed that of those found there now, and also because they contained many populous settlements as well as rivers, lakes, and meadows that supplied all wild and domestic animals with food in plenty, and vast forests that offered a great variety of trees, providing an abundance of timber for woodwork of all kinds. This, then, was the natural condition of the plain which was, however, cultivated by many kings over a long time. An oblong, for the biggest part leveled, was the basic shape, and what was missing from it was added by the trench surrounding it. As for its depth, width, and length, it sounds incredible that in addition to the other structures there should have been such a large, artificial one, but I must pass on what I have heard about it. It was one plethron[38] deep, one stade[39] wide throughout and, because it had been dug round the entire plain, ten thousand stades[40] long. It collected the rivers coming down from the mountains and, because it had been dug round the entire plain and skirted the city on both sides, discharged them into the sea. From its upper part, straight canals, most of them a hundred feet wide, led into the plain and from there to the part of the ditch that emptied into the sea, each at a distance of a hundred stades from the next. It was thus possible not

only to float timber from the mountains to the city but also to transport seasonal produce in canal craft after they had dug cross links
between the canals and the city. And they gathered two harvests
every year by using the waters of Zeus in the winter, and by obtaining
the water that the land needed from the canals in the summer. The
number of the plainsmen fit for army service was laid down as follows: each allotment,[41] which measured ten square stades,[42]
provided a leader; there were sixty-thousand allotments altogether;
those in the mountains and elsewhere in the country supplied limitless numbers of people; they were allocated by villages and settlements to the allotments and their leaders. The leader was also obliged
to provide the sixth part of a war chariot (a total of ten thousand), two
horses and riders, as well as a cart without a seat, drawn by two
horses and carrying a warrior armed with a small shield, who dis-
mounted for battle, and a charioteer, two hoplites, two archers, two
slingers, three lightly-armed stone throwers and three lancers, and
four sailors for the manning of twelve hundred warships.[43] Thus was
the military organization of the kingdom ordered; it differed in each
of the other nine kingdoms, but it would take too long to describe
them all.

"The senior offices and appointments of honor were established
from the beginning as follows: each of the ten kings ruled in his part
of the empire over the men and most of the laws, and could mete out
punishment and death to whomever he chose. But distribution of
power and their mutual relations were governed by the rule of
Poseidon as handed down to them by the law and the inscription
engraved by their first ancestors on an orichalc column in the temple
of Poseidon in the center of the island. They forgathered there alter-
nately every fifth and sixth year to make equal numbers between odd
and even years. During the gathering they consulted on affairs of
common concern, investigated whether someone was guilty of any
misdeed and passed judgment on him. Before they assembled in
court, they exchanged mutual pledges as follows: they hunted the
bulls, ten by number, that freely grazed in Poseidon's shrine, after
having prayed to the god that they might catch the sacrifice that
pleased him, with clubs and nooses, without a weapon of iron;[44] they
led the bull they had caught to the column and slaughtered it there
over the inscription. In addition to the laws an oath was engraved on
the column, invoking harsh curses on those who disobeyed them.
When they had conducted the sacrifice according to their ritual they

consecrated all the limbs of the bull, mixed a bowl of wine and dropped a clot of blood into it for each of them; the rest they threw into the fire with which they cleansed the column. Thereupon, dipping golden cups into the mixing bowl and sprinkling the libation into the fire they vowed to pronounce judgment according to the laws inscribed on the column and to punish whoever had violated any of those laws; not knowingly to transgress any of them in the future and not to usurp the rule of the country nor to obey another ruler unless he ruled according to the laws of his father. Each having given this pledge on his own and his descendants' behalf drank from his cup and dedicated it to the shrine of Poseidon; a meal was consumed and any necessary business seen to; they all wrapped themselves in dark blue garments of the utmost splendor after darkness had fallen and the flame consuming the offerings had almost died down. Sitting on the ground in the light of the glowing embers of the sacrifice they pronounced judgment on each other at night, after all the fires had been extinguished in the shrine, on any complaints of violations of the law. They recorded the judgment they had given on a gold tablet as soon as the day had dawned, and set the tablet and the garments up as a record. There were many other laws determining the duties of each of the kings: the most important one was that they should never make war upon one another, and assist one another should any one of them in some state attempt to destroy the Royal House and that they should jointly, following the tradition of their forefathers, discuss decisions about wars and other enterprises and accord supremacy to the House of Atlas. And none of the kings should have the power of life and death over any of his kinsmen unless more than half of the ten had shown agreement.

"The power of such extent and quality that ruled in these regions was instituted in that country by the god and, so the story goes, given to it for the following reason: for many generations, as long as the nature of the god was active in them, they obeyed the laws and loved their divine kinsman. For their feelings were sincere and generous, in that they practiced gentleness and consideration during misfortune and toward one another; they held everything except honor in low esteem and bore the burden of their vast wealth and possessions lightly; they were not intoxicated with gluttony because of their riches; they therefore did not lose self-control, nor were they blind to what in their sober minds they clearly realized: that all this flourished only because of their common goodwill and morality and that it would perish if they excessively strove for it and overvalued it, and both goodwill and character would be destroyed. Because of this mentality and the continued power of the divine nature, the good fortune we have previously described flourished among them. But as the godlike strain was gradually diluted among them, because it often was mixed with mortal stock,[45] and human nature gained the upper hand, they became evil, unable to bear their riches with restraint. To those who were able to discern this they appeared debauched, because of the greatest treasures they chose to destroy what was most beautiful; but to those who could not recognize a life truly devoted to a state of bliss when they saw it they appeared most excellent and happy the more they were obsessed with the wrongful pursuit of material gain and power.

"And Zeus, the god of gods, ruling according to eternal laws, saw the miserable condition that had befallen this once honorable race and decided to punish[46] them; he summoned all the gods to their lofty abode in the center of the universe, which looks out on everything that grows, and when they were assembled, addressed them as follows . . ."

Here the dialogue breaks off.

What Plato had to say about Atlantis more than two thousand years ago fills little more than twenty printed pages. Thousands of works have up to now been written on this subject and translated into almost every major language. Solon's original text was perhaps the most fruitful contribution to the literature on Atlantis. Far too few among the many who discuss the question are familiar with the two accounts just quoted. Hardly anybody has read these passages containing one of the most astonishing sagas of all time.

Thousands of books may have been written in an attempt to solve the mystery that surrounds Atlantis but the problem remains unsolved and eternally fresh. Nothing has diminished its fascination. There is hardly another nonreligious theme in world literature that has attracted so much strong interest for so long and left such a lasting literary record. It is the scientific aspect that has been neglected.

When we speak of the Atlantic, we very rarely give a thought to the origin of the name. Where did it come from? In other parts of the globe we find India, and the Indian Ocean south of it; we look for and find the Persian Gulf near Persia, the Polar Sea near the pole, the

Baltic near the Baltic countries, the North Sea to the north of Europe. Wherever a sea is called after a country, both are found close together. The only exception is the Atlantic; it is real enough but the country that should have given it its name is missing. This is what Plato has to say about it, precisely and tersely: ". . . but later, when there came violent earthquakes and floods, the entire valiant generation of your people was swallowed up by the earth, and the island of Atlantis was similarly swallowed up by the sea, vanishing in a single dreadful day and in a single dreadful night . . ."

Atlantis has long since disappeared—has been completely destroyed. A lingering echo is all that remains. Two-and-a-half thousand years separate us from the Athens of Plato. What Solon told his friend Dropides about Atlantis takes us back another nine thousand years. So we have here a definite chronology that can be checked and cross-checked. Unlike the age-old myths of the founders of great empires, the first kings of Babylon and China, and the biblical patriarchs, the date of Atlantis rests on as much solid evidence as most dates in history or prehistory. The association of the two subjects of Atlantis and the deluge goes back a very long time. Even if it was not the deluge, as was previously thought, which drowned Atlantis in the waters of the ocean that bears its name, it was, as we shall see later, the same terrestrial cataclysm which produced the deluge. Since Charles Leonard Woolley's discovery of a layer of alluvial clay, about 8 feet (2.5m) thick, buried beneath 40 feet (12m) of desert sand and devoid of archaeological finds, which bears out the descriptions in the Sumerian story of the flood, the deluge has come to be taken more seriously. The Earth has preserved the evidence of the deluge—and the seabed that of Atlantis. Somehow or other there has persisted, among the descendants of those who lived in the lands affected by the flood, an unvarying notion that it really did take place. This has found confirmation and authentic literary expression in Plato's account of Atlantis: a brief, incomplete, but in no way exaggerated testament to past greatness.

It is still an open question whether Plato's account of Atlantis is based on truth or fiction. There is no proof that the country which gave its name to the Atlantic was an island that sank beneath the sea, or a continent that subsequently changed its name. At one end of the scale is belief inspired by intuition; at the other, an uncompromising skepticism leading to total rejection.

What are the established facts?

The conviction that Atlantis really existed is founded on an authentic, documented, and verified text containing nothing that is contrary to the laws of logic or is incapable of scientific proof.

Opposed to this is the suspicion that Plato invented Atlantis as a framework for his theories, hoping to make his authoritarian political ideas more acceptable and impressive by expounding them through this fascinating story. The argument runs that too much of it is frankly incredible, and can only with difficulty be made to tie in with certain scientific conceptions.

Is Atlantis fiction or is it truth? Thousands of years of controversy have failed to resolve this problem. In the end it all comes down to one question: Is Plato's essay on the subject genuine or not?

The *Timaeus* and *Critias* dialogues quoted here contain everything that has been authentically handed down about Atlantis. Nobody doubts that it was Plato who wrote them, and there are valid reasons for attributing their final version to his last years, probably 348 B.C.

Whether or not this last assumption is correct, it is an established fact that a confirmed and historically traceable line of tradition goes back as far as 348 B.C., about 2400 years. But this is only the historical prelude. The story itself goes back to the most ancient prehistory, far beyond Sumer and Akkad, and predynastic Egypt; indeed beyond the beginning of the Holocene epoch of geology.

Plato did not write in the first person. The story is told by the aged Critias. He mentions an even older and more revered man, Solon, the wise lawgiver of the Athenians, who is said to have left to his friend Dropides, a remote ancestor of Critias, written records intended as the basis of a great epic. These originals have disappeared—if indeed they ever existed. Solon himself was not the author of the account. He claimed to have heard it from an aged scribe at Sais, who in turn had referred to much older documentary evidence, Saitic hieroglyphic texts said to be records of the golden age and destruction of the island of Atlantis, 9000 years before. These original texts have been confirmed by a further piece of evidence.

Nine hundred years after Solon, the philosopher Proclus, A.D. 412–485, wrote a detailed commentary on Plato's *Timaeus* dialogue. Here he states that 300 years after Solon's voyage to Egypt, that is about 260 B.C., a Greek by the name of Crantor came to Sais and saw there in the temple of Neith the column, completely covered with hieroglyphs, on which the history of Atlantis was recorded. Scholars translated it for him, and he testified that their account fully agreed with Plato's account of Atlantis, which he knew well. Professor Otto, the Hamburg Egyptologist, points out that there is neither any known Egyptian source for the history of Atlantis nor any mention of the name Atlantis in Egyptian literature. However, this is not a conclusive argument. Atlantis could have been mentioned in the innumerable texts that were lost; for instance in the hieroglyphs on the column in the temple at Sais, which according to the evidence of Proclus were seen by Crantor long after Solon. Perhaps this priceless document is still hidden in the silt of the Nile that covers the cities of the delta. If any Egyptian evidence were to come to light, this would be irrefutable proof that the tradition of Atlantis as asserted by Plato is genuine.

For Critias, having related a "very strange, but true" story of the war between the nations within and beyond the Pillars of Hercules, puts this question to Socrates, conductor of the symposium: "We must therefore find out, O Socrates, whether we can make sense of this material or must look for other ideas to replace it."

Whereupon Socrates answers, "But what, O Critias, would be preferable to it? It is most appropriate on today's festival of the goddess with whom it is connected, and it also has the great advantage of being not a myth, but a true account."

Those who insist that it is a myth accuse Plato of a blatant lie. And yet the evidence all goes to prove that Plato's role was that of an objective chronicler. The more minutely we examine the text for evidence that he deliberately invented Solon's account, the more is this impression confirmed.

This vital, and indeed decisive, question is answered in one of the most significant passages in the text. It has been quoted already, but is repeated here to emphasize its importance. ". . . there was, beyond the strait you call the 'Pillars of Hercules', an island, larger than Asia and Libya together, from where it was still possible then to sail to the other islands and thence to the whole continent on the other side, which encloses the sea truly named after it . . ."

This passage gives a vivid description of the west Atlantic Ocean before the destruction of the island of Atlantis, which lies in its easternmost corner toward southern Europe; there are islands to the west of it, and beyond these a continent encloses the entire sea. Apocryphal though this description may be, it draws in bare outline a faithful map of the western Atlantic: the island-studded seaboard of North America with Bermuda, the Bahamas, and the Antilles strung out in

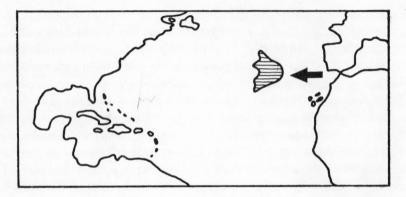

Fig. 2. The approximate position of the island of Atlantis according to Plato's description.

front of it, and the huge, limitless mass of the continent behind this broad island barrier.

Why should Plato have wanted to invent this colorful background for his political ideas? Why speak of islands even farther away than the mythical one, and another continent beyond?

But this is not the whole story. The strangest, indeed the most exciting, feature of these details is the very fact that they contain not the topography of a mythical sea, but an utterly true, realistic description of it. If Plato had wished to invent the outline of a region, he had limitless possibilities. Why did he give a description that in fact is a brief statement of the true conditions of an actual environment? He had heard of it from Critias the Younger, who had heard it from his grandfather, Critias the Elder, who in turn had been granted access to Solon's records of his travels. Solon had reported the astonishing facts he had heard in Egypt and that he could not have invented.

A weighty argument can be advanced to prove the authenticity of this part of Plato's writings. It contains two other statements which Plato could no more have casually invented than he could have invented the brief description of the Atlantic to the west of the island of Atlantis. For if his dating—about 9000 years before Solon's voyage to Egypt—is correct, Atlantis would have prospered at about the end of the Quaternary epoch, that is, at a time when huge masses of water had been converted into sheets of inland ice, and the sea level was about 330–660 feet (100–200 m) lower than it is today. Obviously Plato could not have known of this "eustatic" fall in the sea level. The statement made in the report, that the contemporaneous Attica was only a remnant of an earlier landmass, which included mountain ranges, high hills, and fertile plains, is therefore all the more significant. Figure 3 bears out the assertion made by Critias, that "what had been said about our country, too, was credible and true." It shows the present and the Quaternary coastline; its aspect confirms that the present Attica "as a whole is really like a promontory jutting far out into the sea from the mainland." At that time it was several times as wide, especially in the region of what was later Athens, and joined to Euboea and the Peloponnese by land bridges. And thanks to the eustatic fall in the level of the sea the mountains appeared almost 330 feet (100 m) higher than today, so that the Acropolis, which today

Fig. 3. BOLD COAST LINE: Present sea area.
THIN COAST LINE: Sea area at the end of the Pleistocene.
ACROPOLIS: Height above sea level: today 500 ft (156 m); 5000 years ago 800 ft (250 m).

is 500 feet (156 m) above sea level, was then about 800 feet (250 m) above it, and therefore created the impression of being much higher. The flat expanses that now form the bottom of the sea were those fertile plains described by Plato although he certainly could neither have known this directly nor stumbled upon it by accident.

This also proves the authenticity of that part of Plato's account which concerns the inhabitants, erroneously called proto-Athenians, of the region later called Attica, at the end of the Pleistocene Age.

Could we associate them with a level of civilization roughly equivalent to what Plato describes? He speaks of a comparatively rural, provincial civilization. The quarters of the guards of the citadel were built of wood and clay, the ramparts were palisades or made of Cyclopean boulders. This closely supports the current views held about the life of contemporaneous Aurignacian man, who already knew how to build wooden longhouses of surprising size. A description can be found in Gert von Natzmer's book *Die Kulturen der Vorzeit* (*Prehistoric Civilizations*, Safari, 1955):

"The remains of decayed wooden posts in the ground are almost indestructible . . . which made it possible to prove the existence of wooden houses that had crumbled to dust tens of thousands of years ago. From the arrangement of the holes in the posts it was possible to reproduce the construction of the buildings and even the design of the roofs. . . . It is now known that hunting tribes who inhabited eastern Europe from southern Russia to Austria tens of thousands of years ago erected wooden buildings of large size. These houses were up to 130 feet (40 m) long and divided into numerous rooms, each with their own hearth. Each of these 'longhouses' obviously accommodated an extended family or a clan consisting of numerous smaller families under a single roof. Their general layout suggests that their builders must have used extremely sharp stone axes to be able to work the timber in the required manner. Such tools have not yet been found among these prehistoric hunting tribes. It had also been assumed that they were homeless nomads, but it is now established that they were already settled. Lastly, their communal houses lead to the conclusion that they also had a social order. Only within the framework of such an order was it possible for the life-style they had adopted to develop. . . . These surprising findings show once again that we must not imagine that the life of prehistoric man was as primitive as until very recently it was generally believed to be."

This description, reconstructed from irrefutable discoveries, is in surprising agreement with Plato's account of the life-style of the very early Athenians.

The Aurignacian hunters had a firmly established social order. The very early Athenians, too, were divided into the ancient four castes of priests, warriors, artisans, and peasants. Warriors and priests lived together on the fortified acropolis, or city hill, in simple, spacious, wooden houses, without luxury, next to the equally simple temples of the gods they worshiped. It is quite likely that the life-style of the Chatti, the Cherusci, and the Naharvalani was still unchanged when they fought their wars against the Romans; Herodotus describes similar conditions among the still very primitive Scythians. A tribe that builds longhouses is settled; it therefore understands horticulture and agriculture; a peasant class develops on the strength of a natural division of labor. The peasants do not live on the hill, but on the plain near their place of work—as Plato relates of his early Athenians.

The construction of large wooden houses calls for craftsmanship. Peasants and artisans who are mutually supplementing each others' skills cannot exist in isolation. This again is borne out by Plato's description of the early Athenians, where peasants and artisans lived together "downtown"—probably also in longhouses like those reconstructed from Ice Age finds in southeastern Europe.

Another detail deserves attention. Longhouses as the dwellings of closely knit extended families are unmistakable evidence of a matriarchal social order. This involves the worship of a mother goddess. Such archaic aspects of worship are known from the Upper Paleolithic Age: the Venus of Brassempuy, the Venus of Willendorf, to name only two. And Plato relates that his early Athenians also worshiped a mother goddess in the form of an "arms-bearing temple effigy." The statues of proto-Athena and of proto-Hephaestus stood side by side in their principal temple. This can be interpreted as an indication of a late Amazon stage of gynarchy. Plato's otherwise rather strange information, that in early Athens both women and men engaged in the pursuit of war, is in agreement with this interpretation, and it also applies to the contemporaneous hunting and farming tribes of the Aurignacian type. Consequently, true warrior families, of armed women as well as armed men, lived in clans in the communal houses on citadel hill, in exactly the same way as the Aurignacian longhouse dwellers presumably did.

If we assemble the picture stone by stone and without bias, we will obtain a mosaic of the prehistoric age that matches Plato's description of the early Athenians surprisingly well. They were probably like the "Scythian" Aurignacian hunters of that era, people with a modest rural civilization, but their ethical standards were high and they could justly lay claim to the status of "civilized man." As Gert von Natzmer rightly says, "The term 'Stone Age Man' is, strictly speaking, almost devoid of meaning. It does not indicate that this man was in any way a 'primeval man.' Even the inhabitants of northern and central Europe still lived in the Stone Age two thousand years before the beginning of the Christian era. The same is largely true of the Red Indian civilized nations of Central and South America at the time of the Spanish Conquest. The raw material used by an ancient people cannot by itself provide a yardstick with which to measure the level of its civilization. . . . "

It is true that this prehistoric proto-Attic civilization—and Plato concurs in this—was consigned to the past in a single dreadful night of torrential rain, earthquakes, and devastating floods. Nothing concrete remained of it; everything, even the fertile soil on the acropolis, was washed away without a trace. The Cyclopean ramparts surrounding the shrine and the fortified longhouses were also destroyed.

But another question arises. Was the terrible night, during which earthquakes and floods wiped out the primitive acropolis, perhaps identical with that which sent Atlantis to the bottom of the sea? Were those volumes of water covering early Attica part of the deluge which, as the lore of innumerable nations claims, inundated huge tracts of the Earth's surface? Sufficient objective grounds have been adduced to show that Plato's account contains important and verifiable data which he could neither have invented nor correctly established by inspired guesswork. Its authenticity has been confirmed. What Plato asserts is true; he faithfully passed on the facts he knew.

The discoveries made in eastern Europe were of special significance in this context for they shed a completely new light on the standard of civilization at the end of the Paleolithic Age.

But had Solon really visited Egypt?

Thanks to Plutarch's *Life of Solon*, we do know something about his journeys. He traveled for ten years, between 571 and 562 B.C., and his first destination was Egypt, Sais, and Heliopolis, from where he brought back the account of Atlantis. He then visited King Philocyprus on the island of Cyprus; this visit was commemorated by changing the name of the town of Aepaea into Soloi in his honor. From there he visited Croesus at Sardis in Lydia, and returned to Athens in 561 B.C. Only a year later he was ousted from office by Pisistratus. During the enforced leisure of the last two years of his life—he died at the age of eighty in 559 B.C.—he seems to have written the memoirs of his journeys, perhaps as a basis for a major epic. The account Critias refers to must therefore be dated 560 B.C. This, then, is the beginning of the historically verified Greek Atlantis tradition. It is better documented than many other facts that have been accepted by official historical research.

Life Beyond the Ocean

IN 1836 huge, strange letters were discovered on the rock of Gávea in South America. One of the rocks was sculpted into an enormous bearded man's head wearing a helmet. According to Braghine, the natives call it the "giant Atlas." Bernardo da Sylva Ramos, an amateur Brazilian archaeologist, thinks it likely that the letters are genuinely Phoenician. They are engraved on an almost inaccessible rock at 2800 feet (840 m) above sea level. The text reads in translation:

BADEZIR OF TYRE IN PHOENICIA
THE FIRST-BORN SON OF JETH-BAAL

It is now known that Badezir succeeded his father to the throne of Tyre in 856 B.C. Relics have also been found elsewhere—subterranean vaults at Nictheroy, Campos, and Tijuca, huge ruins of an old castle on a coastal island of Parahyba with enormous halls, long corridors, and galleries. Some experts assure us that their style is Phoenician, others doubt this claim.

The Phoenicians of the ninth century B.C., three hundred years before Solon's voyage to Egypt, kept their secret so well that in Solon's time their descendants had already forgotten what was hidden beyond the ocean. Or could it have been that Badezir had gone on the outward journey, but did not return? At any rate, Hanno, the Carthaginian magistrate, embarked upon his famous maritime expedition to West Africa about 500 B.C., and a hundred years earlier the Pharaoh Necho set out to circumnavigate Africa with Phoenician, not Egyptian, sailors without any mention of the fact that the great secret of the South Atlantic had been revealed centuries before. Both voyages hugged the coast from beginning to end and were completely forgotten. Neither of them could have provided Solon with material for inventing Atlantis and a continent beyond the ocean. For nobody

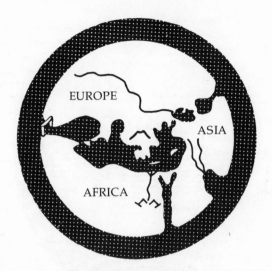

Fig. 4. Herodotus's map of the world. The map at the time of Herodotus (484–424 B.C.), that is, after Solon but before Plato, largely resembled the older map of the Chaldeans: it showed the flat disc of the Earth, approximately circular, in the center of the Okeanos which flowed round it. Olympus, the abode of the heavenly gods, was the center of the world. In the west, the world's end was at the Pillars of Hercules, in the north in the lands of the Cimmerians and the Arimaspi, in the east in the land of the Indians, who live beyond the Persians, in the south in the land of the Ethiopians. There was no space on this map for the huge continent beyond the Atlantic, yet Plato's account of Atlantis contains the first historical report of it.

doubted that it was possible to sail right around the coasts of the Earth's disk. Figure 4 shows the map of the world at the time of Herodotus. The middle region is taken up by the Mediterranean; in the center of the Earth's disk, and therefore of the universe, we find Mount Olympus, the "most venerable abode of the Olympian gods." The land runs out into peninsulas in all directions and is lapped by the waves of Okeanos.

Okeanos divided the bright world of life from the shadowy shores of the dead. In the Nekvia of the *Odyssey* (Book 11) Homer described with all the power of a great myth how the shores of the extreme west of Okeanos appeared to the Greeks' imagination. They lay at the end of the deep river, wrapped in Cimmerian night. Plato and Solon

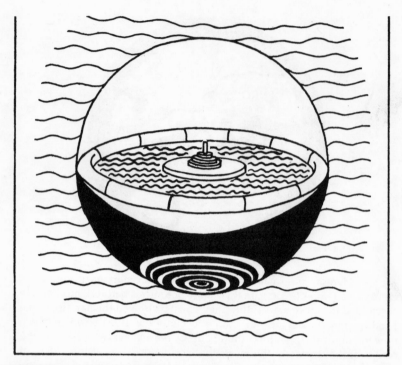

Fig. 5. Scheme of the cosmos of the Sumerians and Babylonians. The world, filled with celestial air, lies in the crystal celestial citadel, which floats on the celestial water. The celestial citadel, supported by the zodiac, resembles a bowl, filled with the water of the Bitter Lake, on which the Earth's disk floats. The sky radiates its light above it, below it is the City of the Dead with the abode of the shades in eternal darkness.

firmly believed this, as did all the Greeks, even the skeptical realist Aristotle. They all believed in the realm of the dead in the west as unquestioningly as in Poseidon's palace in the crystal deep.

But the story that Solon brought from Egypt and that forms the core of Plato's account of Atlantis completely contradicted this traditional view. The description he gives of the western Atlantic is not mythical, but absolutely realistic. A modern cartographer could not give a more concise picture. No Greek philosopher, however, could have entertained the idea of a continent beyond the ocean populated with living people. The image that emerges from the short quotation from the dialogue could not be more alien to the Greek spirit. It contradicts not

only geographical knowledge, but also—and this is more important—the basic cosmological concept of classical antiquity.

The mythical cosmology of the Greeks was derived from
Sumerian-Babylonian models. Figure 5 shows the mental image. The
world, filled with celestial air, is embedded in the crystal celestial
fortress which swims in the celestial water. The fortress is supported
by the zodiac, divided into twelve parts, with the mountains of sun-
rise and sunset. It is filled like a round bowl with the salt water of the
Bitter Lake which the Greeks called Okeanos; in it swims the circular
disk of the Earth. The Babylonians assumed the center to be in their
Ziggurat, the "Tower of Babel." Above it, divided into three parts, is
the vault of the sky; below it is the city of the dead, surrounded by
seven walls and containing the dwellings of the inhabitants of the
nether regions.

The Greeks placed the limits of Hades, the Underworld, in the west
where the sun sinks into the sea. There was no way to reach its shores
save by Charon's ferry. No Greek could have believed in the existence
of real land there. But the Babylonians, the Phoenicians, and the
Israelites would also have considered it heretical even to imagine land
and living beings beyond the Earth's globe.

By late antiquity, groups of scholars had assembled in Alexandria
and in other large cities, who filled whole encyclopedias with all
available knowledge. They formed scientific hierarchies with sacrosanct dogmas, no different from their modern counterparts. One of
these immutable facts was that Earth, in the center of Okeanos, was
the abode of life, and outside it lay nothing but the beyond and the
abode of the dead. This may give an indication of the difficulty that
faced Solon and Plato when they recorded this passage. It may have
been the very reason why neither of them could make up his mind to
commit himself in writing until late in life. Their statements were
certain to be rejected by their contemporaries, and in fact, only a few
had the courage to state their agreement. Among these were the
historiographers Theopompus and Herodotus, the geographer
Poseidonius, and the natural scientist Pliny. The stand they took
enhances both their own reputations and the credibility of Plato's
text. We know today how right they were. That faraway continent to
the west of the western Atlantic island chains described by Plato was
in fact to be rediscovered.

Existence before
the Creation?

WITH PROCLUS'S COMMENTARY on the *Timaeus* and Crantor's confirmation of Solon's account, the chain of the ancient Atlantis tradition is abruptly broken. Nothing of importance has been added to these contributions.

Herodotus makes a brief geographical reference to the northwest African Atlas, said to be the "Pillar of Heaven" and to have given its inhabitants their name. These "Atlanteans" as Herodotus calls them, were reputed to eat nothing that lived and to have no dreams. Only the dead eat nothing that lived, only the dead have no more dreams. Atlantis with all her people is no more.

Aelian mentions a reference by Theopompus of Chios to the existence of a mysterious continent in the far west—the very continent mentioned in Plato's account—inhabited by the Meropeans and ruled over by a mythical queen Merope, a daughter of the Libyan giant Atlas, who carried the world on his shoulders as described in the myth of Hercules. Pomponius Mela and Pliny also mention the arrival of a ship, presumably driven off course across the Atlantic and full of red-skinned people with thick lips, long skulls, and aquiline noses. Perhaps it was the unexpected arrival of these living witnesses of a faraway world that converted Pliny and Mela to the views of Plato.

But this is about all there is, and little enough for nine hundred years. The Middle Ages are a complete void as regards the tradition of Atlantis. This is not surprising. There were two reasons for this lack of interest (Plate 2).

There was the great Aristotle's weighty condemnation of Plato's Atlantis. For the monastic copyists of classical texts, Aristotle was an absolute authority and the greatest scholar of antiquity. The arguments against Plato were weak, but lack of documentary ·evidence made it difficult to show up that weakness. Aristotle's judgment was thus uncritically passed on, and Plato thereby acquired the reputation of a utopian.

But an even more compelling reason why the story of Atlantis was rejected during the Middle Ages may be found in the very spirit of that age. It not only contradicted the geographical view of the world, which differed but little from that of antiquity and offered no scope for assuming the existence of a country in the extreme west, but it also contained a much more serious heresy. The *Critias* dialogue has a date, which for all its vagueness is definite enough. The great war between the people within and those without the "Pillars of Hercules" is said to have been unleashed about 9000 years before Solon's visit to Sais, that is about 9600 B.C. according to our chronology. It ended with those shattering earthquakes that also destroyed the island of Atlantis.

But the Middle Ages had their own era, the Christian era, and they had a date for the absolute beginning of the world, the day of creation. This was taken from the Bible and therefore carried the full authority of divine revelation. Far too much of the Bible was taken literally in those days. The Jews counted their years from the day of the creation of the world. According to the reckoning contained in the *Book of Genesis* (*Bereshith*) the world was created in the year 5508 B.C. No doubts were permitted about this. It was regarded as revelation and was therefore sacrosanct.

Suppose you were suddenly confronted with an ancient account that mentioned a date more than 4000 years before the creation of the world, an account claiming that there existed an island in the middle of the Atlantic inhabited by civilized people at a time when the Earth was not only "without form, and void" but had not yet even been created? In the face of this glaring contradiction of holy writ there could be only one possible reaction: proscribe the text.

Nowadays, there is no problem about discussing these questions. We are no longer taught that we must take the Bible literally from beginning to end. The Hebrew date of the creation is now differently interpreted.

Recent Research on
Atlantis

THE MAN WHO SHATTERED the ancient and medieval concept of the world, and thus initiated a new era, was Cristoforo Colombo of Genoa. He was called Cristobal Colón by the Spaniards, in whose service he made his revolutionary discoveries, but he is best known by the latinized form of his name, Columbus. Many of his contemporaries thought he was a fool, because he fanatically defended the view, ridiculed by the experts, that if one continued to sail westward long enough, one would eventually arrive, through the backdoor as it were, at the easternmost edge of Asia—China and Japan—and from there reach the famous Spice Islands, the Moluccas. The theory appealed to the Spaniards, because the sea route to this region was dominated by their Portuguese rivals, and the land route was irksome because of the heavy transit dues exacted by the Arab states. But not even the Portuguese took the idea seriously, although if true it could have presented a substantial threat to their monopoly of the eastern trade. As a result, Columbus met with general disbelief, and for a long time found no financial backing for his exceedingly risky voyage halfway around the globe. The years passed; only one man, Toscanelli of Florence, supported his daring project, and Columbus was indebted to him for valuable advice and help in obtaining all the information that was available at the time.

We know that this restless man, obsessed by his *idée fixe*, was strongly influenced by the mythical geography of the ancients and the fantastic travel journals of Cosmas Indicopleustes. The route from Lisbon continuing westward via Antilia to Cipangu (Japan) was mentioned in one of Toscanelli's letters to Columbus; the map that was enclosed with it has unfortunately been lost. At long last, his untiring efforts gained Columbus an audience with Isabella of Castile, who made a contract with him at Granada. She fitted out three caravels for him and he set sail from Palos on August 3, 1492, at the age of forty-six. Nobody who witnessed the departure of this small expedition could have foreseen the consequences of this daring enterprise, not even Columbus himself. After months of uncertainty, of waiting, and almost of despair, Columbus landed on October 12 on Guanahani—Watling Island in the Bahamas. He had no idea that he had rediscovered the ancient "New World" that had been described and located 1800 years earlier by Plato, and whose account had been rejected by the scholars of his time.

In 1496 Columbus discovered the American continent at the mouth of the Orinoco, but was convinced that he had arrived in Cipangu (Japan) or Cathai (China). He mistook rows of solemn flamingoes for processions of Buddhist priests. Even on his deathbed he did not know that instead of the east coast of Asia he had reached the eastern shores of a new world. Very seldom has such an original error made such an impact. The gateway to the west was thrown wide open. Discovery followed discovery in rapid succession.

In 1502 the admiral's huge shadow fell across Central America. Tantalizing accounts of El Dorado, the city of gold, began to circulate, and attracted gold miners, adventurers, and knights of fortune. In 1521 Hernando Cortes conquered Tenochtitlan and the powerful Aztec empire, and in 1553 Francisco Pizarro subdued Peru, the land of the Incas. These countries of the far west suddenly moved from the great beyond, as it were, into the field of vision of the then western world and came within its grasp. Mercator's map of the world was published in 1569. Compared with Martin Behaim's globe of 1490 it shows the astonishing progress of geographical knowledge within the space of eight years.

The quest for Atlantis, neglected for more than a thousand years, once more began to occupy men's minds.

In 1553 the Spaniard Francisco Lopez da Gomara, the first to write a history of the newly discovered countries of the West Indies, drew attention to Plato's account of the topography of the western Atlantic. The story, formerly branded as nonsensical and heretical, was now seen to be astoundingly and brilliantly accurate. Da Gomara thought that the new continent of America was either the island of Atlantis itself or the outermost continent beyond the western Atlantic whose existence Plato had foretold. This view has been accepted by a number of famous men, although they have often disagreed on the precise location.

Francis Bacon of Verulam in his *Nova Atlantis* specified Brazil as the continent mentioned in the story of Atlantis. Janus Joannes Bircherod agreed with him. That strange book *Mundus Subterraneous*, published by the Jesuit Father Athanasius Kircher in 1665, deserves special mention. Kircher discerned summits of submerged Atlantic ridges in the islands of the Azores and he drew an astonishingly accurate map of the island of Atlantis—resembling a pear with its stalk pointing southwestward. How Kircher, who did not have the benefit of our modern methods of measuring the ocean floor, arrived at this result must remain a mystery. We must acknowledge his intuitive empathy with Plato's text which, besides his imagination, was the only yardstick available to him (Plate 3).

Kircher, thanks to his strict adherence to the original text, achieved remarkable and lasting results. Other investigators went astray because their interpretation was too subjective. This was the beginning of a tragicomic chapter in recent research about Atlantis. Olaus Rudbeck, for instance, rediscovered Atlantis in Sweden, Bartoli in Italy. George Kaspar Kirchmaier shifted it to South Africa, Silvain Bailly to Spitzbergen. Delisles de Sales preferred the Caucasian-Armenian highlands, Baer suggested Asia Minor, Balch Crete. Godron, Elgee, and later Count Byron de Prorok were certain it was in the oasis of Hoggar, and Leo Frobenius chose Yorubaland. The famous archaeologist Adolf Schulten identified Spain with the island of Atlantis and Tarshish with the real Poseidonis. Richard Hennig, Netolitzky, and others came to share his view. Others thought that the North African Atlas Mountains were associated with Atlantis. Herrman believed he had found it in the Syrtis, and others looked for it, with little more success, in Ceylon and even near Heligoland. Atlantis has been placed in many different locations by those who have dreamed of discovering it, but seldom in the actual spot that Plato described.

Some, however, did follow his account. Cadet, Bori de St. Vincent, Tourenfort, Latreille, the famous Buffon, Lamettrie, Zanne, and Germain, as well as Heinrich Schliemann, the great layman who discovered Troy. As an archaeologist with many striking successes to his credit, his opinion carries special weight, more than those of hundreds of confirmed skeptics or of thousands who were only too ready to give their fantastic ideas full rein.

About sixty years ago the "Affaire Schliemann" again caused quite a stir. In the *New York American* of October 20, 1912, Heinrich's grandson, Dr. Paul Schliemann, published a sensational article about a legacy he claimed to have received from his famous grandfather. This had included a bronze bowl he was said to have found with the superb Treasure of Priam, and which surprisingly bore a Phoenician inscription: "From King Chronos of Atlantis." Schliemann is also reported to have seen in a Tiahuanaco collection in the Louvre in 1883, vases decorated with owls' heads resembling those from the archaic double layers I-II of Troy. If the author was to be believed, these vases contained four-sided, silvery metal plates. Dr. Paul Schliemann, who later disappeared in Russia, apparently built up his theory on this evidence. He also cited two ancient Egyptian papyri allegedly discovered by his grandfather in St. Petersburg, and suggested that Egypt had been a colony of Atlantis. Nor did he forget to mention the Lion Gate at Mycenae, on which an inscription was said to have been found which indicated that the first Temple of Sais was built by Misor, the ancestor of all Egyptians and grandson of an Atlantean priest who had fled from King Chronos with the king's beautiful daughter to the banks of the ancient Nile (Plate 4).

All this—unlike Plato's tradition which is verifiable in detail—is as mythical as the remark of Herodotus about the dreamless Atlanteans on Mount Atlas, or the myth about the god Chronos who, like the emperor Barbarossa in the Kyffhäuser, is said to lie sleeping in a hidden cave on Atlantis.

French researchers have been particularly eager to solve the mystery of Atlantis and have had considerable success. The scholarly Abbé Morieux focused his attention on the hitherto greatly neglected scientific aspect, and in his "four arguments" gave substantial and convincing, if not fully conclusive, grounds for believing that Plato's island really did exist. Lewis Spence's investigations, too, are valuable. On the basis of lava deposits, he put the date of the catastrophe that overwhelmed Atlantis as 13,000 years ago at the earliest, which agrees very well with Plato's summary dating. Spence himself would have liked to move it back even farther to accommodate the theory that Europe was populated by waves of immigrants from Atlantis. A. Braghine's comprehensive description, *The Shadow of Atlantis*, first published in 1939, is also relevant. It supports the theory proposed by earlier researchers, such as Count Carli, that Atlantis was destroyed by the impact of a comet or a meteor, a catastrophe that also caused the flood.

In this context we must also examine the theories published as a result of investigating the puzzling succession of shipwrecks and plane crashes in the so-called Bermuda Triangle. Charles Berlitz's *The Bermuda Triangle* contains accounts of amazing finds on the Bahama Plateau. There has been an unusual number of disasters in this region, but the mystery remains unsolved. Berlitz writes, "From 1968 to the present day, submarine structures have been discovered, particularly in the neighborhood of Bimini, that give the appearance of massive artifacts consisting of tiers upon tiers of huge boulders; these could be streets, terraces, port installations, or collapsed walls. They bear a remarkable resemblance to the stone structures of the pre-Inca period in Peru, to Stonehenge, and to the Cyclopean walls of Minoan Greece. The age of the boulders is uncertain, although fossilized mangrove roots that had grown over them produced carbon datings of about 12,000 B.C. The most famous of all the finds is the 'Bimini Street' or 'Bimini Wall' discovered in 1968 by Dr. H. Manson Valentine and the divers Jacques Mayol, Harold Climo, and Robert Angove. They first saw it from the surface of a very clear and smooth sea; in the worlds of Dr. Valentine it looked like 'an extensive pavement of tetragonal and polygonal stone slabs of various sizes and thicknesses, obviously shaped and precisely fitted together to form a structure that was undoubtedly artificial.' "

Elsewhere Berlitz writes, "Reconnaissance flights since 1968 have brought to light other extraordinary seemingly man-made structures on the Bahama Plateau and on the seabed near Cuba, Haiti, and San Domingo. It is reported that some of these structures far out at sea look like pyramids or huge domes. One of them in the region of Bimini, measures 180 by 140 feet (55 by 43 m) and could be the stump of a pyramid; others appear to be fair-sized pyramids or temple terraces. In Cuban waters an entire complex of marine 'ruins' has already been located and is waiting to be explored." Berlitz mentions the often expressed assumption that the marine structures on the Bahama Plateau are pointers to the sunken island of Atlantis. This apparently contradicts Plato's account. But only apparently. Looking more closely at Plato's text it is seen that he says the island was larger than Libya and Asia Minor together, that it was possible to reach other islands from it, and from there, the continent on the other side. A generous interpretation of Plato's account leads to the conclusion that Atlantis consisted of a very large island and numerous small islands strung out from west of the Pillars of Hercules (the Strait of Gibraltar) to the eastern seaboard of America. These, according to Plato, perished "in a single dreadful day and in a single dreadful night."

During the last two hundred years there has been far more valuable work done on the subject of Atlantis than in the preceding two thousand. But it was not until the nineteenth century that Plato's account regained its former status.

Plato's fate was shared by another eminent Atlantologist, Ignatius Donelly, author of the famous book *Atlantis, the Antediluvian World* (1882). It must be understood that very little accurate evidence was available when he was writing. All the more praiseworthy, therefore, are his attempts to find fresh scientific arguments in support of his theory. His idea was, that before it became submerged, there had been a "connecting plateau" between Europe, Africa, and the New World, across which animal and plant species could migrate in both directions. He demonstrated how such a plateau could have prevented tropical sea currents from entering the North Atlantic, and showed that there was no Gulf Stream as long as Atlantis existed. This last opinion has been advanced quite recently, on different grounds, by Professor Enqvist of Gothenburg and Dr. René Malaise of Stockholm. Dr. Malaise wrote an original and fascinating book called *Atlantis, en geologisk verklighet* (1950).

Professor Hans Pettersson's book *Atlantis und Atlantik (Atlantis and Atlantic)*, is of particular importance. Pettersson, an oceanographer of high repute and great practical experience, leader of two expeditions, reached some interesting conclusions. "The answer to the question whether some large island existed in the Atlantic and was recently submerged is not an outright negative; nor must we exclude the possibility of natural disasters connected with changes of levels that occurred on or near the Central Atlantic Ridge as recently as ten to twenty thousand years ago, that is at a time when the Earth was inhabited by Paleolithic Man. . . . "

This is Pettersson's objective opinion as an oceanographer. His subjective view—which he shared with his archaeologist and philosopher colleagues—"The account of the glory and the wealth of Atlantis, of its princes and warriors, its trade and campaign of conquest, the temple of Poseidon with its roof of ivory and gold, protected by rings of canals and walls is definitely a myth, a figment of the imagination of the greatest thinker of antiquity, Plato"—was mistaken. We have made a detailed study of the arguments for and against Aristotle's old assertion that Atlantis was no more than an invention of Plato's imagination, and have concluded that Plato could not possibly have invented the story in its entirety.

Mythical History of
the Earth?

ADMITTEDLY, THE THEORY OF ATLANTIS still meets with a certain amount of skepticism among most geologists, but not because they necessarily object to the idea that there was at one time land in the Atlantic that no longer exists today. Names like "Gondwana" and "Lemuria" have played their part in learned discussions, although there is no Gondwana Sea or Lemurian Ocean to be found anywhere. The reluctance to associate Atlantis with the Atlantic Ocean is surprising. Perhaps it is due to the swiftness with which this island is said to have sunk beneath the sea. It is this sudden demise that runs counter to the concepts of gradualist geology, to Lyell's theory that changes in the Earth's surface are caused solely by minute forces. These concepts have held sway for nearly a century. The hypothesis of an Atlantic bridge continent which slowly sank beneath the sea in the course of thousands of years might have aroused less opposition for there are, after all, weighty arguments in its favor. But the idea that a large island disappeared "in a single dreadful day and in a single dreadful night" was in such direct contradiction to Sir Charles Lyell's doctrine that it was bound to be universally rejected, and with it the entire theory of Atlantis. The counterargument says, if the island of Atlantis had existed, then some evidence of it would have been found, but there is no such evidence. Nor could it have become submerged in the way it is claimed; large islands do not do this. There have never been geological revolutions of this violence. Historically recorded volcanic eruptions such as those of Mount Pelée and Krakatoa had only local and limited effects. Major drops in the level of the Earth's surface such as occurred along the Dutch coast are out of the question in the open ocean. It is of course possible for small islands, coral reefs, and atolls in seismically active areas such as the Pacific, suddenly to appear and disappear, but a large island of at least 77,000 square miles (200,000 sq.km) would be far too massive and inert to do this. To accept Plato's text complete, with the passage describing the catastrophic destruction of Atlantis, would be an irresponsible reversion to the cataclysm theory of Cuvier and his school. Since Lyell's discovery their views have been considered only of historical interest.

Opinion today, while agreeing that Lyell's theory applies to ordinary geological events, still admits the possibility of extremely rare cataclysms as the exception to his rule. But the theory of Atlantis calls for only one single global cataclysmic event, and the possibility of it is today no longer rejected as categorically as it was a few decades ago.

In addition, it agrees with the theory of convention, the theory of platforms, and in particular Alfred Wegener's theory of continental drift. This revolutionary theory was evolved about sixty years ago. The theory of Atlantis conflicted with it; it is therefore necessary to discuss it and its geophysical principles in greater detail.

The Earth's sphere, on which we live, is covered not by a simple clastic layer of fragments, but by a multilayered mantle. This was already known to Suess, who introduced the now generally used terms "sima" for the bottom layer, rich in silica and magnesia, and "sial" for the top levels of the continents, rich in silica and alumina. These "platforms" float on the underlying denser, plastic-viscous sima and can only move in it slowly, like icebergs in the sea. The secular separation of the platforms of America, Europe, and Greenland has been measured very accurately. It resulted in a gradual widening of the Atlantic, which must previously have been narrower. Wegener thought that in the Early Tertiary epoch no wide expanse of water existed between our Old and New Worlds; there was only a single, homogeneous, original continent, which later separated into its constituent platforms. This idea strikingly recalls the primeval, mythical concept of the land dividing Okeanos surrounding it, illustrated in Figures 4 and 5. If we compare, for instance, the Sumerian-Babylonian map of the world (page 26) with the scheme of platforms drawn up by Wegener, his looks like a modern, more detailed copy of the ancient map. Obviously Wegener could only draw the outlines of the southern continental platforms as he suspected they had been, not as they really were. The Brazilian land mass was contiguous with the African land mass, according to his map, and further north there is no trace of an Atlantic intermediate platform (Figure 6).

The existence of Atlantis would have been simulated only by a Pre-tertiary land bridge between the Canadian shield and the Eurasian platform. When—for whatever reason—the large platforms

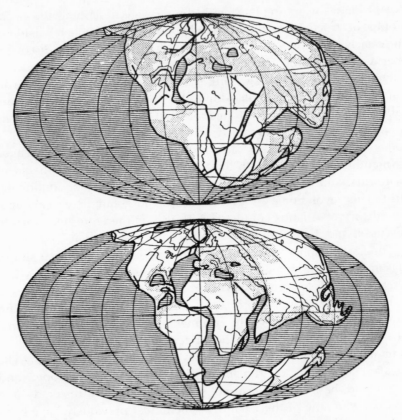

Fig. 6. Map showing Alfred Wegener's theory of continental drift and the origins of the Atlantic Ocean.

drifted apart, this direct land connection was broken; this created the myth of the sunken continent.

Does this refute Plato's account, or is it yet another clash with a new theory?

Alfred Wegener's theory of continental drift is one of the brilliant concepts of modern geophysics. Its acceptance by his professional colleagues is welcome if only because it shattered the dogmatic rigidity that had stifled theoretical geology for decades. Whether or not Wegener's assumption is correct that the continental platforms once formed a single landmass is a controversial point to be decided by geologists and geological historians. It is not necessarily relevant to the problem of Atlantis. Perhaps North America and Europe really were contiguous long before the Tertiary epoch. It is the course of the boundary line that has so important a bearing on the question of Atlantis. Even a brilliant scientist like Wegener could only guess at its true position; he could not rediscover, let alone prove it. He was obliged to draw it with a certain arbitrariness that was bound to allow for inaccuracies. These inaccuracies, in view of the small scale of his maps, could have been on the order of a few hundred miles.

Wegener's main aim was to demonstrate that at one time the eastern edge of North America and the western edge of Europe corresponded as closely as must be expected if we were to accept the revolutionary assertion that they had really been contiguous. He was therefore able to draw the dividing line of his diagrammatic maps only roughly—not as it really ran, but as it would have run had the shelves matched completely with one another along their entire length. But to do this was to anticipate the result it was desired to prove and therefore to disqualify the whole argument.

Civilization
Twelve Thousand
Years Ago?

ARCHAEOLOGISTS, as well as geologists, have rejected the theory of Atlantis. Alexander von Humboldt pointed out the astonishing affinity between ancient monuments on the two sides of the Atlantic, but the only outcome of this was a vague idea that there might have been a land bridge joining the Old and the New Worlds, and the theory conceived by Wegener.

The archaeologists particularly object to those passages of Plato's text which indicate that an astonishingly advanced civilization existed on Atlantis about twelve thousand years ago. The vast population, the fantastic splendor of the royal castles, the magnificence of the temples, the huge walls covered in tin and orichalc, the deep wide canals and other irrigation works—it is the fabulous nature of these details that has led archaeologists to reject the whole account as incredible, a mythical exaggeration. What they overlook is the realistic description of the west Atlantic topography, which proves there is an intrinsic element of truth in the account.

The archaeologists' rejection is also based on a scientific doctrine that states that there could not possibly have been an advanced civilization such as that described by Plato twelve thousand years ago.

Let us begin with the allegedly excessive number of inhabitants. This can be roughly calculated from the details Plato gives of the organization of the Atlantean armed forces: 480,000 foot soldiers, 120,000 horsemen, 160,000 manning the 10,000 heavy chariots and 60,000 light chariots, and 240,000 sailors. These add up to approximately one million men under arms.

An entirely rural population lacking agricultural machinery must depend entirely on manual effort. If the cultivation of the fields, and with it the food production, is not to be endangered, there cannot be a very high percentage of men under arms. Given, therefore, a million men in the armed forces, a total population of at least twenty million and probably nearer forty million is implied.

According to Plato's figures, the large plain in the south of the island alone occupied an area of about 77,000 square miles (200,000 sq.km) and enjoyed the most favorable climate of the Azores. Its fertility would be similar to that of the Sunda Islands. Here a population density of 200–300 per square mile could be sustained before the Europeans arrived and in spite of the absence of agricultural machinery. A similar situation still prevails in India and China today. Numerical comparison shows that the large plain of southern Atlantis alone could have kept at least forty and perhaps even sixty million people supplied with food, with no other methods than intensive irrigation, careful cultivation of the fields, and frequent planting of seedlings. These methods have been known and practiced all over the world for thousands of years. If Atlantis existed and if, as Plato writes, it was inhabited by an industrious peasant population; if its fields and market gardens were well irrigated, then there is no reason to doubt Plato's details of the American military power and the size of the population indirectly arrived at from it.

We come now to the glittering splendor of the walls surrounding the royal city. Those people who enjoyed an abundant supply of metals, the Babylonians, the Egyptians, the Incas, and the Aztecs, would hardly have found anything unusual in these structures. Consider the astonishing riches of the tomb of Tutankhamen, an insignificant young Pharaoh; the metal plating on the Ziggurat of Babylon, which Herodotus himself had seen; the Teocalli of the Aztecs and Toltecs, abounding with gold and silver ornaments and precious stones; the sun temples of the Incas. All this splendor has been found among these nations, and also among the Peruvians, historically a "premetallic" nation. Yet doubts are raised in the case of Atlantis. The civilized inhabitants of pre-Spanish Mesoamerica, who still shaped flint in exactly the same fashion as late Upper Palaeolithic man, by flaking and retouching it, were scarcely less rich in gold.

The amount of gold, silver, and jewels that Cortes brought home from Tenochtitlan was really fantastic. The sunken mountains of Atlantis must have been a direct continuation, via Madeira, of the Sierra Morena in Spain where precious metals abound. One may assume that there were gold and silver veins and rich ore deposits in the

Atlantis mountains too, and this assumption is not invalidated by the barrenness of the Azores mountains. Land that is now 7700 feet (2350 m) above sea level was at that time much higher—10,000–13,000 feet (3000–4000 m)—above sea level. The Azores mountains today are the highest peaks of submerged mountain ranges and therefore too high to contain the metal lodes that may well exist in the submerged strata. The example of ancient Mexico proves that a largely Stone Age civilization like that of the Aztecs at the time of the Spanish Conquest was quite capable of mining and working the precious metals and other very rich ores.

Although no remains of Atlantean smelting furnaces have been brought to light, we nevertheless have evidence that naturally ventilated smelting furnaces were built and used—oddly, where one might least expect to find such evidence. The biblical account of the building of King Solomon's temple mentions smelting furnaces in which was melted the copper for the "molten sea," the "molten altar," the "molten undersetters" for the "pots, shovels, and basons" and for "Jachin and Boaz," the two mighty pillars in the porch of the temple. This large industrial complex was excavated in 1940 by an American expedition in the Wadi-el-Araba, a desert valley south of the Negev in the neighborhood of substantial iron ore and malachite deposits, surrounded by huge heaps of iron and copper slag and unmistakable molds. Nelson Glueck, the leader of the expedition, was mystified by the fact that these industrial plants had been erected in the path of storms from the north instead of a few hundred yards away in the lee of the hills, where there were also freshwater springs. The excavation supplied the answer.

"In the center of an oblong precinct a large structure emerges. The green color of the walls clearly reveals its nature; a smelting furnace. The loam brick walls have two rows of openings—flues. A sophisticated system of air channels forms part of the plant. The whole is a genuine, highly up-to-date smelting furnace built according to a principle that was revived as the Bessemer System by our own steelmakers only a century ago. The alignment of the flues and chimneys is precisely north-south because the prevailing winds and storms from the Wadi-el-Araba had to take over the function of the bellows. That was three thousand years ago. Today, compressed air is pumped through the furnaces . . ." (Dr. Werner Keller, *Und die Bibel hat doch recht* [*The Bible as History*], Econ Verlag 1955.)

A nation whose technical achievements were comparatively primitive was able to construct smelting furnaces in which copper has been shown to have been melted simply because they were keen observers of the forces of nature and put them to good use. Skill and the ability to make use of an opportunity are themselves gifts of nature regardless of a nation's level of civilization. It was these, and not the mechanical aids at the nation's disposal that were decisive. Indeed, such gifts are more likely to be found during the early stages of civilization, when man is closer to nature, than at a later stage. We must also remember that the Atlanteans had before their eyes a prototype of a gigantic, natural smelting furnace; Mount Atlas, the volcano that supported the heavens, and that they worshiped as a god, from whose crater molten lava flowed during eruptions. What was more likely than that such a people, with a good eye for the opportunities offered by nature, should discover the basic principle of a smelting furnace, a method which other nations managed to develop only with the aid of technology?

If we take all this into account we may question the traditional dating of the earliest epochs of metalworking. As far as we know at present there was scarcely any metal used in Post-Glacial Europe and the Near East before 4000 B.C. and little copper before 3000 B.C. Bronze does not appear to have been used before 2000 B.C. Compare the relatively poor quality of the artifacts of the Mesolithic Age with the high quality products of the late Magdalenians. The former include fishing rods and harpoons carved from reindeer antlers and bones, crudely carved geometrical microliths, blades, scrapers, and gravers of the Tardenoisians and Capsians. Among the latter are laurel-leaf blades, spear points, saw blades, extremely carefully carved microliths, delicately finished harpoons, and fishing rods made of horn and bone. Such a comparison reveals, contrary to the prevailing idea of an uninterrupted progress of civilization, a regression of the later Mesolithic artifacts from the earlier Late Paleolithic ones. This has been acknowledged and the Mesolithic epoch has been described as a "hiatus" or intermediate period, a temporary setback coming between the two widely differing cultural epochs of the Glacial Late Paleolithic and the postglacial Neolithic Age. This setback can only be interpreted as a consequence of a disturbance of life which also manifested itself in a wide variety of findings. Archaeological evidence confirms, not the hypothesis of undisturbed cultural progress, but the opposite: the aftereffect of a profound upset contemporaneous with the transition from the glacial to the postglacial climate. These two synchronous events may, indeed must, be causally connected. The disturbance that left its mark on the artifacts produced must have been caused by a change of climate, and not the other way round. A change of climate so radical that it caused ten-thousand-year-old land glaciers to melt must inevitably have had a profound effect on the living conditions of the people existing in that period of transition. And it is equally clear that such an enormous upheaval, which fundamentally changed the climate of the whole world, cannot have come about in the natural course of everyday events, but was almost certainly caused by a catastrophe.

A catastrophe on such a scale would have destroyed the heritage of the advanced civilization of the late Paleolithic era that preceded it to the extent that the only relics left would be regarded as almost negligible by modern archaeologists. A similar fate, which we must hope will remain in the realms of theory, could overtake our own era. Let us suppose that a nuclear war breaks out. Hydrogen, cobalt, and carbon bombs very nearly extinguish life in the centers of civilization; the cities are reduced to dust, the paper records of our achievements are burned to ashes. . . . What will happen? The few survivors on the fringe areas that have escaped the horrors of nuclear war will have the enormously difficult task of building afresh on the ruins of the past—probably from a very low level. After many thousands of years scholars of the future will compare the few finds preserved from the time preceding that long-forgotten catastrophe with those from the centuries immediately following it; they, too, will regard these earlier relics as somewhat more advanced than those that followed, but will nevertheless be unable to accept them as evidence that something had existed in the remote past—which to them is our present age—that could be called an advanced, highly sophisticated civilization. In spite of all our technological achievements, of which no trace will be left, we would be unlikely to come out much better in their judgment than late Paleolithic Man does in ours today.

Something like this does appear to have taken place. A prehistoric catastrophe radically destroyed the very center of civilization. It affected the fringe areas of the continents much more strongly than the heartlands; these central areas were less influenced by that very ancient advanced maritime civilization, and it is there that the comparatively primitive artifacts have been unearthed.

The ocean floor has not yet given up its secrets. The chance of recovering metallic artifacts or other evidence of a submerged civilization with deep-sea dredgers and core barrels is remote. We do not know accurately enough where to look, and it is most likely that the objects we would hope to find in some prehistoric Pompeii about 10,000 feet (3000 m) below the sea would be buried under a hard layer of ash and lava.

Admittedly, no remains of the legendary treasures of silver, gold, or orichalc have yet been found, but the search has not yet been very intensive. Nevertheless Pettersson, in his critical appraisal *Atlantis and Atlantic*, confirms that there have been some findings. "A weak pointer in this direction was a single link of a thin copper chain dredged up with the mud at a Monaco station southwest of Santa Maria" (an island of the Azores Group).

This accidental find also supports the archaeological evidence which indicates the existence of a higher level of civilization at the end of the Late Paleolithic era more strongly than one would be inclined to expect on the basis of the purely linear idea of progress. The significance of the arguments in favor of the existence of a large Atlantean island and its catastrophic destruction is therefore all the greater.

Were the Atlanteans a civilized nation?

We could regard the ability to erect the huge buildings Plato describes as evidence for this assumption. In the Mississippi valley and in other areas of North America are to be found huge, strange earthworks dating from prehistoric times. They are "Monmouths," built in the shape of animals such as snakes or jaguars, and are as large as hills. Nobody knows who made them. But they are there.

Other examples of primitive building techniques that have attracted far too little attention are the terracing and irrigation of entire provinces in China, Indonesia, India, and Peru. The loess regions in China, the rice empires in Southeast Asia—all these are the result of manual toil without any agricultural machinery. Here too, primitive methods were and still are being used to shift millions of tons of soil quickly and seemingly without effort.

The Atlantean earthworks described by Plato are no more astonishing than the achievements of peasant communities throughout the ages, using the most primitive tools and working in their steady, diligent way. Nothing Plato says is exaggerated. What is imposing is not the quantitative aspect but the mental effort that created these structures. The conception of this system of irrigation and canals is absolutely superb. It achieves enormous success with strikingly little effort, which is the strongest evidence of the high level of intellect, culture, and civilization the authors and executors of such plans must have attained. These plans are wholly attuned to the mentality of prehistoric and pristine man, which was concentrated on rural life. Fertile soil was the first raw material from which man fashioned large structures. The first civilizations, therefore, originated where this basic building material was abundant, for instance in the alluvial lands of the Nile, the Euphrates and the Tigris, and the Mississippi.

Surely there can be no doubt that the large plain of Atlantis was as rich in this precious material as were the more familiar regions in which the earliest civilizations of mankind were evolved.

Light from the
West?

DURING RENAISSANCE TIMES it was classical Greece and Rome that were regarded as laying the foundations of the most advanced civilization of mankind. Then other civilizations began to be rediscovered: that of ancient Egypt, the even older one of Mesopotamia, the "onionskin" civilization on the hill of Troy, the palaces of Minos on Crete. Fresh information was constantly coming to light and opinions had to be revised. One fact, however, remained unchanged: all these ancient civilizations flourished in eastern Europe and in the Middle East. It was readily accepted as being of the natural order of things, that human civilization should reach its zenith in these regions. But is this really the case, or is it only an illusion?

Remains of prehistoric civilizations that do not fit into this pattern were, and still are, being discovered elsewhere. They include the gigantic animal hills in the Mississippi valley, the timber and bone civilization on Novaya Zemlya, the mysterious structures on the shores of Lake Titicaca, and many others. Nobody knows what is hidden in the inaccessible forests of the Matto Grosso, the Toltec jungle, and the Green Patch along the Amazon. Will it be possible to fit everything that may come to light into the hypothesis that these areas, too, were reached by the light of civilization that came from the East?

There is no lack of evidence that new and more highly developed types of man, the Cro-Magnon race of *homo sapiens diluvialis*, lived on the European continent between 20,000 and 10,000 B.C.

Prehistoric skeletons and artifacts have been found in particularly large numbers in the wide valleys of the Guadalquivir, the Tejo, the Douro, the Charente, the Dordogne and Garonne—all flowing into the Atlantic. Where did these forms of life originate?

In a ten-thousand-year-old skeleton found in the "Tomb of Palli

Aike" in Tierra del Fuego in 1969–70 we again meet Cro-Magnon Man, so we have recent confirmation of the spread of this race to South America.

We would have expected the finds to be concentrated in the heart of the continent if this race had been settled in Europe, for instance, but in fact the opposite is the case. According to the finds in these areas, Neanderthal Man is the proto-European. Cro-Magnon Man must have come from the west, sailed across the Atlantic and landed at the river mouths, and penetrated inland along the rivers. Figure 7 shows these hypothetical routes of immigration. They are marked by the burial sites of the Cro-Magnons, which differ radically from those of the Neanderthalers. The artifacts have greater artistic value, the weapons are more effective. It is likely that the Cro-Magnons, with their superior weapons, pushed the Neanderthalers back toward the Alpine retreats.

The driving of the Neanderthalers back to the hinterland, a process that can be reliably reconstructed from the results of excavations, must have taken place over thousands of years. These excavations confirm the theory that the Cro-Magnon race came not from the east but from the west. If we admit their western origin, however, we must further conclude that they came from a country situated to the west of Europe.

There is a striking resemblance between Cro-Magnon man, as revealed in the reconstruction, and the Red Indian type of man. Like the Red Indians, the Cro-Magnons are tall, big-boned, muscular, athletic, and agile. Their huge skeletons would suggest that the Cro-Magnons were splendid representatives of the Redskins. Where did these aboriginal Red Indians who came to diluvian Europe originate?

There are only two possibilities. Either they came from North America or Mesoamerica 2485 miles (4000 km) away, or from Atlantis, only 930 miles (1500 km) away. The areas that are rich in Cro-Magnon finds are the very regions that are stated by Plato to have been subject to the rule of Atlantis. If these early civilized men were pioneers from Atlantis who arrived in Europe, which at the time was largely covered by ice, then the remains of their civilization that they left behind in these fringe areas could not possibly be representative of the level of attainment that Atlantis itself had reached. It would be only glimmerings, small offshoots of the civilization that penetrated the virgin territory of Europe, where game was abundant and hunting the main activity. These ancient invaders no doubt took advantage of this

Fig. 7. Settlement of southwestern Europe
The arrows indicate the leading direction of the advance of the Cro-Magnon race into the interior of the continent from the river mouths, confirmed by finds of skeletons and of Late Paleolithic artifacts. They all arrived from the west, from Atlantis across the Atlantic. Cave paintings depict them as red-skinned people, "primitive Red Indian."
Broken Line: limit of the continental shelf. *Solid Line:* present coastline

abundance in the same way the white pioneers took advantage of a similar situation on the North American prairies during our own era. The slaughter of the mammoths reminds us of the senseless killing of herds of bison in America.

Primitive hunting tribes are still to be found today in the Australian outback, in the primeval forests of Central Africa, in Sri Lanka, Borneo, and along the Amazon. Should we conclude from this that conditions must therefore be the same in the rest of the world? Ituri

pygmies, Botocudos, or Australian aborigines who have never left
their reservations and had no contact with higher levels of civilization
might reasonably be expected to draw this wrong conclusion.

Is it not equally wrong to assume that the primitive remains of the
late Quaternary era in Europe were characteristic of the rest of the
world? These remains do not, in themselves, provide any serious
challenge to the view that the level of civilization in the country from
which the Cro-Magnons came was much higher.

Anyone who has seen the superb cave paintings of Late Paleolithic
Man must marvel at the perfect representation, the strength of the
artistic expression, and the magic of the overall effect. Could the
creators of these works of art—and there is little that matches them in
quality—have been naked savages? Painting was not their only skill.
The famous laurel leaf points of the Magdalenians, the superbly
shaped mallets and daggers were not, as in the Neolithic era, products of a semimechanized grinding process, but were individually
fashioned out of the flint by hand. Great skill was needed to make the
most of the natural properties of the stone. If we try to do what these
so-called savages did ten or twenty thousand years ago, we can ap-
preciate the measure of their skill. To relive the far distant past in this
practical way is a good method of evaluating its creations.

Admittedly, Columbus in his caravels encountered a primitive
civilization of "gentle savages" on Guanahani. But Cortes's conquistadors were utterly amazed when they came upon the fringe civilization of the Totomacs on the coast. In comparison with this, and with
the flourishing civilization in the high valley of Anahuac nearby, the
splendors of their Spanish and Portuguese homelands paled. It was
they, and not the Red Indians, who were the barbarians. There may
well have been a similar difference between the life led by the Atlantean pioneers in Europe—the Cro-Magnons—on the one hand, and
the luxurious splendor of the cultural center of Atlantis, with its resemblance to Tenochtitlan and Babylon, on the other.

On Java and Bali, long before the coming of the white man, there
was a native civilization that was intellectually, spiritually, and artistically sophisticated and was backward only in technology. But in
nearby Borneo, barbaric head hunters were gaining the upper hand.
In one island, as in Europe at the end of the Ice Age, man had not
progressed beyond the stage of hunter and food gatherer. In
neighboring islands, at the center of the Indonesian civilization, was a

flourishing culture with striking achievements to its credit. Might it not have been so with Atlantis?

If we seek in the European fringe areas for evidence of the civilization of Atlantis, what do we find? We find that relevant remains are comparatively rare in the ritual caves of Southern France and Spain. But the layout of these caves, and the implements contained in them date back to far more archaic periods and may well be remains of these times. If we take an impartial view, we cannot say that the rarity of such remains is in itself evidence that no such civilization existed on Atlantis.

There is a great deal of mystery about the way in which native civilizations develop, springing up here and there in isolated, localized growths. Oswald Spengler rightly stressed their vegetative nature. They flourish only in their specific habitat, where they find the unique conditions necessary for their equally unique existence.

Advanced civilizations are also luxuriating growths. They need opulence and are stifled by poverty. A plentiful supply of food is essential. They can therefore only develop where more food can be grown than is necessary for bare survival. The Nile valley, fertilized and irrigated by the holy river itself, is such a region; so is the fertile alluvial plain of the Euphrates and the Tigris, and also the loess regions of China. In all these, abundance of food could be grown, and they were all cradles of a sophisticated civilization.

Ice Age Europe did not come within this category. Its narrow fertile strip was wedged between the Alpine glaciers in the south and the gigantic ice cap in the north, which occasionally covered the whole region down to the latitude 52°. It was sodden with melted ice and water collected in lakes and ponds and accumulated on the moors. It looked more like the Siberian tundra than like Europe as we know it today. It may have been an ideal hunting ground, but it was no country for gardeners and farmers. It supported huntsmen; it could not support an advanced civilization which requires a settled life on fertile soil. This diagnosis has been confirmed by the remains that have been found.

A different situation existed on Atlantis. Here was a privileged country blessed by a bountiful nature: an ideal climate, an ideal situation surrounded by a warm sea, hot sun, abundant rainfall, and almost tropical fertility.

PART TWO

REALITY, NOT MYTH

The Gulf Stream
and Isotherms

SCIENTIFIC PROOF and accurate records of effects which can still be checked today, and cannot be traced back to any cause other than the existence of a large island in the Atlantic, enable us to revive Plato's account as the true drama of mankind.

Our arguments until now have been lacking in one vital factor: we have not determined the exact nature of Atlantis. Was it a large island, or was it perhaps some other form of land—a bridge continent, or a continental drift?

We already have one argument to advance. Plato's topographic information has been astonishingly justified by the rediscovery of America. His details of locality, position, and dimensions can be trusted. He states unequivocally that Atlantis was a vast island—in Alfred Wegener's language, a small continental platform. This is a fact of decisive importance. If the island had been comparatively small the chances of finding it, or of conclusively proving its former existence would be almost nil. In areas of seismic activity the emergence and disappearance of volcanic islands is an everyday event. The Pacific is full of typical examples, but the Atlantic can also provide instances. In 1931 two small islands emerged near Fernando de Noronha and disappeared again before the interested powers could start to quarrel over them. If Atlantis had been an island like these, or like the island of Sabrina, which emerged for a few hours in the 1880s, then the attempt to investigate it would have had to be abandoned before it had been begun.

A large island, however, is a far more stable formation of soil and rock. If it rises above sea level and does not remain a shallow bank beneath, and is in a suitable position, then it can have specific, persistent, and long-term effects upon the sea that washes its shores. And if it sinks beneath the waves, this event will make a major impact on the Earth's history.

To understand these statements we need to ask an apparently simple but in fact very important question: what, from the geologist's point of view, is an island?

An island is a fragment of a platform. Usually it is broken off the edge of a large, hard, granitic platform and is therefore thinner than the platform itself. Whereas the latter is immersed in the highly viscous sima base to a depth of 25 to 37 miles (40–60 km) and, according to Alfred Wegener, can drift horizontally at secular rates, islands are not so deeply immersed in the sima. Wegener likens the continental platforms to icebergs floating in the sea and islands to corks bobbing on the surface. For this reason, and also because they are much smaller, islands follow local variations in the sima level much more quickly and noticeably than the heavy, massive, very inert large platforms. Given certain conditions, an island can sink. A continent cannot. This is an important distinction. A sunken island can no longer be seen above the surface of the sea; it is completely submerged.

The islands of the Sabrina type, or the two nameless ones that made a brief appearance near Fernando de Noronha, are islands in name only. On closer investigation, they turn out to be not fragments of a platform, but temporarily risen domes of submarine volcanoes, or some other elevation of the sima floor of the ocean. Atlantis, however, was a true island, a small, relatively thin fragment of platform, presumably splintered off from the Eurasian twin platform as it drifted eastward during the Early Tertiary epoch.

Such true islands are always rooted below the bottom of the ocean, a few miles inside the sima mantle. Like the Azores, they are often the summits of huge submarine ridges. Floating islands do not occur naturally.

A large island, a solitary piece of land in the middle of the ocean, obstructs the free flow of ocean currents. The larger the island, the more far-reaching is this obstruction.

Gales and storms rage over the vast expanse of the ocean and create the rhythmic motion of the waves. The stronger the winds become, the heavier the swell. And in addition to these movements of the waves, caused by winds of varying direction and strength, there are the less frequent but constant currents caused by winds that blow steadily from the same direction—the so-called trade winds. These currents are regular and are confined to the surface of the ocean.

What is the cause of the trade winds?

The Earth rotates around its north–south axis, and transmits the greater part of this motion to the atmosphere surrounding it. Some of

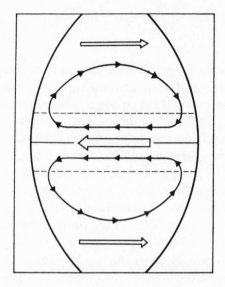

Fig. 8. Circulation of the water in an ideal sea basin. Through the interaction between the tropical Easterly Trades and the west winds prevailing at higher latitudes, two water vortices symmetrical to the equator are set up between the two adjoining continents. The energy requirements of this circulation is met by the solar radiation and the Earth's rotation. Because of the irregularity of the coastlines the real water circulation diverges from the ideal scheme to a varying extent. *Straight line (center):* equator. *Broken straight lines:* tropics.

the momentum is lost, and the atmosphere lags a little behind in the equatorial belt, where the speed of rotation is the greatest—1300 feet per second (400 m per second). This atmospheric lag produces a steady east wind, which is prevalent throughout the entire tropical zone, except for the doldrums directly on the equator.

At higher latitudes the rotational speed of the Earth decreases, so that the atmosphere carried along by meridional transverse forces of the tropical air begins to run ahead. In these zones of changing wind directions it is the west winds that are prevalent.

These regular currents of air produce parallel currents on the surface of the ocean. The easterly trades drive the tropical waters steadily westward and in the higher latitudes an easterly current arises, and both combine into a closed circulation system, illustrated in Figure 8. Whenever an ocean basin is surrounded by continents, there will be a circulation of water on its surface. (These circular currents are not as regular as might be supposed from the diagram, but in essentials it is correct.)

The Atlantic Ocean is just such a basin, bordered by continental platforms on both sides, and it is traversed by these regular circulating currents.

One of them is the so-called Gulf Stream Drift, better known simply as the Gulf Stream. Its familiar blue expanse of water is hundreds of miles wide and it crosses the cooler gray waters of the Atlantic from west to east between the latitudes of 34° and 43° north. If a large island were situated in the middle of the Gulf Stream, then the waters of this great current, which now flow toward northwestern Europe, would be deflected by the west coast of the island and would flood back to the west in a wide arc.

The effect that this would have upon northern regions can be described by climatologists, which may provide a clue as to whether such an obstacle to the Gulf Stream ever existed. We may follow the trail back to the remote past, but a successful conclusion for our search depends on the island's having been situated dead in the middle of the Gulf Stream and nowhere else. Plato's account lacks precise details about the location of Atlantis. All we can gather from it is that it was situated somewhere in the eastern Atlantic, roughly at the latitude of Gibraltar. There are no references to the Gulf Stream.

We can, however, examine in detail the history of the climate of northwestern Europe, which is notoriously dependent on the Gulf Stream with its current of mild water washing the western seaboard of this region. Has this always been the case? Or was there a time when the Gulf Stream was blocked and deflected by an obstacle in mid-Atlantic, now submerged, but at that time above the surface of the ocean?

Let us for the moment confine our investigations to one point: at what period, if any, in the history of the Earth have climatic conditions in northwestern Europe been of a character that might well be attributed to a blocking of the Gulf Stream?

Strictly speaking, the Gulf Stream is that part of the huge circular Atlantic current that originates in the Gulf of Mexico and crosses the ocean twice, traveling in all a distance of 12,430 miles (20,000 km). It forms a complete circle and its energy is maintained by heat and wind. The current begins its westward drift in the tropical Atlantic. The strong easterly trade winds whip it up, driving it from the region between Guyana and Guinea toward the eastern apex of the triangular platform of South America—in other words, toward Brazil. Figure 9 shows how this landmass divides the current that is flowing toward it. Situated at a latitude of about 10° south, it diverts an appreciable portion of the waters coming from the South Atlantic west-northwestward into the North Atlantic. There they combine with the parallel drift of the northern trade winds beyond the equator. The volume of water flowing toward the coast of Central America is therefore considerably increased by the addition of water from the South Atlantic. The result is a very powerful current with more water flowing in it than in all the rivers of Earth combined.

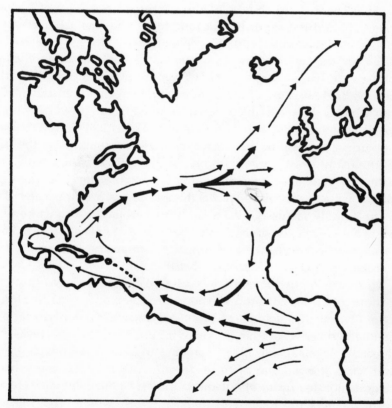

Fig. 9. The Gulf Stream. The Gulf Stream originates as a westward current of warm tropical water between West Africa and South America, enters the Caribbean and the Gulf of Mexico with the Easterly Trades; it is then deflected and leaves the east coast of North America as a warm easterly current which flows past the Azores and the British Isles as far as northern Norway.

Driven by the easterly trade winds, the current, azure because of its higher salinity, extends along the northern coast of Brazil farther and farther toward the northwest. It breaks through the arc of the Antilles and enters the Caribbean through the narrow gaps between the Lesser Antilles. Here it is boxed in for the first time. To the north are the Antilles, to the South are Yucatán and Mexico. The waters are imprisoned in a shallow structural basin, from which escape is not easy.

The current is progressively slowed down and becomes appreciably warmer as it enters first the Caribbean and then the Yucatán Basin. Gradually it fans out and becomes shallower. In the Gulf of Honduras it warms up considerably before it squeezes through the narrow Yucatán channel. At this point the almost circular Gulf of Mexico opens up, and the arc of its coastline forces the sluggish current to change its direction through an angle of about 90°.

The current, now bearing its name, leaves the Gulf with difficulty through the very narrow Florida Strait, past Cuba and the large Bahama Bank. Because of the low rate of flow within the Gulf, where the current is deflected, the water appears stagnant. The current takes a long time to escape, and during this time it remains in the shallow Gulf under the heat of the tropical sun. Here the waters of the current, already warm, become hotter and greatly enriched with salt. Halophile blue algae gives it a luminous azure color, and the high salinity increases the density, weight, and viscosity of the water. The hydrologically mature Gulf Stream thus becomes a distinct body of warm water. In spite of its greater density, it at first remains lighter, because of its much higher temperature, than the less saline, less viscous, gray, cool waters of the North Atlantic.

This warm, light current of the Gulf Stream enters the North Atlantic through the Florida Straits, where it is sometimes called the Florida Current. Initially, it hugs the east coast of North America and is gradually diverted by this coastline from a north to a northeasterly direction. It remains shallow, confined to the surface of the ocean, and has a temperature of never less than 68°F (20° C) even in the coldest months, up to about the latitude of Philadelphia. Here the current enters the region of prevailing west winds. The westerly trades deflect the current in an east-northeast direction, driving it to the open ocean. Fanning out under the force of the west wind, the Gulf Stream flows as a blue, warm expanse between gray, cool waters into the North Atlantic.

As it flows it becomes progressively broader and stronger, merging along its edges with colder, less saline water. At the latitude of the Azores it is nearly 500 miles (800 km) in breadth. It gradually becomes heavier as it approaches the west coast of Europe, where it is cooled by the surrounding water, and sinks deeper and deeper. But the saline, viscous body of warm water remains intact. West of Europe the main current flows 2500–3300 feet (800–1000 m) below the surface of the sea.

This downward flow acts as an accelerating force. It is the true motive power that carries the warm water body on its long journey across the Atlantic. The gradual cooling, and consequent sinking of the current, acts as its power supply. It rolls at a gradient of about 1 in 5000 across the Atlantic ocean. It laps the west coasts of Ireland and Scotland, flows into the Irish Sea and the English Channel, and skirts western France and Spain.

As it nears its final destination, the current fans out more and more and becomes cooler. The Scandinavian peninsula deflects a narrow branch into the Norwegian trench, the Kattegat, and the Danish archipelago. But its main body drifts along the Norwegian fjords, around the North Cape, and as far as the Barents Sea. At this stage, the current has lost the last vestiges of its warmth and impetus and has sunk to the bottom of the sea, where it becomes a cold undercurrent. But in the arctic waters to the west and north of Spitzbergen it surfaces again. As the East Greenland current, cold and of low salinity, it flows southwestward along the icy coasts of these great northern islands, bearing the cold winds with it. Nothing is left to remind us of the Gulf Stream.

This is only a brief summary of the workings of the mighty Gulf Stream, seven times longer than the huge Amazon. The rate of flow in its Florida section is about 100 million tonnes per second. If all the rivers of the world (metric tons) were combined they would not produce anything like this rate of flow. Along the edges of this vast body of water, sharp variations of temperature are to be found. Differences in water temperature of up to 53.6° F to (12° C) have been measured from an ocean liner whose bow is in the Gulf Stream and whose stern is outside the warm water. The cohesion of the warm water body of the Gulf Stream is astonishing. It is of immense and unique importance as the "warm water heating system of Europe."

The climatic effect of the Gulf Stream is not, however, confined to providing warm water. Even more important is the property to which it owes the name of "King of the Storms." For this huge, compact body of warm water carries mild, rain-bearing winds in its wake. The anticyclones follow in its track and determine the weather in western Europe. When the Meteorological Office forecasts a spell of bad weather, a depression bringing rain and storm, it is from the north-west that this area of low pressure comes. The warm waters of the Gulf Stream combine with the humidity of the warm winds that drive it along and bring mild, wet weather to western Europe, as far as the extreme north of the continent.

It is to these two important factors that the area bathed by the Gulf Stream owes its unique Atlantic climate.

Climate can be measured and categorized by its mean air temperature adjusted for sea level. This is recorded in the form of monthly and annual average values and provides a clear picture of both the climate and its seasonal changes.

In the west of England the characteristic temperature for January, the coldest month, is 41° F (5° C). In Labrador, at the same latitude but on the other side of the Atlantic, it is −50° F (−10° C). This 59° F (15° C) makes a very appreciable difference. It shows how very greatly western England benefits from the warm current of the Gulf Stream in comparison to Labrador, which is untouched by it. In July the air temperature reaches 62.6° F (17° C) in western England but only 50° F (10° C) in Labrador. The annual mean is 50° F (10° C) in the former, 32° F (0° C) in the latter. In Labrador the air temperature varies by about 77° F (25° C) annually. The comparable figure in the west of England is only 53.6° F (12° C).

Thus, Labrador, unaffected by the Gulf Stream, has a typical continental climate, with extreme variations of temperature; it is in fact a subarctic region. England, at the same latitude, has a much milder, equable, maritime climate as a result of being warmed by the Gulf Stream.

This bounty brings great material benefits. In northeastern America a crop like rye, nonresistant to frost, can only be cultivated up to 50° north: in Norway it can be cultivated up to 20° higher latitude. This is also true of wheat and potato crops, and the northern limits beyond which horses, mules, and sheep cannot be kept. Those inhospitable regions in which the arctic dog sledge is the chief means of transport begin at a latitude of 55° north in eastern America, but in Norway they do not start till 70° north.

All the climatic effects that make life easier, that are needed for the production of food and the accumulation of wealth, are brought by the Gulf Stream to uniquely blessed western Europe. There is no doubt whatever that this region developed its civilization before eastern America solely because of the effects of the Gulf Stream.

We can clearly see the influence of climate if we use the methods of measurement that have been developed by climatologists. They are simple and easily understood. The characteristic value is that of the air temperature adjusted to sea level to eliminate the effect of the surface profile. A distinction is made between daily values, obtained through direct readings, and mean monthly and annual values, calculated by averaging the daily values. The mean monthly and annual values are particularly suitable for our purposes. They are a useful means of categorizing various climates, and provide valuable information about the global distribution of air temperatures.

Drawing a line to connect up all those places with the same mean annual temperature gives an isotherm (Greek iso = the same, therme = heat). The course of these isotherms provides direct information about patterns of climate. This is what is needed to answer the question of how the Gulf Stream affects the climate of northwestern Europe. Figure 10 shows the isotherms of the North Atlantic region. As expected, their general direction follows the Gulf Stream, and the mean annual air temperature rises spectacularly from west to east.

This general law is strikingly illustrated by the 32° F (0° C) isotherm, shown on the map. As its name indicates, it links the places whose mean annual temperature coincides with the freezing point of water. Its course is of special interest in the context of our subject.

The 32° F (0° C) isotherm leaves the east coast of America at the latitude of about 50° north, cutting across Newfoundland. There it reaches the vicinity of the Gulf Stream, which pushes it abruptly northward across the southern tip of Greenland. It crosses the Scandinavian peninsula at increasing latitudes and not until it is within the Arctic Circle, at about 75° north, does it at last turn sharply southward.

This pronounced bulge of the 32° F (0° C) isotherm far into the north above northwestern Europe clearly shows the privileged one-sided position given this area by the Gulf Stream.

What would happen if the Gulf Stream suddenly failed? It would mean that the climate of northwestern Europe would undergo a radical change. The climate would become the normal one for that latitude. The isotherms would run from west to east more or less parallel to the lines of latitude as they do in North America and Asia. The 32° F (0° C) isotherm would run between the latitudes of 45° and 50° north. The northward bulge of the 32° F (0° C) isotherm would disappear, and with it the climate that northwestern Europe enjoys. Such a drastic change in climate as measured by the course of the 32° F (0° C) isotherm is offered only as a hypothesis. But if the climatic conditions postulated by such a change could in fact be shown to have occurred, that could be regarded as evidence that the Gulf Stream was not flowing along northwestern Europe.

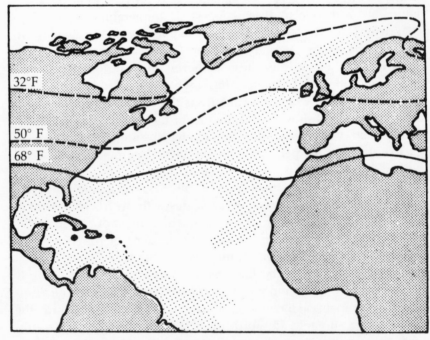

Fig. 10. Isotherm pattern of the North Atlantic today. The North Atlantic isotherm pattern is represented by the 32°, 50° and 68° F (0°, 10°, and 20°C) isotherms. The last-named follows the main body of the Gulf Stream, then the African branch returning to the South, and finally crosses the Atlas on the North African coast. The 50° F (10° C) isotherm roughly follows the British branch; the 32° F (0° C) isotherm outlines the marginal effect of the northern branch. Result: the isotherm pattern is entirely determined by the Gulf Stream.

The blue waters of the Gulf Stream are most certainly responsible for the climatic fate of northwestern Europe. It is possible that the course of the isotherms will provide the key to the problem. The trail leads from the Atlantic of the present day back to the Atlantic of the remote past, far beyond the few thousand years of our recorded history.

The Gulf Stream and
the Quaternary Era

THE CAUSAL RELATIONSHIP between the favorable climate of northwestern Europe and the unobstructed flow of the Gulf Stream across the Atlantic is fully confirmed. As long as the waters of the Gulf Stream continue to reach them, these comparatively high latitudes will continue to enjoy the same mild climate and high mean annual temperature that they have enjoyed throughout recorded history.

But the possibility remains that in earlier epochs the climate of this region was much colder and more inclement. We must turn to the paleoclimatologists for help in the next stage of our search.

Has there at any time been a sharp fall in the temperature of northwestern Europe? If so, could this—taking into account our knowledge of climatic conditions—be accounted for by the failure of the Gulf Stream to reach its shores? Could it be stated with certainty that this was the cause of the drop in temperature? Is it possible to determine at what period the change took place?

Scientists of many disciplines have successfully collaborated to give a picture, vivid both in outline and in detail, of the climatic changes that have taken place during the recent history of the Earth.

The outlines and characteristics of the different epochs have been determined by geologists and paleontologists working on fossils. Infinite care has been taken in their dating. The contributions of the Swedish research workers, de Geer and Sernander, deserve special mention. Pollen analysis has established a valuable basis for determining the nature of the dominant plant life of the different epochs, and from this conclusions can be drawn about their pattern of climate.

The following brief table does not claim to be complete—for this would be outside the scope of our present inquiries—but it does claim to be accurate.

THE CLIMATE OF THE PREHISTORIC ERA

Period	Sub-period	Beginning about	Type of climate
	Present	2000 B.C.	decreasing warmth
Quinternary	Postglacial	5000 B.C.	optimum climate
	Epiglacial	10,000 B.C.	sub-boreal (raw, cold)
Quaternary	Würmglacial	20,000 B.C.	typically glacial

To give life to this dry table we must take a journey back into the past.

We move quickly through the Iron Age into the "good old days" of the Bronze Age—designated good on account of its climate, if for no other reason. The Europe of that time was covered with a green blanket of oak, beech, and hazel forests that extended far up to the north. In this green landscape the advanced civilizations of the Hallstatt period had their heyday. It is probable that Europe owed its cultural flowering to this wonderfully mild climate.

Next is the Neolithic period, blessed with the best possible climate, of which the paradise of the Bronze Age was only a pale shadow. It was not by chance that the sudden flowering of early European civilization coincided with this most favorable of climates. Splendid forests, abounding with animal life, grew everywhere. Men had a wide variety of food from which to choose. The kitchen refuse dumps of the Kjoekenmoedding are evidence of this. The geologists have named this subperiod the Litorina after its predominant fossil, the marine snail *Litoria litorina,* which is typical of the associated deposits in the Baltic Sea.

Going back farther, the golden green oak gives way to the somber pine, birch, and aspen. The climate is less hospitable. Still another step leads to the cold, sub-boreal phase of the Epiglacial period. This has been called the Yoldia period after its leading fossil, the arctic marine shellfish *Yoldia arctica.* The birch has vanished. Where, in our journey back through time, we saw lush, green oak forests growing under a warm sun, we now see no trees but stunted polar osiers. There are white dryas flowers on the edges of the retreating snowfields, and moorland and pools as far as the eye can see. The dryas can survive on little light, but they only flourish during the brief four-month growing period. Everywhere there is scarcity and stunted growth instead of luxuriant abundance, tundra instead of forests and flowers. In the distance gleams a white wall of ice that appears to be advancing from the north, threatening the last vestiges of life with extinction.

The farther our journey takes us into the Earth's past, the more immense this glittering sheet of ice becomes. It advances southward and covers Scandinavia. It forms a frozen bridge across the belt of north Europe; it thrusts out inexorable tentacles of ice that bury Slesvig in north Germany, and Ireland and Britain as far as the southwestern corner of Wales, under a solid blanket hundreds of yards thick. North America presents the same picture. On both sides of the Atlantic there is only ice, nothing but ice. Northwestern Europe does not enjoy a better climate than northeastern America. We have journeyed back to an era in Earth's history when our present beneficent climatic conditions in northwestern Europe did not exist.

The climatic advantages in northwestern Europe are caused by the Gulf Stream. The absence of these advantages may provide us with evidence of the reason why the Gulf Stream failed to flow. It becomes a distinct possibility that during the time when northwestern Europe did not enjoy a privileged climate in comparison with North America, the Gulf Stream might really have been blocked by a barrier somewhere in the Atlantic, which prevented it from reaching the west coast of Europe.

What do we now see if we halt our journey back in time? We are at the transition stage between the Quinternary and Quaternary eras (also called the Pleistocene, Diluvial, or—less happily—the Ice Age or Glacial period), the threshold between the fourth and fifth geological eras. We have entered a strange world. Ice covers the earth; a limitless expanse under a hazy, overcast sky, with no horizon in sight . . .

> First was the time when Ymir raged,
> Sand was not yet, nor sea, nor salty wave,
> I found no earth beneath nor sky above,
> All was a gaping void—and grass nowhere . . .(Völuspá)

The geologists call this epoch the Würm Glacial Period. It was the fourth and last of the successive advances of ice which alternated with warmer periods. Throughout this epoch northwestern Europe enjoyed no climatic advantages over eastern America.

This statement is sufficient for our investigations. We have shown that during the Quaternary era there was a connection between the climate of northwestern Europe and the course of the Gulf Stream. This book is not a geological or paleoclimateological textbook. It does not pretend to provide extensive information about climatic fluctuations in prehistoric times. Whether climatic conditions were due to astronomical causes such as a variation in the plane of the Earth's orbit, a motion of the apse, a change in the obliquity of the ecliptic, or whether they were due to cosmic factors, such as the passage through a dark nebula, are questions that will not be dealt with here.

It is enough to state that during the Quaternary Age of the Earth there was about the same cover of ice to the east and the west of the Atlantic. Both continents were buried under huge ice caps that occasionally reached as far as latitude 50° north. This is the vital point. The location of the fluctuating boundary between the icebound and the ice-free regions is immaterial. The limits of glaciation have left their most prominent signs in the form of piled-up debris of rock. This is known as the belt of terminal moraines, and its position is firmly established. It runs across the New and the Old Worlds, roughly parallel to the latitude. A corresponding boundary between the open sea and the pack ice runs across the North Atlantic.

Figure 11 shows its approximate position. During the periods of extreme glaciation it ran between the latitudes of 45 ° and 50 ° north, but it is not so much the precise latitude as the general course of these limits of glaciation that is of vital interest.

This course corresponds unmistakably to the course of the isotherms in a "normal" climatic situation: that is, a climatic situation that is not subject to the influence of the Gulf Stream.

What is the significance of the correspondence between the line of the isotherm and the line of the limits of glaciation?

Permanent sheets of ice could persist only where the mean annual temperature of the air remained below the freezing point and where the annual fluctuations of temperature remained small. The mean annual air temperature must have been higher than 32 ° F (0 ° C) where the permanently ice-free region begins.

It is legitimate to make this assumption, because in the regions with which we are concerned—northwestern Europe and North America—the change from ice-capped land to ice-free land took place very gradually. In other regions, for example in the Andes of South America, thick glacier ice may have moved over steep precipices and extended far into the warmer areas. In these instances we cannot associate the 32 ° F (0 ° C) isotherm with the limits of glaciation. Even in the case of our own region, however, it must be stressed that the limits of glaciation in the Quaternary era can only be taken as a rough guide to the course of the 32 ° F (0 ° C) isotherm during that period. It is very possible that in some places masses of land ice advanced beyond the 32 ° F (0 ° C) line and in other places remained short of it. But it is a fair assumption that the permanent ice sheet came to an end where the mean annual air temperature was close to the melting point of ice. Obviously this does not enable us to draw a sharp boundary line, but what matters is not the exact location of the ice boundary, but its general course and that of the 32 ° F (0 ° C) isotherm associated with it. This general course can, and has been, determined by the remains of the Quaternary terminal moraines which are still extant.

Terminal moraines are always to be found piled up in front of the extreme limit of the ice sheet, along the boundary between glaciation and green land, which runs roughly between the isotherms above

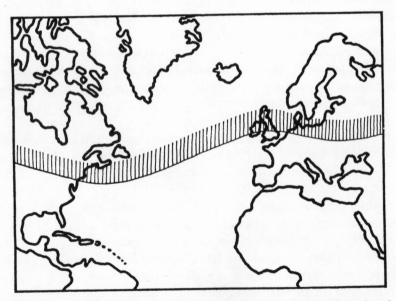

Fig. 11. The limits of glaciation during the Quaternary Age. The belts of terminal moraines found in Canada and Europe indicate the southern limit of the advance of the inland ice sheets, which reached about the same latitude on both sides of the Atlantic. It clearly shows that during the Quaternary period northwestern Europe did not enjoy a better climate than northeastern America.

32 ° F (0 ° C) and those below. There were frequent changes of climate in the Quaternary Age. Glacial periods alternated with interglacial and interstadial eras. Every fluctuation in climate resulted in a correlated shift in isotherms. When we speak of Quaternary isotherms, therefore, we must state whether we are referring to those of the glacial or of the interglacial periods. The most typical climate of the Quaternary epoch is glacial and the most typical isotherms are those of maximum glaciation. For the purposes of our investigation, we will use the term "Quaternary isotherms" for the isotherms of maximum glaciation. The course of these isotherms, and in particular the course of the 32 ° F (0 ° C) isotherm reconstructed from the belt of the southernmost terminal moraines, provides us with a sufficiently accurate and detailed picture of the pattern of the diluvial climate.

From this we may draw conclusions about the Quaternary climate in the same way that we may draw conclusions about the Quinternary, present-day climate from the course of the Quinternary 32 ° F (0 ° C) isotherms.

We are now in a position to compare the isothermal pattern of the two epochs.

Figure 11 shows the course of the Quaternary 32 ° F (0 ° C) isotherm within the glaciation limits. The course is radically different from that of the present 32 ° F (0 ° C) isotherm; it lacks that highly typical northward "bulge."

For ease of comparison, Figure 12 shows both isotherms on one map, and from this it can be seen that there is a striking difference between the climates of these two epochs in the Earth's history. This diagram shows at a glance that throughout the Quaternary epoch the northwest of Europe did not enjoy the favorable climate that it does today; like northeastern America at that era, it was buried under an enormous sheet of land ice.

The favorable climatic position of northwestern Europe is a result of the Gulf Stream. The absence of this climatic advantage during the Quaternary epoch implies that the Gulf Stream was unlikely to have reached Europe during this whole long period. It is hardly conceivable that there can be any question of error here. Ireland in the Quaternary epoch was an arctic, inhospitable country covered by a sheet of ice. Today, with the Gulf Stream washing its shores, the winters are mild and even semitropical. There is a remarkable and undeniable difference between the Quaternary and the Quinternary

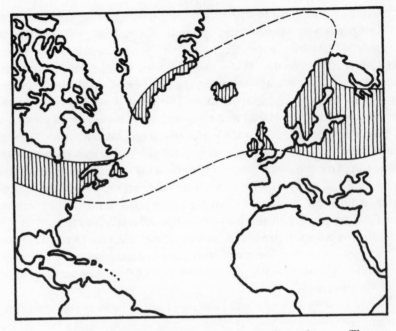

Fig. 12. Quaternary and Quinternary 32° F (0° C) isotherms. The upper, Quinternary, 32° F (0° C) isotherm, the same as in Fig. 10, exhibits its typical "bulge." Equally typically this bulge is absent from the lower Quaternary 32° F (0° C) isotherm, the same as in Fig. 11. The hatched land areas, especially northwestern Europe, are the beneficiaries of the Gulf Stream. This is clear evidence that the Gulf Stream cannot have reached Northwest Europe at any time during the Quaternary era.

patterns of climate. It constitutes virtually incontestable proof that the Gulf Stream, to which Ireland owes its name of the Emerald Isle, cannot have existed then.

If the marked change in climate cannot be challenged, it may still be questioned whether it was due to a cause other than the existence of the Gulf Stream. The nonexistence of the Gulf Stream does not, in itself, explain the origin of the enormous sheets of ice in Canada and Scandinavia, and the oddly periodical fluctuation of the ice cover. There can be no doubt that other terrestrial as well as cosmic factors contributed to these events. Figure 12 does not claim to illustrate all the problems of the Ice Age. It is concerned only with one part of the problem. Setting aside all other contributory factors, can it be maintained that the specific form and extent of the diluvial glaciation of northwest Europe follows solely from the nonexistence of the Gulf Stream?

Any other possible factors, whether terrestrial or cosmic, that contributed to glaciation must have had one feature in common. They must have affected the isotherm pattern of the entire northern hemisphere and not just of a part of it. Let us take the possibility of a general drop in temperature caused, perhaps, by the Earth passing through a dark nebula that absorbed and attenuated the sun's radiation. Such an event would have resulted in a parallel southward shift of all the isotherms of the northern hemisphere. A partial cooling of the northern hemisphere owing to some other cosmic cause must have had precisely the same effect on the pattern of isotherms. Suppose that the Gulf Stream reached northwestern Europe during the Ice Age in the same manner as it does today. It would then be easy enough to reconstruct the Quaternary pattern of isotherms for this hypothetical case.

Figure 13 illustrates the Quaternary pattern which has been obtained by a southward shift of the Quinternary isotherms. The 32 ° F (0 ° C) isotherm exhibits that typical northward bulge except that it has suffered a 10 ° southward shift because of the assumed partial drop in temperature.

This purely hypothetical course of the Quaternary 32 ° F (0 ° C) isotherm would also have determined the position of the glaciation belts and the walls of the terminal moraines. In North America these would be roughly between latitudes 40° and 45° north. Glaciation in northwestern Europe would not have extended beyond 65 ° north. The British Isles, and Norway up to the latitude of Trondheim and Namsos, would have remained ice-free. In fact, the ice sheet covered the whole of the British Isles and the continent almost up to the latitude of present-day Berlin. The existence and the extent of this ice sheet can be proved beyond question by the moraines that it left behind. It is also equally certain that terrestrial or cosmic factors contributing to glaciation would not, in themselves, be sufficient to explain the absence of the temperate weather now enjoyed by northwestern Europe—an advantage that can be seen from the pattern of isotherms in the northeastern Atlantic whenever the Gulf Stream flows but is absent when it doesn't. There are other plausible possibilities for explaining this marked characteristic.

The only possible explanation for the true position of the glaciation limit in northwestern Europe is the absence of the Gulf Stream during the entire Quaternary epoch. Only the failure of these warm waters to reach Europe could have led to the Scandinavian icecap—which could still have formed even had the Gulf Stream arrived—spreading right across the British Isles and northwestern Europe.

So the absence during the Quaternary epoch of the advantageous position enjoyed by northwestern Europe today could have been due to the nonexistence of the Gulf Stream at that time. What have the paleogeographers to say to this?

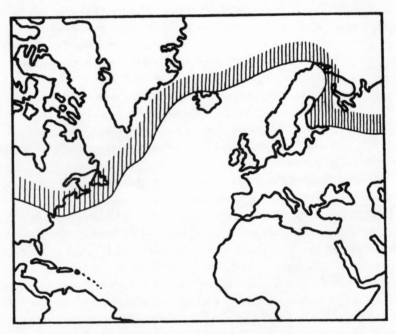

Fig. 13. A paleoclimatological objection refuted. Could the glaciation of Northwest Europe have been caused by a general global or cosmic event rather than by the absence of the Gulf Stream? The Quaternary 32° F (0° C) isotherm then would have run about 10° farther south parallel to the present one. The glaciation limits would have been as shown in the illustration, and the British Isles and Norway ice-free. The comparison with the actual limits of glaciation (Fig. 11) shows that these could be established only in the absence of the Gulf Stream. It follows that the Gulf Stream could not have reached Northwest Europe during the Quaternary Age.

The Gulf Stream is a seawater drift that has been set in motion by the trade winds. These winds are the direct results of the loose coupling between the rotating Earth and its encircling air. There is no doubt that the Earth rotated during the Quaternary period. Nor is there any doubt that the trade winds blew then just as they blow today, the easterly trades in the lower latitudes, the westerly trades in the higher. The circulation of water caused by the trade winds and shown in Figure 8 is also valid for the Quaternary epoch. Then, as now, warm tropical water was driven westward and in the northern section of the cycle the drift water was deflected first northward and then toward the east, reaching Europe via the east coast of North America. The Stream is as old as the Atlantic.

There is not the slightest reason to suppose that there was no water separating Europe and America during the Quaternary epoch. In all probability the sea opened at the beginning of the Tertiary era when the large platforms, for whatever reason, drifted apart. Certainly by the end of the Quaternary era the large platforms were in a very similar position to that of today. They began to drift, and largely ceased to drift, during the preceding era, the Tertiary. The Atlantic of the Quaternary age, like the Atlantic of today, extended from the North to the South Polar Sea and was bordered on both sides by continental platforms. Then, as now, warm tropical waters were driven westward by the trade winds; then, as now, the northeastern tip of Brazil diverted the greater part of these drifting waters into the North Atlantic and guided them toward Central America. And here, too, most of the geotectonic structure had long been completed. Extensive covers of lava indicate that this probably took place during the early Tertiary era. The structural basins between the mainland and the arc of the Antilles were probably also formed during that period as a result of the enormous pressure exerted by the platforms. The Quaternary Gulf Stream would have followed a similar course to the Gulf Stream today.

But let us assume that the Gulf of Mexico, which today reaches a depth of 10,000 feet (3000 m), was not in existence at that time, and that the east coast of America was formed by what is now the Antilles. The stream of warm tropical water would only have suffered a minor parallel displacement to the east. It would still have come from Pernambuco and its main body would have continued to the north—not, as today, to the south—of the Antilles. The Gulf Stream would have been the Antilles Stream. The shallow zone between the

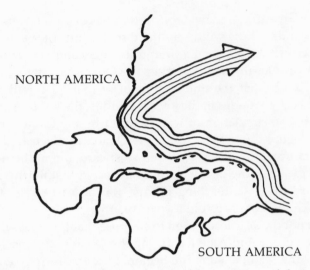

NORTH AMERICA

SOUTH AMERICA

Fig. 14. Antilles current instead of Gulf Stream? Even if the structural basin of the Caribbean and of the Gulf of Mexico, presumably formed in the Early Tertiary, had still existed at the end of the Quaternary Age, an approximately equivalent Gulf Stream would have been produced along the arc of the Lesser Antilles and the Bahamas and flowed eastwards into the Atlantic.

Antilles and the Bahamas would have taken the place of the Gulf of Mexico. The current would have been deflected in the bay immediately north of Florida. Figure 14 shows how these slightly modified conditions would have affected the current. The tropical waters would still have had the chance to have become even warmer and more saline and would still have flowed into the gray North Atlantic as a great blue salty band.

A detailed investigation into the orogenetic conditions of the Antilles arc has recently been carried out. This has provided reliable evidence that the structural basins of the Caribbean and of the Gulf of Mexico originated during the Pliocene era, the last phase of the Tertiary epoch. In the Quaternary epoch, the oceanographic situation in the region where the Gulf Stream originates was very much the same as it is today, with one exception. This exception is the general lowering of the level of the sea during the Quaternary Age as a result of the absorption of a large volume of water by the polar ice caps. But even this drop of about 300 feet (90 m) had no noticeable effect.

It is likely, however, that the Atlantic Ocean was not quite as wide as it is today. The Gulf Stream would therefore have had a shorter distance to cross and its waters would have been even warmer than they are today when they reach Europe. These two factors might well have canceled each other out. The effect of the Gulf Stream on the climate of northwestern Europe would not have been weaker in the Quaternary age than it is in the Quinternary. If, indeed, the Gulf Stream ever arrived at northwestern Europe at all.

The glaciation of western Europe shows that it did not arrive.

And yet there is no doubt at all that a southerly and a northerly trade wind drift existed throughout the whole Quaternary epoch. And there is no doubt that warm tropical waters flowed along the coasts of Brazil, Central America, and North America up to the latitude of the prevailing west winds. Therefore it follows that the Gulf Stream entered the North Atlantic and flowed eastward across it along the latitude of 40° north in the wake of the west wind during the Quaternary Age as it does in our own era.

But it never arrived off Europe, at the other side of the Atlantic. What happened to it? Surely we can only conclude that somewhere in the middle of the Atlantic its path was blocked and it was deflected from its course.

We have at last arrived at something that provides a very solid basis for further inquiries.

Echo from the Atlantic

OUR SEARCH FOR EVIDENCE has yielded a sensational result. A current mightier than that of all the rivers on Earth combined flowed during an entire geological era into the Atlantic but not out of it. It did not lose itself in the Atlantic as the river Tarim loses itself in the arid zone of Central Asia. There can be only one satisfactory explanation for its failure to reach the west coast of Europe: it encountered a material obstacle on the way; a sizable, solid barrier blocked it, deflected it, perhaps even turned it back.

Where could this barrier to the flow of the Gulf Stream have been situated?

The map of the ocean shows that it no longer exists on the surface. This tallies with the fact that as a result of its disappearance after the Würm (Wisconsin) Glacial epoch there was a radical change in the climate of northwestern Europe. It was then that the Gulf Stream arrived for the first time. For the first time the coasts of northwest Europe were bathed in warm water, and the warm, rain-bearing winds began to erode the land ice and force it gradually back to Gotland. The barrier that had previously blocked the passage of the warm water and the rain-bearing winds to Europe must somewhere and somehow have disappeared at this time.

Not long after it veers away from the east coast of North America, the Gulf Stream attains the formidable width of 370–500 miles (600–800 km). To block it effectively, the barrier must have been 500–620 miles (800–1000 km) long, measured at right angles to the current. The Gulf Stream flows in a generally easterly direction; presumably the barrier ran from north to south. It must have been an enormous mass rising from the bottom of the sea to above the surface. We cannot yet say how wide it might have been. Let us assume a length of about 620 miles (1000 km) a width of perhaps 248 miles (400 km)

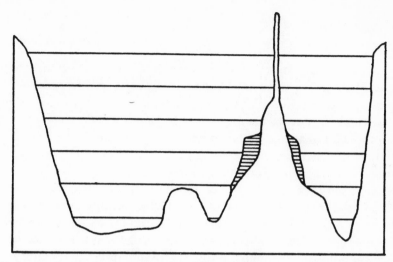

Fig. 15. Relief of the Atlantic seabed (cross section at 40° N), elevation 600 × (1 cm = ⅝ mile = 1 km). From left to right: North American mainland, Atlantic Ridge (in the hatched background the submarine land mass), Spanish basin, continent of southern Europe.

and a depth of something under 2 miles (3 km) down to the bottom of the sea. The volume would then be well over 240,000 cubic miles (1 million cu. km). Such a mass of solid material cannot possibly have dissolved; it cannot have disappeared without trace. Recognizable remains must still be in existence somewhere. Where else but on the bottom of the Atlantic Ocean beneath the area crossed by the Gulf Stream? Let us look at the seabed of the Atlantic. The oceanographers provide some exact and detailed information.

Figure 15 shows a simplified section of the basin of the northern part of the Atlantic emptied of its water. The Atlantic consists of a huge basin, about 9900 miles (16,000 km) long and on average 3400 miles (5500 km) wide. It covers an area of 38 million square miles (98 million sq. km) and contains 84 million cubic miles (350 million cu. km) of water weighing more than 3×10^{17} tonnes. Of this unimaginable volume of water the Gulf Stream forms only a part.

Throughout the last hundred years oceanographers have been keenly interested in measuring the depths in the Atlantic and assessing the profile of the seabed. Vast sums of money have been spent, and great effort has gone into this research. The history of this sector of deep sea exploration makes fascinating reading.

It began with a Swedish expedition that was launched about 1860. Its sounding equipment was very primitive compared with that of today. Wyville Thomson and William Benjamin Carpenter continued the investigations with a typically British systematic approach. Their ancient, rather ramshackle little ship *Lightning* was very nearly lost in the process. But their efforts attracted the attention of their government, who provided them with a powerful, seaworthy vessel, the *Porcupine*. Their results encouraged other explorers, and in 1872 the famous *Challenger* expedition set out on a voyage that was to total 8000 miles. It took 370 soundings and 255 temperature measurements and carried out 129 trawls. A surprising fact came to light from these first precise and systematic investigations. The floor of the Atlantic is not level but exhibits a marked relief. The simplified diagram in Figure 15 gives a rough idea of this relief.

Later voyages were made by the British *Hydra*, the U.S. *Dolphin* and *Gettysburg*, the German *Gazelle* and *Meteor*, among others. Innumerable data were collected, from which a useful overall picture emerged. *Meteor* alone took more than 10,000 echo soundings in accordance with Behm's method. H. Stock's comprehensive report, *The Scientific Results of the German Atlantic Expedition 1935*, reveals that the huge basin of the Atlantic is divided into two parts by a very long, massive submarine ridge extending from Iceland in the north to the Antarctic shelf in the south. The western basin has an average depth of 21,000 feet (6500 m), the eastern basin of 15,000 feet (4500 m). Occasionally there are depths exceeding 23,000 feet (7000 m).

The ridge between the two basins has been named the "Dolphin's Back" in honor of the U.S. survey ship *Dolphin*, but it is also known as the "Atlantic Ridge," or, less aptly, the "Atlantic Plateau." It rises on average about 9000 feet (2750 m) from the seabed. Figure 15 shows a section—very simplified and grossly exaggerated in elevation— through the North Atlantic at about the latitude of 40° north. It reveals a structure of surprising width—about 186–248 miles (300–400 km) at the 13,000 feet (4000 m) level of depth, which looks like a submarine folded mountain range.

In one place, at about 30° west and 40° north, this ridge widens out into a strange structure, a huge sunken landmass which has the appearance of a great submarine mountain. Figure 15 shows it clearly in section, and a glance at the map also reveals this complex. Out of it rise sharp peaks that pierce the surface of the sea and appear as land. These peaks are the Azores, and some of them, the Pico Alto for instance, reach a height of up to 20,000 feet (6000 m). Some are active volcanoes, others are extinct.

This land under the sea is called the Azores Plateau and it is of vital importance to our investigation because it is situated just south of the present path of the Gulf Stream. The majestic eastward flow of this mighty current is today virtually unimpeded, because the tiny islands offer very little obstruction.

This is the only region where the Gulf Stream crosses the Atlantic Ridge. Perhaps it is no coincidence that the ridge is noticeably broader here. Furthermore, the seabed is very near the surface of the sea at this point. Here is the focal point of our investigations. Here ends the trail that began in the Gulf Stream. We followed it through the pattern of Atlantic isotherms, through the glaciation limits during the Quaternary epoch, and on through the hypothesis of a diluvial barrier island in the Atlantic and have finally come to this unique spot.

Making a leap of the imagination let us assume that for some reason or other the level of the North Atlantic suddenly drops by 10,000 feet (3000 m), and that we are able to watch this happening from a aircraft. What can we see?

At this spot, and at this spot only, there emerges a huge landmass with high mountains and steep cliffs. It rises up in the very place where the Gulf Stream flows over the Atlantic Ridge. The waters break against the slightly curved western coast of this big island that has risen from the sea. They can go no further. They send up huge showers of spray and then retreat, eddying in a wide arc around the Sargasso Sea and flowing westward. Figure 16 shows their course.

It is, perhaps, not the entire current of the Gulf Stream that is so deflected, but only the greater part of it. Some of the warmer waters will perhaps flow around the northern tip of this barrier island, thereby shifting slightly northward the cold Labrador current from the west. But the Gulf Stream as we know it, with its warm water and its warm humid air, does not reach to the north and east of this island barrier. Northwestern Europe does not feel the moderating oceanic effect; it is no longer protected from the bitter cold of the continental climate. There comes an era of intense glaciation, and this region, like North America at the same latitude, is shrouded in ice.

This actually occurred during the fourth, or Quaternary, geological age. Figure 16 does not represent a mere hypothetical situation, but actually reconstructs the situation in the North Atlantic at that time. The "Barrier Island X" that took shape in our imagination is this real barrier island in the Atlantic. And at the end of the Quaternary era this real barrier island became the submarine massif on the Atlantic Ridge.

We have found the object of our search.

In order to avoid all possible misunderstanding, we must emphasize that this imaginary description of the emergence of the submerged barrier island has only been used as an experimental model. Professor Pettersson in *Atlantis and the Atlantic*, uses the same illustrative method. But neither in that book nor in this is there any suggestion that this Atlantic barrier island actually emerged as a result of a lowering of the sea level and disappeared again when the level rose. In fact it was the opposite that happened. The level of the sea has remained more or less the same. It was the ocean floor, together with the island platform that it supported, that sank. This island platform, therefore, became the submerged Azores Plateau of today.

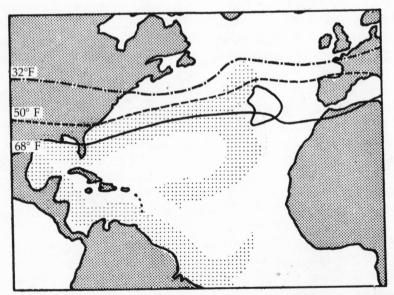

Fig. 16. Gulf Stream and isotherm pattern in the diluvian North Atlantic. The isotherms are generally parallel to the latitudes. It was the island of Atlantis, not western and northwestern Europe, as today, that enjoyed a better climate than the east coast of America.

We can confidently repeat the statement: in the region of the Azores we have found the only place in which a former island, now a submarine massif, could have blocked and deflected the flow of the Gulf Stream.

Figure 16 shows how the Quaternary isotherm pattern was influenced by the presence of Barrier Island X in the Atlantic. The 32° F (0° C) isotherm runs roughly parallel to the latitudes. It leaves the northeast of America at about 45° north, gradually turns northward following the course of the Gulf Stream, and forms a slight bulge where the weak northern branch of the warm current struggles to hold its own against the cold waters of the Labrador current. At a point about 30° west the isotherm reaches 50° north, and here it remains, all the way eastward toward the ice-covered west coast of Europe. This Quaternary limit of glaciation has been theoretically reconstructed in conformity with the location of the terminal moraine walls. The reconstructed climatic pattern fully corresponds to the actual situation in the Quaternary era. The total glaciation of northwestern Europe presupposes the existence of an Atlantic barrier island blocking the flow of the Gulf Stream.

This much is certain and it is vital to the solution of our problem. Here we have evidence that during the entire Quaternary Age there was a great landmass of about 154,400 square miles (400,000 sq. km) in area in the region of the Azores, which lay in the path of the Gulf Stream and deflected the greater part of its waters westward.

For some reason this landmass sank about 2 miles (3 km), causing the broadening of the Atlantic Ridge below the sea and no longer being visible above the surface. When was it that this barrier to the Gulf Stream became submerged?

This question is no longer very difficult to answer. The barrier existed during the Quaternary Age and came to an end with the end of that era. So the sinking of Barrier Island X is contemporaneous with the end of the Quaternary or Diluvial Age. *Nomen est omen.* It is the very history of the Earth itself that creates the identity between the catastrophic end of the barrier island and the diluvium—the deluge.

We can be reasonably sure about the time when the Earth moved from the fourth into the fifth geological age. Until very recently, however, subjective estimates have been more plentiful than objective assessments. The views of the geologists differ considerably from those of the paleontologists. If we take as large a number as possible of reliable individual estimates and obtain their mean value, this will give us a fair idea of the prevailing views of contemporary experts. The table below lists eight well-authenticated values in order of magnitude. They range between 20,000 and 8000 years. The sum of the eight estimates is 103,000 years and the mean value is 12,875 years.

END OF THE GLACIAL PERIOD

Author	Object	Years ago
Lugeon	Erosion of the Rhone Gorge	20,000
Heim	Deposits in Lake Lucerne	16,000
Stock	Formation of the Aare Delta	15,000
Lewis Pence	Deep sea lava in the Azores region	13,000
J. Hug	Silting up of the basin between Lakes Zurich and Walensee	12,000
Brückner	Deposits in the Lütschine Delta	10,000
Woodward	Recession of the Niagara Falls	9000
Winchel	Displacement of the Mississippi	8000

This mean value agrees remarkably with what is currently the most popular "optimum" value of 12,000 years. It was obtained by de Geer, who estimated the time separating the Quinternary epoch from the present day by counting the bands in the Swedish varved clay. De Geer's optimum differs from our mean value by just under eight percent. An element of uncertainty can never be eliminated from this sort of investigation, and if this is allowed for, then the agreement between the mean value and the optimum value can be regarded as very satisfactory.

If we then date the transition from the Quaternary to the Quinternary Age at 12,000 years ago, or around 10,000 B.C., we are doing so on the authority of contemporary geologists and paleontologists. We are at the same time fixing the date when Barrier Island X, which had hitherto prevented the Gulf Stream from reaching the coasts of Europe, sank beneath the Atlantic.

So we have come to a point in time that marks the end of one geological age and the beginning of the next; when the land ice sheet began to melt and retreat; when the warm water and rain-bearing winds brought by the Gulf Stream were no longer deflected back to the west by the Atlantic island barrier, but flowed freely eastward because the barrier had sunk beneath the waves.

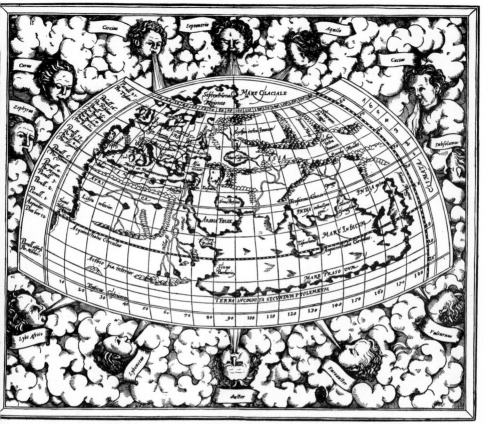

Plate 2. Ptolemy's map of the world in the Middle Ages (according to
the *Cosmographia* by Sebastian Münster 1540) shows the "Old World,"
still quite similar to the ancient Ecumene, as one half of the Earth's
sphere, no longer as a flat disk.

Plate 3. Maps of Atlantis. *Top:* Sebastian Münster (1540) identified the "Insula Atlantica" with the recently discovered South American continent. *Bottom:* Athanasius Kircher in his *Mundus Subterraneus* (1678) located the sunken island of Atlantis in the Atlantic, near the Azores.

Plate 4. Figments of the imagination: maps of the island of Atlantis. *Top:* The modern Greek writer I. Kampanakis drew the island of Atlantis as a submerged "bridge continent" between the Old and the New Worlds. *Bottom:* Dr. Paul Schliemann, a grandson of the discoverer of Troy, placed the lost continent of Atlantis on the "Dolphin's Back" in 1912.

Plate 5. Step temples on both sides of the Atlantic. *Top:* Reconstruction of the Marduk temple in Babylon (about 600 B.C.) with the Temple of the Convocation (Esagila) on the left and the stage tower (Etemenanki) in the walled temple courtyard. *Bottom:* Reconstruction of the temple complex of Copán (Honduras), about A.D. 200–500. The "relationship" between this Maya temple and the Marduk temple in Babylon is striking. The stage tower could have been brought to Mesopotamia and Mesoamerica by the intermediary of the more ancient Atlantean civili-

Plate 6. Step pyramids in Egypt and Mexico. *Top:* The famous Step Pyramid of Sakkara built by King Djoser (Third Dynasty) about 2900 B.C. It was once the center of a huge walled temple complex. *Bottom:* The sun pyramid of Teotihuacan is the purest example of the architecture of the step pyramids in Mexico; they could be climbed from outside like the Chaldean stage towers.

Plate 7. Top: The step Temple of the Inscriptions at Palenque resembles the Egyptian pyramids not only outwardly but also in that it housed a royal tomb, in which among other items a superb jade mask was found (Plate 9). *Bottom:* Temple towers in South India.

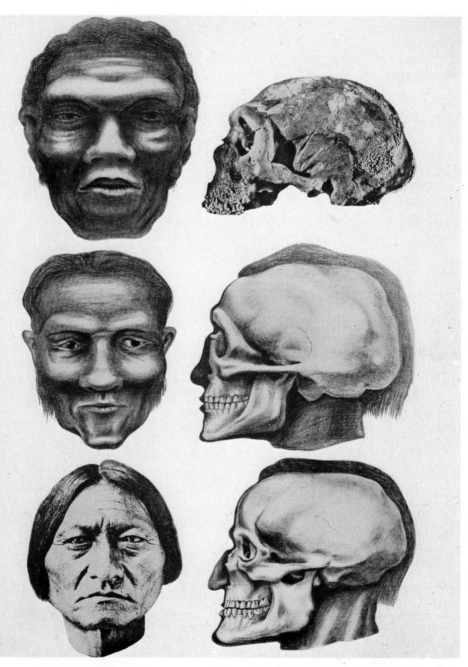

Plate 8. Reconstruction of the Ice Age types of man: *Top:* Neanderthal man, representative of the Lower Paleolithic civilization. *Middle:* Aurignac man, beginning of the Upper Paleolithic Age. Presumably a type that immigrated from the East (pre-mongoloid?) (Brünn or loess hunter race). *Bottom:* Cro-Magnon man. Distributed first in western, later in central and northern Europe during the Upper Paleolithic Age. Somatic resemblance between the Cro-Magnon skull (right) and the recent Red Indian head (left: head of the Sioux Chief Sitting Bull).

Plate 9. The jade mask from the royal tomb in the Temple of the Inscriptions at Palenque.

Plate 10. This young Basque could be a great-grandson of the man with the jade mask (Plate 9). The bold outline of the typically aquiline nose, the expression of the eyes, and the shape and position of the mouth are strictly comparable.

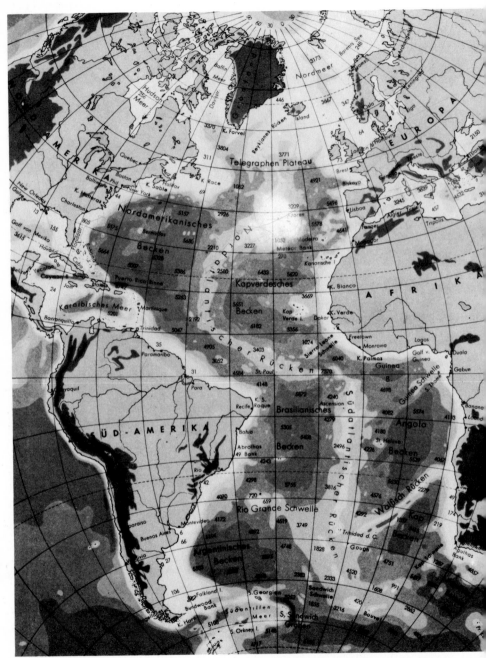

Plate 11. This depth chart of the Atlantic clearly shows the North and South Atlantic Ridge, with its typical broadening, the Azores Plateau, the sunken landmass of the large island of Atlantis.

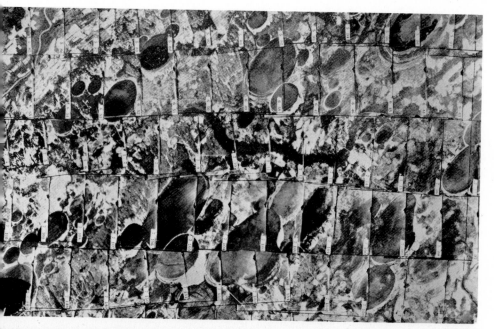

Plate 12. Top: The aerial photograph of the impact of the Carolina Meteorite (according to D. W. Johnson) shows a typical section of the crater field, with many peatified, partly overlapping impact craters. A document of vital importance to the reconstruction of the Atlantic catastrophe. Bottom: The huge meteorite crater of Arizona, perhaps caused by a satellite of Asteroid A.

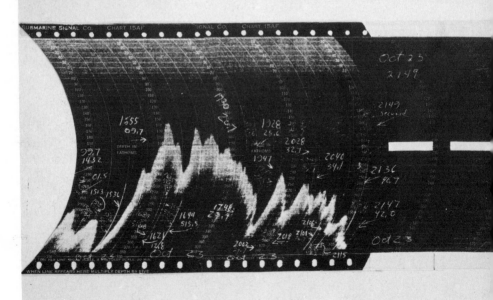

Plate 13. Top: Azores landscape; volcanic character; typical highlands, comparable with the present Andes; about 10,000–13,000 ft (3000–4000 m) above sea level before the large island subsided. *Bottom:* Negative photostat of an echogram: Depth values automatically recorded by echo soundings during a crossing of the Atlantic Ridge at 32° N (southern edge of the Azores Plateau)—"echoes from Atlantis."

Plate 14. Loess landscapes: the Loess region of China is very rich in typical alluvial landscapes, which are evidence of the "aquatic" origin of the stratified bank loess, famous for its "terrace cultivation." *Top:* Loess terraces in Shensi. *Bottom:* Paddy fields in South China.

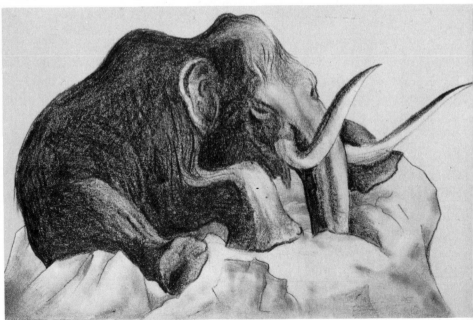

Plate 15. Two reconstructions. *Top:* A mastodon, a huge, tapir-like proboscidian, which became extinct probably as recently as 150 years ago. *Bottom:* The mammoth reconstructed as it was found in the frozen mud in the bed of the Berezovka river in Siberia; the reddish-brown woolly coat is clearly in evidence.

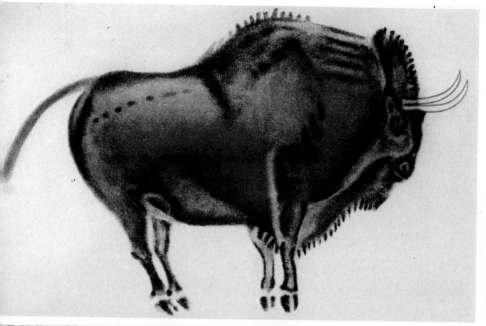

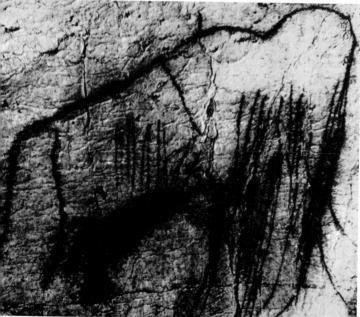

Plate 16. Bison. Ice Age art, Altamira Caves, Spain.

Plate 17. This is how Ice Age man saw the mammoth. Representation in the style of late Aurignac man at Cabrerets, France. Overemphasis on the characteristic features such as shaggy coat, trunk, and fat humps on neck and head. Striking agreement with the Siberian reconstruction; a sign of the uniformity in the animal kingdom and of the glacial environment between the Pyrenees and the Chukotsky Peninsula.

Plate 18. Astronomical initial: The Mayas concealed their advanced astronomical knowledge in such symbolic representations. The initial introduces a series of glyphs in the Palacio of the temple at Palenque. The fantastic animal carved inside the ring is the "carrier of the period," symbol of an astronomical period of revolution; the man supporting the "ring" represents a "god of numbers," the associated factor of multiplication. Both together represent a precisely fixed unit of time.

Such astronomical reliefs covered entire walls. Their scientific deciphering has yielded an unexpected view of the astronomical knowledge of the Mayas and of their almost incomprehensible calendar mania, of their fixation on celestial mechanical periods, and above all, of the age of their calendar, going back more than 10,000 years.

We have uncovered the traces of the greatest cataclysm on Earth that has been experienced by man. For there can be no doubt that this catastrophe of 12,000 years ago is the most terrible event that has ever taken place in all the dramatic history of mankind.

We have dug deep into the depths of Quaternary time and into the waters of the Atlantic and we have struck it rich. We are now in a position to compare our own findings with Plato's account of Atlantis.

Plato gives us three facts that can easily be compared with ours: the location of Atlantis, the size of Atlantis, and the approximate date of its destruction.

As for the location, there are two passages in Plato's account that, taken together, provide an approximate location.

". . . there was, beyond the strait you call the 'Pillars of Hercules,' an island, larger than Asia and Libya together, from where it was still possible then to sail to the other islands and from there to the whole continent on the other side. . . . This island . . . perished through an earthquake . . . the ground was . . . not . . . thrown up high, but washed away all around it and disappeared below the sea. As happens with islands that are small compared with the previous landmass, only the bare bones, as it were, have remained. . . ."

We may gather from this that Plato's island was situated somewhere between Europe and the string of West Indian islands that are at roughly the same latitude as Spain. The expression beyond the Pillars of Hercules implies that the island was fairly close to Europe, that is in the eastern Atlantic. If we move westward in the same latitude as Spain, we encounter submerged land in the eastern Atlantic in only one area—the region of the Azores. The second passage from Plato's text also points clearly in this direction. It states that the water washed the fertile soil away, leaving only the bare bones, the shoals, behind. Nowhere else in the eastern Atlantic at the latitude of Spain do we find such residual islands except in the region of the Azores. Only here do we find a huge submerged landmass, the Azores Plateau of today.

Plato does not give a precise location. But his account was adequate for his purposes, and it is adequate for a reconstruction of the true position of the sunken island. It was clear to Athanasius Kircher and the other early researchers, that if Plato's account was to be treated objectively and all its information utilized, then there was only one region in the North Atlantic where Atlantis might be found—the region of the Azores. This fact, so plain to them, must also be decisive in our own investigation.

This area is precisely the point of intersection between the Gulf Stream and the Atlantic Ridge. There can be no doubt that Barrier Island X was situated at this point where it deflected the Gulf Stream back to America before it was submerged.

The second point is the size of the island.

Plato describes the island as "larger than Asia and Libya together." Plato's Asia is the Asia Minor of today, and Libya, according to Plato, is the part of North Africa that was known to the ancients. In view of the lack of geodetic knowledge in antiquity and preantiquity, we cannot get very much help from Plato's statement about the size of the island. All we can deduce from it is that the island must have been a large one. But Plato's general statement is supplemented by a passage giving details about the large plain in the southern part of the island. The area of this plain is given as 3000 by 2000 stades. Six million square stades in equivalent to 77,000 square miles (200,000 sq. km). If we assume that this large plain occupied about half of the entire island, we arrive at a total area of 154,440 square miles (400,000 sq. km). An estimate derived from the pattern of the seabed contours in the Azores region results in a size not very different to this.

The third point is the date when the barrier island sank.

By taking the mean of eight geological estimates we have arrived at the date of about 10,000 B.C., which agrees well with de Geer's optimum estimate for the end of the Quaternary Age. Plato's ancient Egyptian authority makes a confident declaration: "We must above all remember that nine thousand years have passed since that . . . war we described . . . was fought. . . ." This war, according to Plato's text, ended with the earthquake that sank Atlantis. The dialogue between the priest of Sais and Solon took place about 570 B.C. According to tradition, then, Atlantis was submerged around 9500 B.C. This proximity to the date of 10,000 B.C. on which we have fixed is surely as good an agreement as one could possibly hope for.

We have thus been able to compare the results of our own independent inquiries with Plato's account in three important ways. In all three cases Plato's account agrees with the information that we have arrived at by means of an objective scientific inquiry.

Atlantis and Barrier Island X were situated in the same area—the Azores region of today. Their size was similar—at about 154,144 square miles (400,000 sq. km). They became submerged at about the same date—around 10,000 B.C. We can draw only one conclusion from this: Barrier Island X was none other than Atlantis itself.

We come by means of our scientific investigation to a solution that thousands of books on Atlantis have been unable to give us. We have found the spot where Atlantis sank 10,000 feet (3000 m) below the sea to which it gave its name. The Gulf Stream, which now flows past the tiny islands in this area, contains the secret of the Atlantic and of the island of Atlantis. When *Meteor* sailed around the Azores and sounded the ocean bed time after time to determine its depth from the echo—did anyone on this survey ship realize what it was that they were hearing? Those highly sensitive microphones on board the ship were recording something very mysterious, very strange—echoes from a world drowned long ago, echoes from Atlantis. Those sound impulses from the Behm transmitter were the first call for 12,000 years by living men to the forgotten island beneath the waters of the Atlantic. And the echoes were the island's answer. The echoes were duly recorded, but probably nobody on the *Meteor* grasped the full significance of this answer.

Depth soundings were taken, and Atlantis was found.

The Mystery of
the Eels

WE HAVE NO MONUMENTS, no tangible remains by which the Atlanteans can speak to us. All these relics sank beneath the sea with their island. But if concrete evidence is lacking, there are other witnesses to take its place.

What man had forgotten was indelibly imprinted on the memory of an animal species whose development had been very different to that of man. Paleontologists put the origin of this species in the so-called Cretaceous Age. It is the eel. The European eel harbors a secret which is closely linked with the sunken island of Atlantis. These creatures have a habit that seems to be pointless and is passed on from eel to eel as a powerful and unvarying instinct, inherited from one generation to the next. Twice in its lifetime the eel crosses the huge basin of the Atlantic; the first time as a colorless larva about the length of a matchstick, the second time as an adult ready to breed.

Not only does this habit appear to be senseless, for no plausible reason can be found for this peculiar behavior, but it also puts the survival of the species in danger. During the years of swimming the high seas the swarms of eels are far more exposed to attack from their enemies than during their stay in fresh water or shallow seas. This makes the business even more mysterious. Why is the eel unable to give up this habit and thus avoid both danger and great physical effort?

Ever since the time of Aristotle, scientists have been intrigued by the mystery of the eel. But Aristotle could have found the key to unlock it if he had not rejected Plato's account of Atlantis. Neither he nor any of the later scholars could offer any valid explanation for the fact that only female eels are found in European rivers. The absence of detailed observation of these strange aquatic creatures did not mean that there was any lack of learned hypotheses about them. J. Schmidt

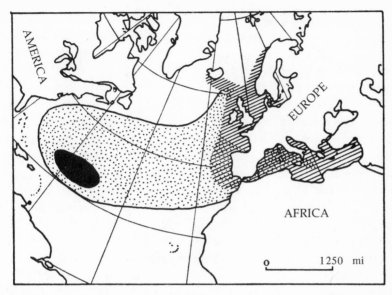

Fig. 17. Distribution of the European eel. *Black:* spawning grounds. *Dotted:* grown larvae. *Hatched:* sexually mature eels. The map shows that unlike the Indonesian eel, the European eel has to cover a very long distance back to its spawning grounds.

was the first to observe the eel closely and to map its migrations, but this did not enable him to give any biological explanation for the incomprehensible, instinctive action of the species.

The following facts however, have come to light.

The eel begins its life in the seaweed jungle of the Sargasso Sea. This is an area of warm water the size of Central Europe that lies to the west and southwest of the Azores region. Sargasso means seaweed, and the Sargasso Sea is very aptly named. Buoyed up by sluggish currents, huge plants of up to 1000 feet (300 m) in length float about in these limitless forests of Sargasso weed. They do so today and have done so ever since the Atlantic first came into existence. Masses of seaweed and algae converge on this area from all the coasts that are washed by this slow-moving current. In the center the water is almost completely stagnant and the plants are matted into an impenetrable tangle.

In this seaweed paradise the eels mate. The American eel spawns in the western part of the Sargasso Sea and the European eel in the eastern. Tiny transparent larvae hatch from the fertilized spawn. Even at this early stage in their lives they are imbued with this mysterious wanderlust. Gradually they wriggle out from the seaweed jungle to the edge of the eddy, and from there they are borne on the warm current of the Gulf Stream eastward toward the distant shores of Europe. The voyage lasts three years. The larvae that do not fall prey to the innumerable predators that feed on them, slowly grow into greenish-brown snakelike fish. The migrating swarm includes both males and females. When it reaches the coast it splits up. The male eels remain in the sea, the young females enter the lower courses of the European rivers. From there they swim upstream, surmounting all natural or artificial obstacles, and even on occasion making their way over land. This strange separation of the sexes lasts for two years. At five the eel is sexually mature, and it is only then that the two halves of the swarm meet again. The young males wait at the river mouths for the females to come back down the rivers and then the return journey to the Sargasso Sea begins.

The reunited eels return to their early home in immense swarms. They are blind and deaf to everything that is going on around them. Near the coast they are attacked by hungry seabirds and on the high seas by dolphins and predatory fish. They swim at a great depth, making use, perhaps, of the cold undercurrent that flows in the opposite direction from the Gulf Stream. They cover the long journey in the relatively short time of one hundred and forty days. All that has survived of the "wedding procession" disappears into the depths of the seaweed tangle. There, mating takes place, followed by the death of the old fish and the hatching of the larvae. The old cycle has ended and a new cycle has begun.

There are two factors in this life cycle that are very difficult to understand. First, why this complicated migration twice across the ocean, with all its attendant dangers and the risk it brings for the survival of the species? Second, why do the female eels alone enter the freshwater rivers, why do they not remain at sea with the males?

The second question has been answered. Female eels become sexually mature only in fresh water. The chemistry of the process has not yet been determined in detail, but the fact has been established. This explains why the female eels are compelled to swim toward some landmass which contains large freshwater rivers. But the answer to this question presents us with yet another puzzle. The West Indies are much closer to the Sargasso Sea than is Europe. Yet the larvae of the European eel swim not to this nearest land, but eastward in the opposite direction to distant Europe, although this takes them three years and exposes them to great dangers. It can be argued that the larvae are driven by their inherited instinct to choose the longer way because they can drift with the Gulf Stream and need make no great effort. All they have to do is to entrust themselves to the warm current of water and it will take them eventually to the nearest continent. This might explain why the female larvae commit themselves to the Gulf Stream, why they make the long journey to Europe to enter the fresh water in which they become sexually mature. But the male larvae have no such compelling biological urge. Why should they accompany the females and share their dangers? If the urge to become sexually mature were the sole motive for the migration then it would apply to the male larvae as well as the female. But it does not. Yet the male larvae migrate as well. The primary impulse seems to be, not the specific urge to sexual maturity, but a general urge to drift in the warm waters of the Gulf Stream. That they should possess this instinct is not in itself so very surprising. What is strange is that the instinct should be so strong that it leads them to swim all that distance to the continent of Europe.

It is the length of this journey that makes the second mystery in the life of the eel so difficult to solve. The female eels require a stay in fresh water in order to mature sexually; they choose the fresh water on a faraway continent; the nearer West Indies cannot be reached by drifting with the Gulf Stream. Can we find any explanation for the development of this peculiar characteristic of the eel?

Figure 18 shows at a glance how the mystery of the eel can be explained. Here is the solution not only of the problem of Atlantis, but of the eel, which is closely associated with it.

The map shows a general view of the western Atlantic before the island of Atlantis sank beneath the waves. The Gulf Stream breaks against the west coast of the island, which deflects it and forces its main mass back into a gigantic eddy that circles around the region of the Sargasso Sea. The eastern arc of this circular current touches Atlantis and its many rivers; the western arc reaches Central America and North America, with its abundant supply of fresh water.

This circular current was the habitat of the eel before the cataclysm which ended the diluvium, submerged the barrier island, and changed the whole course of the current. The whole mode of life of the eel was adapted to this habitat. All it needed to do was entrust

itself to the Gulf Stream and drift along in it. The vast eddy of the
Gulf Stream would carry the eel from sea water into fresh water and
back again. It provided the eel with a convenient method of traveling
between salt water and fresh water. It is not so very surprising then,
that a species of fish with such a habitat should have developed the
characteristic of the young females requiring fresh water to reach
sexual maturity. Fresh water could be reached very easily. Perhaps it
provided better protection from seabirds, which do not go far inland
from the coastal strip, and from the large predators of the open ocean.
The young females, so essential to breeding, would need protection
above all. Perhaps the eels, at that time so well adapted to their
special habitat, were so numerous that the continental rivers could
not provide food for them all, and the dependence on fresh water was
exclusive to the females. Whatever the reason, there is no doubt that
the dependence on fresh water made sense, and did not endanger the
species in the conditions that existed before the sinking of Atlantis.
They no longer exist today, and this is why the life of the eel has
become such a mystery to scientists.

But when we look at Figure 18, this puzzle is solved. In the dense
seaweed jungle of the Sargasso Sea around which the Gulf Stream

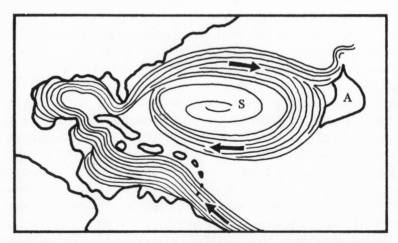

Fig. 18. The eel habitat in the North Atlantic during the Quaternary era
was the large island of Atlantis (A). Because Atlantis induced the Gulf
Stream to circulate around the Sargasso Sea (S) it was a factor in the life
of the females, as the much more distant western Europe is today.

flows, the eels safely mate. The seaweed becomes the graveyard of the old fish and the playground of the newly hatched larvae.

The warm, sluggish current carry the young eels around the jungle of the Sargasso Sea. If danger threatens, the tiny transparent creatures have a safe, convenient hiding place. This same warm current takes the growing eels effortlessly to river mouths near and far, east and west. There the urge for fresh water arises in the young females, and they swim up the rivers, farther and farther inland, where they are safe from most of their enemies. They are, after all, predators themselves, and can survive after they have grown so large as to lose the advantage of transparency.

While the young females are frolicking in the fresh water until their approaching maturity drives them back to the sea, the young males are swimming in the sea until they hear the call of the females. Perhaps this is through the gamones, with which aquatic animals can scent each other and communicate across incredible distances. So they come together, and the great wedding procession forms, and they drift on the warm water current back into the protection of the seaweed jungle to mate, to spawn, to die, and to begin afresh.

This cycle of the eel's life was broken when its means of transport, the Gulf Stream eddy, and the barrier island that maintained it, ceased to exist. And now we see the reverse side of the normally beneficial functioning of instinct.

Instincts are not open to reason. Instinctual animals cannot learn from experience. Eels have been ruled by instinct since the Cretaceous Age. They are unaware that Atlantis no longer exists, that the current circling around the Sargasso Sea is broken. And even if they did know it, they could not change their instinctual life cycle.

From time immemorial the eel larvae have entrusted themselves to the Gulf Stream, and they must continue to do so, even though it no longer carries them around the protective seaweed jungle, but bears them across the ocean to the distant shores of Europe. Countless eels perish on the way. But they must go to Europe because the Gulf Stream flows there and has flown there in a one-way course ever since the submersion of Atlantis. For the same reason the wedding procession must return across the ocean, in spite of the hazards and losses of the journey. This is why the eel swarm, blind and deaf to all around it, strives with all its might to return to the safe haven from which the Gulf Stream has borne it away. Because only there, safe in the jungle of seaweed, protected from its enemies, can the eel mate and spawn. The newly hatched brood needs protection if it is to survive. To ensure this protection, the eels must risk this long return journey across the ocean.

The instinct is designed to safeguard the offspring and thus the continuance of the species. And so the beginning and end of the life cycle of the eel must remain, as it always has been, based on its protective habitat in the Sargasso Sea. These safe breeding grounds are all that remains of what was once a perfect adaptation to habitat. And this small residue is only maintained at the great cost of countless individuals sacrificed during the outward and return crossings of the Atlantic. It is the price the eel has to pay for the loss of the island of Atlantis.

So the mystery of the eel is no longer a mystery when we take into account the changed conditions to which this ancient and harmonious life cycle has fallen victim. The eel has, it seems, a better memory than man. It cannot forget the land in the east. Every larva, every one of the courting eels, bears silent witness to Atlantis.

PART THREE

ATLAS—ATLANTIS

Mount Atlas

THERE IS NO MYSTERY that cannot be solved provided we can find the key. The mystery that shrouds the ancient Atlantean civilization is no exception. The key lies in the very word "Atlantis."

The sunken isle of Atlantis, the ocean to which it gave its name, the people who lived on the island—all these have in common the mythical symbol of the giant Atlas, who held up the heavens. His name appears to differ slightly from that of the island and the ocean, but the genitive in classical Greek—Ατλαντου—shows that it has the same etymological root. In the name of this mythical giant we shall find the key that will lead us to an understanding of the Atlantean civilization.

The oldest reference in the literature that has come down to us is found in the first book of the *Odyssey* where there is a description of the mythical island of Ogygia and the nymph Calypso, daughter of the giant Atlas. "The island is well wooded and a goddess lives there, the child of the malevolent Atlas, who knows the sea in all its depths and with his own shoulders supports the great columns that hold earth and sky apart. . . ."

If this last line, which is of particular importance, is translated literally it reads as follows: "Who himself has the great columns that keep earth and sky apart. . . ." We have here a description of a primitive phenomenon, undoubtedly based on a concrete fact, which later became transformed into the mythical symbol of Atlas, supporter of the heavens.

In his fourth book of travels, dedicated to the muse Melpomene, Herodotus writes of the extreme northerly tip of Africa: ". . . then, also after a journey of ten days, I came to another salt hill and a spring and people living around it. A mountain called Atlas borders on this salt hill. It is narrow and rounded and reputed to be so high that one cannot see its summit because it is always, summer and winter, wreathed in clouds. The local inhabitants say it is a pillar of the heavens. . . ."

This mountain is the so-called High Atlas in northwest Africa. It has two peaks more than 13,000 feet (4000 m) high. It has been called the Atlas range since the time of Polybius. According to the late Hellenistic version of the myth of Hercules the giant Atlas had his abode there. Heros, in search of the Apples of the Hesperides, encountered Atlas there and shared with him the famous adventure with the globe.

We know that Mount Atlas was not called by that name until a comparatively late date. According to Strabo the natives called it Dyris; according to Pliny they called it Daran. The association of the ocean beyond the Pillars of Hercules with the name of the island Atlantis has been proved to date from a much earlier time. The ocean was called the Atlantic long before the North African mountains were called the Atlas range. So the ocean cannot have derived its name from the mountains, but it is the latter, and particularly the main peaks, that were given a new name. Why was this?

The quotation from Herodotus provides the clue. The size, the wreath of clouds, and the overall impression of the high mountain in North Africa were very reminiscent of another such mountain—the original Mount Atlas which rose from the island of Atlantis and gave its name to the ocean surrounding it. The original Atlas sank into the Atlantic; the mountain in North Africa took over its name. The Azores, sparse relics of a once large island, provide us with proof.

Athanasius Kircher came to the correct conclusion more than three hundred years ago, when he realized that the nine islands that make up the Azores are in fact none other than the peaks of the highest mountains on what was once the island of Atlantis. On the island of Pico in the Azores there rises a mountain called Pico Alto—High Peak. It reaches a height of 7600 feet (2320 m), and even today it is an imposing sight. If we add to this a submerged depth of 10,000 feet (3000 m), that would give the original mountain the formidable height of 17,600 feet (5300 m), 1700 feet (500 m) higher than Mont Blanc, the highest mountain in central Europe.

Imagine a giant mountain the size of Mont Blanc on the precipitous coast of a subtropical island. This is what the ancient mariners might have seen as they sailed westward toward the Island of the Blessed, away from the coast of the inhospitable barbaric continent in the east: a sacred mountain that really did seem to be rearing up from the waves of the ocean into the heavens above. Like Mount Atlas in North Africa, it was always shrouded in steaming clouds. It was, in fact, emitting these clouds, because like Pico Alto today, this original Atlas mountain was an active volcano.

Steam rose from the crater as it rises today from the main crater of Mount Etna. Sometimes the clouds covered its summit; at other times they rose up in the shape of a mushroom, mingled with the clouds of the sky, and thus linked together the three life-giving elements of water, earth, and air. We understand now the source of Homer's mythical image of the giant Atlas who knows the depth of the sea and has the column that holds heaven and earth apart. For this giant mountain rises steeply and suddenly above the surface of the water as if it has indeed risen from the very depths of the sea. From its summit it emits a cloud that appears to hold up the heavens. The mountain is an enormous column that holds heaven and earth apart.

Here, then, is a reconstruction of the primeval image from which the mythical symbol of Atlas was derived. When the greater part of the mountain sank beneath the sea, the symbol was transferred to the High Atlas mountain in the northwest of Africa.

The island of Atlantis, which gave its name to the Atlantic Ocean, had in its turn received its name from the high mountain that domi-nated it and symbolized it. Myth has endowed it with its first king—the firstborn of Poseidon, god of the sea, as a parallel to Atlas, bearer of the heavens.

In the Nahua dialects, spoken by the peoples west of Atlantis, "atl" means water. From the name given to the South American cordilleras—Andes—one might conclude that "anti" could have meant a high mountain range or a high mountain. On such a hypoth-esis the name Atlantis would combine the two meanings of water and mountain. "A mountain rising from the water"; "a mountain in the midst of the water." Either of these phrases would admirably describe the real appearance, especially from the east.

The original bearer of the name, the true source of the mythical Atlas, is the smoking mountain rising up to the sky from the waves of the sea, with its column of cloud supporting the heavens. This mountain gave its name first to the island and then to the ocean surrounding it. In mythical politics and cosmology this awe-inspiring image is personified in Atlas the first king, and in Atlas the giant holding up the sky.

But this is only one of its effects. There is another that is very much more far-reaching. Mount Atlas is presumably the prototype for the pyramids and other ritual buildings in those countries to the east and west of the Atlantic, which were illuminated by a ray of light from Atlantis, either directly or by reflection.

Many observers have remarked upon the striking similarities between the religious architecture of ancient civilizations. The most outstanding example is the pyramid, and we can speak of a "pyramid belt." This embraces the multistory pagodas of China, the East Indian temples along the Nile, their less well-known copies in Libya, the megalithic structures of northwestern Europe, which are only superficially more primitive, the nuraghes of Sardinia, the Erse-Scottish crannogs and brochs, the talayots on the Balearic Islands, and—west of the Atlantic—the teocallis of the Mayas, Totanacs, Toltecs, Aztecs, and other aboriginal inhabitants of America. All these can be traced back to the primeval symbol of the gigantic mountain rearing up to the sky, the home or the temple of the gods.

An attempt to illustrate this very ancient connection is made in Figures 19–21. Figure 19 demonstrates a striking structural motif, which up till now has not been adequately explained. All these religious edifices are derived in the first place from a structure consisting of several steps. Attempts have been made to explain this by assuming that the ancient builders had only mastered the technique of building to a limited height. To erect higher structures they were obliged to pile one story on top of another. In some cases this explanation is probably true. But why was the stepped construction so often retained when the technique of building higher in one stage had been learned? This objection applies in particular to the relatively squat temple pyramids of Mesoamerica, which resemble terraced hills. It would certainly have been no more difficult—in fact it would have been easier—to erect them with a continuous slope rather than in steps. Nevertheless, the original form was retained, seemingly because the prototype was characterized by several stories.

The structure of the volcano Atlas embodied the original form of religious buildings in prehistoric times. The right half of the illustration shows a diagrammatic cross section of the steps in the volcano; the different steps have been defined by different hatching. Volcanic vents pass through these steps, particularly along the boundary layers. These are shown in black on the diagram. The central conduit leads to the main crater in the center of the volcano. The surface view of the volcano is shown in the left side of the diagram.

If we compare this with a Mesoamerican step pyramid, with the picture of the Sun Pyramid of Teotihuacan in Plate 6, for example, the resemblance immediately strikes us too forcibly to attribute it to coin-

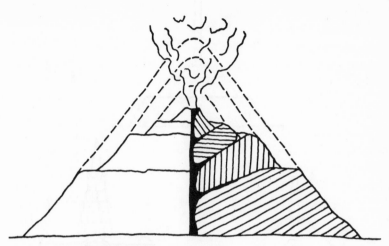

Fig. 19. Atlas, carrier of the heavens, as the prototype of the step pyramid. It can be concluded from the generally volcanic character of the Azores archipelago that the present Pico Alto was a high step volcano, built up of several eruptions, before the submergence of Atlantis. *Right:* cross section through the stepped layers; the conduits (vents) are black. The step volcano is the prototype of the stepped ritual structures, from which the various types of building in India, Mesoamerica, Mesopotamia and Egypt can be derived.

cidence. Such a comparison suggests that the layered religious edifices could have been derived from the layered volcano. And the holiest of all volcanic mountains was Atlas, bearer of the heavens, on the island in the center of the world.

Figure 20 illustrates diagrammatically the architectural reproduction of the original model, and its modification—a layered step mountain supporting a pillar upholding the sky.

Two types of building are clearly derived from this. First is the archaic hero's tomb, the tumulus, which later developed into the templum or temple. Its most important features correspond to those of the megalithic tombs of northern Europe. Building materials and the design of buildings must inevitably depend on natural conditions and resources. A classical example of this is contained in the twenty-third book of the *Iliad*, "The Burial of Patroclus." The dead hero, carried away to the gods and the great beyond, is laid to rest inside an artificial hollow mountain. Why is this?

Beyond the ocean that separates the Old World and the New

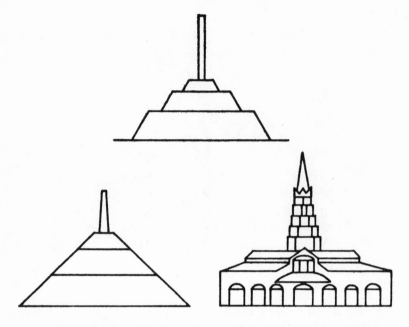

Fig. 20. The stepped ritual building is an architectural copy and reduc-
tion of the prototype (cf. Fig. 19); its architectural symbol is the
mountain carrying the heavens, that is, the mountain with the
heaven-supporting pillar. The following types are derived from the
formal architectural design (top):

a) the archaic hero's grave (tumulus with cairn or pillar), a mound
raised around a passage grave, sometimes in several layers, with a
pillar, pointed rock, etc. (left).

b) The ritual design of Christian churches evolved from the ancient
hero's grave; the formal resemblance of the "mountain carrying the
heavens" (cf. Fig. 19) is not always clearly apparent; the example on the
right, St. Sernin's Cathedral at Toulouse (1096), still has the typical step
design of the base (church), with the "pillar supporting the heavens"
(spire) built upon it.

Cathedrals, too, are built over graves. St. Peter's is the cairn on the
tumulus of Peter, the prince of the Apostles. It started with the crypt,
and above it rose the small chapel, the artificial hollow mound, with the
pillar, the little tower. But the Christian churches are not the only
examples; mosques, too, are hollow mountains, and the minarets flank-
ing them are the pillars supporting the heavens. The pyramids, which
sheltered the mummies, were likewise associated with the pyramidion
which crowned them, not by accident but by necessity; the tapering
column of smoke emitted by Atlas is reproduced in the Egyptian obe-
lisk, in the North German, Celtic, and British menhir (a word which
resembles the Italian *minaretto* perhaps only by coincidence), and in the
soaring spires of Gothic cathedrals.

World—a New World that in fact may well be older than the other—
kings and chieftains were also buried under hills. The totem pole is a
structural symbol in the style of the obelisks and the menhirs. It is a
striking symbol of those forgotten religions which are now unintelligible to us. Here, unless we are greatly mistaken, we meet for the
second time relics of Atlantis.

Religious buildings often served as fortified refuges during times of
unrest as far back as the early Neolithic Age. Figure 21 shows the
famous "Hausberg" of Stronegg, a village in Lower Austria. Here we
see the unmistakable Atlantean terrace design, closely related to the
Step Pyramid of Sakkara, the biblical Tower of Babel, and the Sun
Pyramid of Teotihuacan. This type of profile leads eventually to the
Chinese pagodas and to the even more extreme form, the Dravidian
step temples (Plates 5–7).

Yet another significant motif can be traced back to the now
semisubmerged giant mountain. The Pico Alto, whose peak still rises
7600 feet (2320 m) above the sea, has been an active volcano from time
immemorial. Smoke rises from its crater. The fiery reflection of the
glowing lava within lights up the clouds of smoke, and these glowing
clouds are in turn reflected on the snowy peaks, which blaze like
burnished gold. The ancients would have said that when the god
within the mountain stirs and speaks to mortals in a voice of thunder,
then the summit of the mountain is bathed in golden light.

Even this golden glow was reproduced on the artificial mountain.
Herodotus reports that the temple of Marduk on the peak of
E-temen-an-ki was completely covered with gold. The pyramids
wore metal crowns. Pagodas and stupas were decorated with gilt-
pointed roofs. The gold used so lavishly on the Aztec temple
pyramids amazed the Spanish conquistadors and aroused their
greed. Even the Christian cathedral of Milan, a dream spun from
marble pinnacles without number, has a luminous golden peak—the
Madonnina. Why have so many religious buildings been capped by
this golden metal? Because their prototype was a burning mountain
long since forgotten; a glowing summit that could be seen far out at
sea, and that served as a beacon for the mariners who sailed
thousands of years ago to the Island of the Gods in the waters of the
Atlantic.

The crater of the volcano emits not only a fiery glow, but also
smoke. The glow has been reproduced on the buildings; the
smoke—one is tempted to say—has been reproduced in the rituals

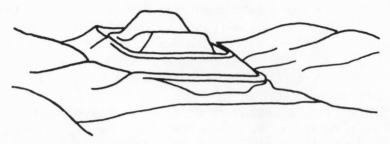

Fig. 21. The "Hausberg" at Stronegg, Lower Austria, is the type of early step structure found in Germany, Austria, France, Hungary, Sweden (Old Uppsala), and North America. These structures served as ritual buildings and refuge keeps. The formal similarity with the prototype (Fig. 19) is unmistakable.

that took place in the buildings. The Aztec temple pyramids provide a horrifying example of the use of the smoke motif in ritual. These supported altars on which the offerings to the god were burned. In Phoenicia and Carthage the burning mountain became a burning god, the terrible Moloch (Melek or god-king), to whom the firstborn were sacrificed. The Old Testament states clearly that fat and meat were sacrificed to God as burnt offerings on the altar. In ancient Greece and Rome hecatombs were burnt on altars. Christian altars, which no doubt have their origin in the ancient sacrificial altars, serve for a symbolic offering. The cloud that announces the presence of God, and that seems to have been an essential element in the dialogue between God and man since earliest times, is symbolically represented by the use of incense.

The Europe of old had another symbol for the world: the tree of life—or of knowledge, or fate, or time, or space. Can this not be regarded as a later version of the smoking mountain which supports the heavens? The world rests on its slender trunk; twigs, branches, and leaves spread out like clouds. It cannot be interpreted as a pillar supporting the heavens and it is totally different from a treetop, which could represent only the star-studded sky. This symbol belonged to the megalithic civilization which grew up in the areas where the land ice had retreated. Men of the red-skinned Cro-Magnon type settled on this virgin land and erected these strange vast structures. Avenues of huge stone pillars point the way to coasts long since vanished. They point to the sea, to the west where lay their own first home.

Yggdrasill, the mysterious tree of life, is typical of the pre-Germanic Europeans in the east. Equally representative, and equally inexplicable, is the symbol of the Feathered Serpent in the west. This is associated with the god Quetzalcoatl of the Mayas and Aztecs, the god Kukumac in Guatemala, and the god Kukulcan in Yucatán. The smoke, which emerges either from the water or a hole in the ground, symbolizes earth or water; the feathers enable it to hover and to fly. But what is it that rises writhing and twisting from the crater of the mountain and soars upwards to the sky? What is it that comes from the earth and the primeval waters? It is the smoke from the volcanic mountain hovering and then rising to the sky; the smoke that distinguishes the holy mountain from ordinary dead or sleeping mountains and imbues it with godlike power. The Feathered Serpent is the symbol of the supreme god in the New World. The myth states that he came to the continent from Tlillan-Tlapallan, an island in the eastern sea of America.

The god whom we must call Atlas—or more strictly, Atlants—because we know only this Hellenic version of his name, may with justice be claimed to be lord of all four elements: of the water out of which his giant body grew; of the earth over which he towered, godlike; of the air into which his pillar of smoke rose and supported the cloud blanket of the sky; and of the fire, which was his personal metaphysical element. If ever an ancient people had reason to believe in an all-powerful god, it was the people of the island of Atlantis. We know no older civilization. We may assume that this ancient monotheism, which many prehistorians are convinced is the oldest type of religious belief, forms part of the heritage of Atlantis.

This primeval god seems to have been primarily a god of fire and his most terrible weapon was the thunderbolt. Zeus used it against the giants and titans, Marduk against Tiamat, and Thor against the powerful giants. The earliest thunderbolt was not a flash of lightning, but a rock that fell from the sky, made deep holes in the ground, started terrible fires, tore up trees from their roots—a meteor or one of the lapilli ejected by active volcanoes. In prehistoric times they were probably regarded as identical. A large meteorite which fell from the sky thousands of years ago was immured in the Kaaba and is still the center of worship for the cult of Mecca, which is much older than Islam. The Magna Mater of Pessinum was a meteoric rock. What came down from the heavens must have come by god's hand. Cosmic bombs were worshiped no less than terrestrial ones. Only a very mighty, awe-inspiring god could use such terrible weapons to destroy his enemies. A god who compels mortals to worship him by hurling giant rocks is a god who will demand sacrifices regardless of human life. Such a conception is irreconcilably opposed to that of the loving father, but it accords with the Vulcan-god, whose body is the great boiling mountain that spews out fire and thunderbolts. It is easy to see why it was felt necessary to propitiate this irascible god with such inscrutable ways. He had to be pacified; gifts had to be made to him to avert his wrath, and it was hoped that the free offering of such gifts would prevent him from forcibly demanding them. From time immemorial the ways of the god of fire have been studied and imitated in the form of burnt sacrifices. The creatures sacrificed were slain with symbolic thunderbolts and burnt as in the flow of lava. The abhorrent custom of human and animal sacrifice on the altar of burnt offerings is almost certainly derived from the original natural model of the burning god-mountain.

It can be no accident that Atlantis was situated in the center of this arc of horror which, with its outward manifestations of pyramids and similar structures, encircled almost the entire globe. It seems to have been here, on this island that has become mythical, that this most abominable form of ancient ritual originated. It radiated westward to the Aztecs, who captured 20,000 to 40,000 sacrifical slaves every year and offered them as a mass sacrifice to their blood-gods; it radiated eastward to Tyre and Carthage, Etruria, Rome, and Greece. The ancient Israelites, no less than the Babylonians and Assyrians, made burnt offerings, and human sacrifice was also practiced in pre-Buddhist India. Wherever red or brown-skinned people worshiped their gods on step temples or pyramids, there burned the flesh of their sacrifices.

Other peoples, more remote from the Atlantean influence, followed other customs. The Scythians speared those whom they sent as messengers to the gods. The Germanic tribes that came from Scythia hanged their sacrifices. Tribes living in marshy regions drowned them in the morass. Not all ancient peoples subscribed to the custom of propitiating the fire god of heaven and earth with burnt offerings and human sacrifices. Was it a premonition of their own destruction by fire that impelled the Atlanteans to anticipate a thousand times their own inescapable fate?

The blue waters of the Atlantic Ocean roll over the sunken land. We ask our questions and it remains silent. But the breath of the fiery god still issues from Pico Alto as it did ten thousand years ago. He lives on still in the depths of the sea and in the souls of the heirs of Atlantis.

Country and Climate

THERE ARE ONLY TWO PIECES of evidence available for a reconstruction of the island of Atlantis, the isobaths and the brief topographical information in Plato's account.

Modern charts of the Atlantic give the depth measurements in the form of uninterrupted contour lines, but their accuracy should not be taken too much for granted. Depth values can be determined only indirectly from soundings taken by survey vessels. These values combined still provide only a summary picture, but to stress this is not to question the accuracy of these measurements.

In the vast majority of current echo soundings, all that is determined is the transit time of the sound pulses. Nobody can state with confidence that the pulses always return exactly vertically; they may sometimes be reflected by a neighboring steep slope. Where the ocean floor is strongly profiled, this uncertainty is particularly relevant. Even the individual measured points are not reliable. Still less so is the depth chart, obtained indirectly by drawing more or less arbitrary lines between the measured points. The depth profile is not in itself an adequate basis for detailed investigations. As far as possible, the depth chart for the Azores region needs supplementing by Plato's account. Figure 22, which largely agrees with the depth chart, is based on this method of combining the two pieces of evidence.

The reconstruction has been drawn mainly from the 10,000 foot (3000 m) isobath. It requires no great stretch of the imagination to recognize the description of the island in the resultant picture. A huge landmass rises from the azure depths of the sea. The present settlements on the Azores islands are raised to heights above 10,000 feet (3000 m). Huge mountain ranges soar into the sky. A well-tilled plain stretches far away into the southwest. The overall picture is very much what Plato's text has led us to expect.

The large island extends in a north–south direction for almost 685 miles (1100 km). Its northern and northeastern flank is fringed by a great range of snow-capped mountains. They rise to a height greater

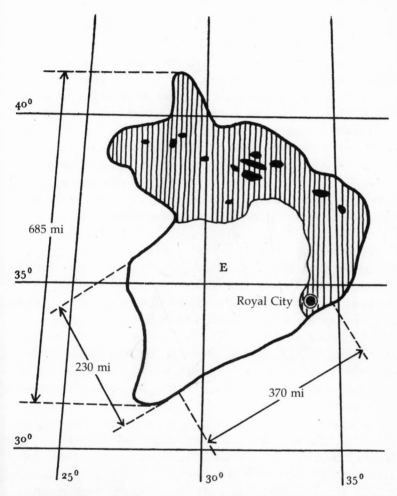

Fig. 22. Large-scale map of Atlantis, 1:10,000,000. The outline plotted from the isobaths obtained by soundings shows a large island extending 685 miles (1100 km) from north to south, sufficient to deflect the Gulf Stream from its eastward course. A range of high mountains towered over the northern portion with ten tall peaks, among them Mt. Atlas (today Pico Alto), which was then more than 16,400 ft (5000 m) high. The southwestern part of the island, which enjoyed a Gulf Stream climate ideal for vegetation, comprises the "Great Plain" (E) mentioned by Plato and occupying an area of about 77,000 sq. miles (200,000 sq. km). The Royal City, according to Plato, is situated near the southeast coast. *Hatched:* mountainous area.

than the 10,000 feet (3000 m) of the Alpine region. Crowning the serrated crest of the range are ten peaks. The highest, Pico Alto, is a giant almost as high as Ecuador's Chimborazo. It is situated roughly in the middle of the range and it rears up in several steps. Its fire shines in the sunlight. Day in and day out a banner of cloud flies from its summit, rising high into the sky in the form of a pillar, which seems to be supporting the blue expanse of sky. The stars appear to orbit around it. Here is the giant who carries the heavens on his shoulders, who has given his name to the island and to the ocean.

This mountain range well deserves Plato's words, "The mountains surrounding it were highly praised at the time, because their numbers, height, and beauty far surpassed that of those found there now, and also because they contained many populous settlements, as well as rivers, lakes, and meadows that supplied all wild and domestic animals with food in plenty, and vast forests that offered a great variety of trees providing timber for woodwork of all kinds. . . ."

It may be objected that in fact the Himalayas are much higher and more massive than these mountains described by Plato. But the Himalayas, like the Andes and the Rocky Mountains, were not within the world as the Greeks and the ancient Egyptians knew it, so Plato could not have used them for comparison. The mountains he knew would be those of North Africa and the Balkans. Neither of these regions can boast a mountain range comparable with that which rose steeply from the sea in long-forgotten times on the northeastern coast of the island of Atlantis. The isobaths show us the shape of this range. And the map shows that these high mountains sheltered the flat southern half of the island from the cold northerly winds borne by the arctic current. Today, these cold winds and currents are pushed farther north by the main body of the Gulf Stream. But in those days, when the Gulf Stream was deflected by the island, the arctic currents could have come nearer to its northern coast. The high mountain range would have protected the southern plain from rain, storms, and snow. In the same way, the high Alpine range protects northern Italy today from the snow and cold characteristic of the climate to the north of the Alps.

The large plain in the south and southwest of Atlantis would have enjoyed a position similar to that of Lombardy today. Estimates based on the isobaths give the extent of the plain of Atlantis from northeast to southwest as about 370 miles (600 km) and the average width as 230 miles (370 km). In Greek measures this would be the 3000 and 2000 stades mentioned in Plato's text. "To begin with, the whole region was said to be very high above and steeply risen from the sea, but the whole plain surrounding the city was in turn completely enclosed by mountains, which came down to the sea; the plain was uniformly flat, oblong, measuring in length three thousand stades and in width, rising from the sea, two thousand stades. This part of the whole island lay to the south, sheltered from the north wind. . . ."

Figure 22 illustrates this passage of Plato's text. Insofar as is possible in so complicated a case of submarine reconstruction, the isobaths confirm his account so strikingly that text and illustration provide a clear idea of the nature of the long-submerged island.

The island of Atlantis was an antediluvian barrier to the Gulf Stream. We have proved its antediluvian existence by means of the effect it had on the sea current and therefore upon the diluvian pattern of climate in northwestern Europe. It straddled the crucial area of the Atlantic.

The currents of the Gulf Stream flowed into the bays on the west coast of Atlantis. On that side of the island the seabed rose more gently than in the east, where the land platform came to an abrupt end, and the mountains reared up in an unscalable vertical wall. On the other side, however, where the great plain merged into a gently sloping beach, conditions were just right for a prehistoric Waikiki.

The Gulf Stream provided a never failing supply of warm blue water and brought a mild, damp climate to the whole coast. Water and air temperatures were probably identical, in this hot, damp region, exposed only to the mild west and southwest winds—a paradise for warmth-loving, sun-hungry people.

Yet the climate was subtropical rather than tropical, mild rather than excessively hot, because of the cool air coming from over the mountains in the north. On the northern and northeastern mountain flank the atmospheric moisture resulting from rising bodies of cold air was precipitated in the form of rain, snow, or sleet. The Gulf Stream, diverted by the west coast, pushed the isotherms northward toward the pack ice cap. Icebergs drifted southward from this cap and cold water currents flowed toward the northern tip of the island. This explains the abnormal crowding together of the isotherms, a crowding which indicates an extremely steep climatic gradient. In only 15° latitude the climate changes from subtropical warmth to arctic cold.

The cold water current reaching the northern coast brought with it bodies of cold air. These brought rain and snow to the high mountains, which sheltered the southern plain, and the rain and snow accumulated in the form of glaciers.

Streams flowed from the mouths of these hanging glaciers, and when the mountain wind blew, the melting water flowed in great abundance down the mountainside. Springs welled up from the ground. Their clear water poured over the rocks, collected in the forests, and on reaching the valleys broadened out into rivers great and small. This extremely favorable orographic and hydrographic condition is an inevitable result of the geographical position and the pattern of climate produced by the interaction between the Gulf Stream and the arctic current. It accords well with the tradition that had been faithfully handed down over the years to Plato's informant. ". . . . The rains in the course of the year made the soil particularly fruitful. Because unlike now, as it flows over the cold ground, the water was not lost, the fertile soil soaked up the rain and stored the water in its clayey ground, letting it flow from the heights down to the valleys, creating copious springs and rivers . . . (the mountains) . . . contained many rivers and lakes . . . (the large canal) . . . collected the rivers coming down from the mountains. . . ."

To obtain a clear picture of the pattern of climate, let us look at the isotherm map of this region (Figure 23). At a scale of 1:20,000,000 it gives an outline of the island, with the isotherms at ten-degree intervals shown by broken lines. At the left they are mostly running parallel to the Gulf Stream, and are deflected by the range of high mountains in the north. The warm west wind is dammed up by the western slopes of the mountains, and this produces a northward bulge in the isotherms. This bulge, on a very much smaller scale, is similar to that brought to northwestern Europe by the warm flow of the Gulf Stream today. Beyond the island of Atlantis, the isotherms drop rapidly again, and gradually return to the course of the parallels of latitude. The bulge in the isotherms shows how climatically favored was this Gulf Stream barrier island, even more so than the Hawaiian archipelago.

The pattern of the isotherms clearly shows the effect of the dammed-up and deflected Gulf Stream on the mean temperature of the island. Heat builds up at the west of the island, and in this region air and water are abnormally warm for this latitude. But in the east of the island they are much cooler—normal for the latitude. It is not impossible that the mountain area jutting out northward into the cold currents could have had a climate as harsh as that of Patagonia, for this

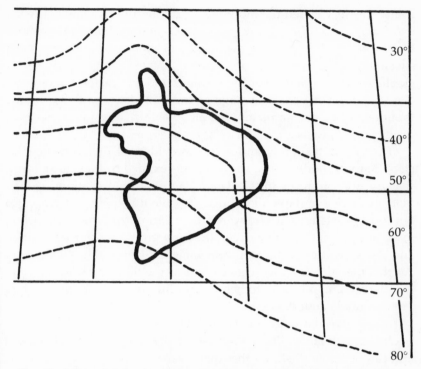

Fig. 23. Map of Atlantis showing isotherms, 1:20,000,000. The Gulf Stream coming from the west causes the isotherms to converge and produces a similarly privileged climate as that enjoyed by northwestern Europe today. The air temperature of Atlantis ranged from moderately cool (annual mean 50° F—10° C) to tropically humid (annual mean 77° F—25° C). The Gulf Stream barrier island of Atlantis was at the time the most climatically favored area in the Atlantic. This beneficial climate produced a truly Elysian fertility, providing the basis for the development of an advanced civilization before it could develop on the continentsl less benefited by the climate.

was an island of great climatic variations. It may well have contained as many different types of climate as a continent, from the sub-boreal to the tropical. And the variety of climate would have been reflected in the great abundance and variety of forms of life, both flora and fauna. Plato wrote: ". . . . in the olden days, before the land perished, its mountains were high and covered with soil, and its plains, now described as stony ground, consisted of fertile humus.

Dense forests covered the mountains . . . the soil also bore many tall fruit trees and offered the flocks and herds abundant pasture. Moreover, the island was a rich source of timber for building and it sustained large numbers of animals domestic and wild, many elephants among them. For there was abundant grazing not only for all the animals that live in swamps, ponds, and lakes as well as on the mountains and on the plains, but also for this largest and most voracious of all beasts.

"The island also grew and amply provided all the aromatic substances, roots, herbs, trees, various gums exuded by flowers and fruit that the soil produces today. There were the mild fruit and cereals that provides our staple diet, pulse (to give it its generic term), also needed to sustain us. There were trees bearing fruit that yield drink, food, and oil but are perishable; they are grown for our delectation and pleasure after meals as a welcome stimulant to the sated palate. All this the island, which was bathed in the light of Helios, divine, wonderful, and a beauty to behold, produced in superb quality and immeasurable abundance. . . ."

This, it may be objected, is an imaginary paradise created by a poetic flight of fancy. But the isothermal map, which is purely factual and can be verified, shows that this Elysian topography corresponds very well with that of the sunken island.

Certainly Mount Atlas, and possibly all ten of the high peaks, was an active volcano. It can be assumed that even in the Early Tertiary Age their flow of lava was copious. Rivers of fire would have rolled down the slopes, flooded the great plain in the southwest and covered it with a thick layer of lava—as has happened in many other places throughout the world. Weathered lava produces clayey, quartzitic strata resembling loess in their high fertility. They contain large quantities of mineral salts and of almost every trace element that is required for the healthy growth of plants. The loess of China and of northwestern Hungary has a composition similar to that of weathered lava. The immense fertility of these regions is beyond question. For thousands of years they have been intensively cultivated. Although never fertilized, they still yield the most abundant crops. The detritus of volcanic lava contains not only large reserves of mineral salts, but apparently also special growth substances and stimulants. Its suitability as a soil for plant cultivation can be studied in the Hegyalya region of Hungary and on the slopes of Mount Vesuvius and Mount Etna. Only on old volcanic soil can such luxurious growth be found;

nowhere else do the plants give out such an intoxicating scent, no other type of soil grows such luscious fruits. Hungarian Tokay and the Sicilian and Neapolitan wines testify to the special quality of the soil produced by the furnace of the Earth.

Atlantis was a volcanic country and a volcano was its god. Its soil was of weathered lava; its fertility was outstanding. Active volcanoes give out water vapor and carbon dioxide—the two substances used by plants to supply their carbohydrate content. The moister the air, the denser its carbon dioxide envelope. The quicker a plant grows, the higher will be its yield of oil. Carbon dioxide enhances the scent of flowers, results in a stronger setting of fruit, and greatly increases crop yields.

It is not only the ideal climate, but also the promixity of Mount Atlas that accounts for the fertility of this island so blessed by the gods. It is understandable, perhaps, that many critics have believed it to be a figment of the poetic imagination. Two of Plato's details, in particular, have been questioned. One is the reference to the "mild fruit" and the other is the phrase "trees bearing fruit that yield drink, food, and oil all at once."

What can the 'mild fruit' refer to? If it had been the grape, from which the god Dionysus was the first to press out the intoxicating liquid, then Plato would have used the specific Greek word. Nor can it be any of the field crops of classical times—pulse, barley, or wheat. These are explicitly listed. So are the "highly perishable" gifts of a particularly tasty type of fruit. So it cannot have been that. Perhaps the combination of the words mild and fruit points to something that is as mild as fruit and yet has a greater nutritional value. Could it have been the banana? It was Kuntze who suggested that the wild banana bush, *Musa paradisiaca* or *Musa sapientum*, was bred into the seedless cultivated variety during the Quaternary Age. This is quite possible, but even without such an elaborate explanation Plato's reference may well be confirmed as a description of a banana. A type of banana called the pacoba was recently discovered in Brazil, which is within the immediate cultural ambience of Atlantis. It grows wild, regularly forms seeds and therefore does not need to be artificially propagated by means of cuttings. This very demanding, warmth-loving plant would have found on the southwest plain of Atlantis the climatic conditions that it required. Here in the region of the 68–77° F (20–25° C) isotherms, where the Gulf Stream was deflected by the coast, annual variations in temperature must have been negligible. Warmth, moisture, and a steady, unvarying temperature are the three conditions that the banana requires to flourish.

Plato's "mild fruit" has not been easy to identify. But there is no such difficulty about the nameless tree whose fruit yields drink, food, and oil all at once. This can only have been the coconut palm (*Cocos nucifera*). Like the banana, it is a typical tropical plant, and extremely sensitive to any drop in temperature below the minimum that it will tolerate. It is no longer found today in the parts of the world that were known to classical antiquity. Perhaps this was the case even in Plato's day. If so, this would account for the fact that neither he nor the Egyptian priest was able to give a name to this plant that grows on the coasts of Africa and southern Asia, but not north of the Guinea arc. But where the banana can grow the coconut palm is also at home. Both of them flourish on the West Indian archipelago today. So they must have done on the southwestern plain of Atlantis.

Where palm trees wave in the warm breeze and bananas grow in abundance, the shoots of bamboo will surely also be found. These, and other giant reeds, are the favorite food of the great pachyderms. And in such a climate the mangroves may well have sent their huge aerial roots through the tangle of swampy undergrowth as in the Amazon delta across the sea. Orchids provided brilliant patches of color in this symphony of green. The hippopotamus and the crocodile were at home there. And so, of course, were the elephants.

Today, these giant beasts are to be found only in India and central Africa. But in the lifetime of Herodotus they were still to be found in northwest Africa. He writes; ". . . . this land (of the Maxyans) however, and the rest of Libya towards the west has many more wild animals and forests than the land of the herdsmen. For the eastern part of Libya, which belongs to the nomads, is low-lying and sandy up to the river Triton. But from there to the west, the land of farmers is full of mountains, forests, and wild animals, enormous snakes, lions, elephants, bears, vipers, and horned asses. . . ."

Today, the large animals are, perhaps, doomed to extinction. But in the Quaternary Age they flourished. In South America there were mastodons; in Europe there were protoelephants, the arctic version of the mammoth, together with other varieties. It is perfectly natural to assume that not only elephants—presumably the African variety— lived on this large island with its great variety of climate, but also other now rare creatures. These could have included mastodons, as well as tapirs, hippos, and rhinos and other representatives of this once numerous genus. The humid, tropical coastal belt in the south-west of Atlantis would have suited them perfectly. We know enough now about comparative climatology, and about the habitat of prehis-toric beasts, as well as of still surviving species, to make this assump-tion. The Egyptians and the Greeks did not have this knowledge, and what seems obvious to us would have appeared very strange to them. They knew nothing of the Indian elephant, and they therefore be-lieved that this "largest and most voracious" of all the beasts was to be found only on the African continent. This, in Plato's terms, meant only Libya. It would be incredible to them that such a creature should be found on a faraway island in the middle of the ocean. Surely this could be only myth and not reality.

But this detail, too, was handed down in the tradition. It is scarcely possible that Plato could have invented it.

The People of
Atlantis

DO WE KNOW ANYTHING MUCH about the human inhabitants of the Atlantis region in the Early Quaternary Age? No, not very much. In the western region there is a total lack of authentic skeleton finds. We can only assume that a red-skinned people similar to the American Indians lived there then, as the Caribans, the Guatemaltecs and Mayas do today. There is no means of proving either the presence or the absence of such peoples in the Quaternary Age. In northwest Africa, too, virtually nothing has been found, and we are obliged to fall back on the assumption that during the Quaternary Age this region was inhabited by the Mediterranean race thought to resemble the ancient Libyans, the modern Berbers, and the extinct Guanches. In appearance they resemble the Indian-type people on the other side of the Atlantic at least as much as they resemble the neighboring Hamitic peoples of northeast Africa.

All the tribes that we have mentioned have certain marked features in common—a sharp profile, an aquiline nose, and black hair—usually wispy and growing back from a receding forehead. The modern Indio has these features and so did his Mayo ancestors. They are depicted on many reliefs, and they would appear to be constant racial characteristics. The cave paintings in Spain and western France do not show Quaternary man as realistically as they show Quaternary animals. In the pictures of humans there is an almost expressionist emphasis on certain features. Probably these were the features that the artist considered to be particularly representative and desirable.

The males were always tall, long-legged, and powerful. They are depicted as muscular and athletic, as runners and hunters. They are brown-red in color. Probably this really was the color of their skin. The cave paintings to the east of the Atlantic depict similar essential characteristics as those of the American Indian races to the west—a link across the ocean that cannot be ignored.

There are strong reasons for attributing these beautiful early paintings to the non-European nation of the Cro-Magnons. We have already pointed out the likelihood that this race came to Europe from the west, either from, or by way of, the island of Atlantis. According to Lewis Spence's theory, early western Europe was populated by successive waves of migrants of this non-Neanderthal type. We are not, at the moment, concerned with either proving or disproving this theory. The number of relevant finds is small. Isn't it possible that the "invaders" were not large hordes of nomadic peoples and tribes, but small, organized hunting expeditions sent out from the highly civilized island? Europe at that time was barbaric and wild and very sparsely populated. It would have provided excellent hunting grounds.

In either case, whether hunting excursions or waves of migration, there is no doubt that the Cro-Magnons were very distinct from the ancient European races, Neanderthal and Aurignac Man. With their superior weapons they pushed the latter back into the Alpine redoubts and gradually exterminated them. They colonized Europe from the west, and this colonization must have taken place before the island of Atlantis became submerged, during the period of transition between the Quaternary and the Quinternary Ages. In the unfortunate absence of authentic Atlantean relics, we must act on this assumption to attempt a mental reconstruction of Atlantean Man.

Fleshing out the bony outline of a Cro-Magnon skull, and making use of the best available anthropological knowledge, we would describe these Atlantean men as of the proto-American Indian type. They bear a greater resemblance to the modern Indios than they do to any other type of man. It only needs a glance at the face of Sitting Bull to see this.

Can one put proto-American Indians and Cro-Magnons in the same category? The anthropologists will certainly object. Let us try to meet their objections with the help of a book edited and approved by anthropologists, Herbert Wendt's *Ich suchte Adam* (*I looked for Adam*). "During the seventy years that have passed," he writes, "since Chester Stock speculated on the footprints found at Carson City, numerous human skeletons and relics of civilization have been discovered throughout the American continent from Minnesota to the Strait of Magellan. These proto-Americans belonged without exception to the species *Homo sapiens*; they combine the characteristics of Cro-Magnon Man with Mongoloid and Red Indian traits, and can be dated fairly accurately with the aid of the radio carbon and the fluorine test. None of the skeletons has been in the American ground longer than twelve thousand years. . . ."

These proto-Americans were clearly contemporaneous with the last Atlanteans. They are the unmistakable ancestors of the present-day Red Indian races. Their skeletons reveal features resembling both the Cro-Magnonlike Atlanteans and the modern Red Indians, and they therefore occupy an intermediate position between the Cro-Magnon types found in Europe and the Red Indians of America. In these skeleton finds we have a link between the Atlantean type and the lands west of the Atlantic, which complements the link we have found between the Atlanteans and the continents of the Old World. A picture is beginning to emerge of Atlantis as a world power that sent its pioneers out into the world and passed on its own racial characteristics. According to the evidence of the cave paintings, the Atlantean Cro-Magnon people were reddish-brown in color. They may well be claimed to be the prototype of the redskin race and therefore of the proto-American Indians.

Red-brown skin is an unmistakable racial characteristic of the Red Indian—a full-blooded, strong, athletic human type. Let us now examine the symbolic meaning of the color red among the ancient prehistoric peoples who inhabited the pyramid belt, the regions into which the early Atlantean civilization radiated.

Red is the color of imperial emblems, and of princes and cardinals. Images of gods are painted in red, as are images of heroes in victory processions. The Egyptians used scarlet makeup, as is shown by the statue of Ra-nefer (Fourth Dynasty). The Roman Catholic Church uses purple for special occasions. Again and again the color of blood is associated with the idea of supreme power, triumph, and glory.

Were the "first humans" red-skinned? Is this why the first created man was called Adam, which means "the red," as the first soil is called Adamah, the red? Verse 4 of chapter 6 of Genesis contains a curious statement: "There were giants in the earth in those days . . . the same became mighty men which were of old, men of renown. . . ."

Did those giants really exist? Does this verse refer to Meganthropus, of whom a piece of lower jaw with three teeth was found on the island of Java? Can we conclude that there existed a huge primitive man, or a giant ape similar to the Gigantopithecus of Africa?

Must we go back to the dim light of prehistory to discover what was meant by those giants, those "mighty men which were of old"? There

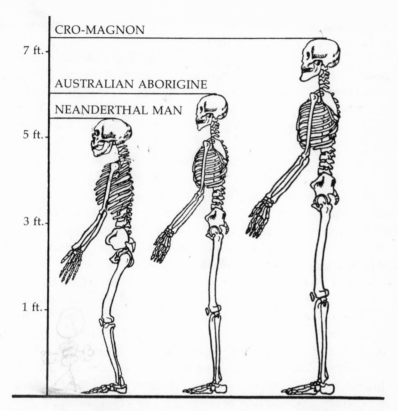

CRO-MAGNON

AUSTRALIAN ABORIGINE

NEANDERTHAL MAN

7 ft.

5 ft.

3 ft.

1 ft.

Fig. 24. Thére were giants in the earth in those days. . . . The comparison between the diagrammatic skeletal outlines of a diluvian Neanderthal man, a recent Australian aborigine, and a diluvian Cro-Magnon—
that is the Atlantic racial type—shows that the Atlantic race was gigantic compared with early and recent types of man. (Measurements according to Hermann Klaatsch.)

is no need to search so far back. All we need to make sense of this
strange verse from the Bible is to compare the reconstructions of the
Cro-Magnon skeletons with those of the Neanderthal skeletons.

Figure 24 shows three types of skeleton drawn to scale. On the left
is diluvian Neanderthal man; next comes a modern Australian
aborigine, representing a normal primitive race; on the right is a
Cro-Magnon.

The average height of the European Neanderthal man was less than
5 foot, 3 inches (160 cm). They were plump, strong-boned pygmies.

The Cro-Magnons grew to 6 foot, 7 inches and more (200 cm) and their bones were just as strong. Compare their skeleton with that of the Neanderthal and the aborigine and they will look like Goliaths.

Most myths have a basis in fact, and the myth of dwarfs and giants is no exception. The illustration shows the historical dwarf, the Neanderthal man, on the left, and the historical giant, the Cro-Magnon man, on the right. There really were giants on earth in those days.

Neanderthal man is usually regarded as an offshoot of the family tree of modern man and is dated back 50,000 to 100,000 years. This may well be correct, as may be the assumption that he was exterminated by the races of the Late Glacial Period. The latter—which included people of the Cro-Magnon and the Aurignac types—belonged to the species *Homo sapiens*. But the dwarfs and the giants must for a time have coexisted. Was there no intermixture of the two races? Is it not possible that some relics of these proto-Europeans have been preserved in their Alpine refuges? Neanderthal man lives on in fairy tales, in which we find dwarfs living in mountain caves. So do the ancient bear hunters, who are truly human in spite of their anthropological designation. For all their savage life-style, they were at least as wise as their cousins of the two diluvian races that have been endowed with the adjective "sapiens." But the latter had the advantage in bodily size and had developed more lethal weapons.

It was not only the Neanderthal race, which in fact comprised a whole group of tribes, that was small in stature. All the other races were equally small, with the exception only of the Cro-Magnon and Aurignac peoples, who were presumably closely related. This is evident from the lower Paleolithic bone and utensil finds. The Acheulean mallets were designed to be used by small hands, and so were the artifacts of earlier dates. The swords and daggers of the Bronze Age, from Hallstatt to the chamber tombs of Mycenae, have remarkably slender hilts. For a long time they were thought to be weapons used by women. Even the suits of armor of medieval Germans are too small for a man of normal height today.

Gigantism would appear to be an "asylum" symptom. It is associated with the terminal phases of a civilization in the same way as its opposite, dwarfishness, is associated with the beginning of civilizations. The Cro-Magnons, those ancient European pioneers of Atlantean racial stock, were broad and tall and massive in appearance. They belonged to the end phase of a civilization. According to the myths, the deluge was sent by the angry gods as a terrible punishment for the arrogance and wantonness of mankind. There is in these myths an unmistakable note of indignation about the decadence and depravity of those who were then rulers of the world. *Genesis* 6, verses 5–7, says, "And God saw that the wickedness of man was great in the earth, and that every imagination of the thoughts of his heart was only evil continually.

"And it repented the Lord that he had made man on the earth, and it grieved him at his heart.

"And the Lord said, I will destroy man whom I have created from the face of the earth; both man, and beast, and the creeping thing, and the fowls of the air; for it repenteth me that I have made them."

The flood which destroyed so large a part of civilization was a punishment for the rulers of civilization, the giants of Atlantis. They were the "mighty men which were of old," who had kept all the peoples around them in slavery.

If we compare the biblical story of the Flood with Plato's narrative, we will see a striking similarity between the motives given for the destruction of civilized man. It is hardly likely that this is accidental. The wickedness of mankind is said to result from the gradual extinction of the powers of his divine ancestors owing to miscegenation with the "daughters of the Earth." Was this the unforgivable sin that weighed so heavily that the whole world had to be punished? Or were there others?

Atlantis—World Power

FIGURE 25 SHOWS how the island dominates the Atlantic. A prehistoric Albion. This island is the center from which its influence spreads in all directions to all the coastal regions that can be reached by sailing across the ocean and even as far as the Mediterranean sea. Atlantis was a world power.

There is a very ancient myth, far older than the epics of Homer, of the Phaeacians and of Scheria, a remote island at the furthermost end of the western sea. Can we see in this myth a glimmer of Atlantis? There are certain similarities between the palace of Alcinous described by Homer and the Atlantean temple of Poseidon described by Plato. Was Plato, consciously or unconsciously, influenced by the *Odyssey* that he knew so well? Or are both accounts based on a common origin? We cannot tell.

What did Poseidonis really look like? Did it resemble the city on the mythical island of Scheria? More likely it resembled the port on the shore of Lake Titicaca, which lies today 12,500 feet (3800 m) above sea level. This harbor town was never completed and from time immemorial has been in ruins. According to Posnansky, Rolf Müller calculated its age with the aid of certain structural measurements. Combining this with other relevant data, such as the oldest historically verified value of the obliquity of the ecliptic, which plays an important part in this context, he arrived at a date of about 9500 B.C. This agrees exactly with the date given by Plato. Tiahuanaco was situated on the Pacific side of South America. Was it nevertheless part of the empire of Atlantis? Could it perhaps be that mariners from Atlantis, like the daring Norwegians of the Kon-tiki expedition, were carried along on the Humboldt Current? Could they have reached Easter Island? The strange giant heads on that remote isle have many features similar to those of Aurignac Man in ancient Europe.

Of the many questions that still await an answer, the question of language is perhaps the most promising to tackle. Is it conceivable

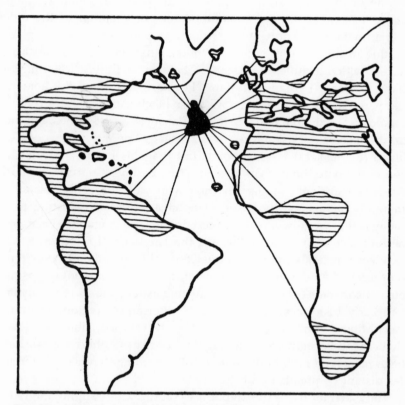

Fig. 25. Atlantis—center of the world of Red-Skinned Man. At all points where various authors have claimed to have found "their" Atlantis, arguments in favor of an alleged cultural link with this very ancient center were advanced. The map demonstrates the range of this long extinguished beacon of the Red Indian world which illuminated the ancient civilizations, and therefore shows roughly the size of the first empire claimed for the Redskins.

that any modern idiom still retains some lingering and recognizable traces of some *lingua franca* of Late Paleolithic times? Etymologists specializing in this field will probably disagree.

But let us persist. In what area would lie our best hope of recovering such very ancient linguistic fossils? Not among the Indo-European family of languages. They are far too recent. A more promising field is one of those random splinter languages that do not fit into any conventional schemes, and there is just such a misfit in Europe, the language of the Basques.

One of the greatest authorities on comparative philology, F. N. Finck, has called Basque an indubitable continuation of the older Iberian, which we know of only from inscriptions on coins. He places Basque in the same category as "other languages of the Caucasian Race," which includes Cossaeans, Chaldeans, Hittites, Mitanni, Lycians, Carians, Lydians, Mysians, Pisidians, Isaurians, Lycaonians, Cappadocians and Etruscans. All these he classifies as "group of the unknown." The Roman name for the Basques was Vascones, but they call themselves "Euskaldun," which means "people who speak Eskuara (or Euskara)." Finck points out that this Eskuara is not only connected with the Roman Vascones (the Basques), but also with the Ausci, an ancient Aquitanian tribe who were probably related to them. What makes the Basque language so very interesting to us today is that we now know that certain Siberian languages bear some resemblance to it. One of these is the language of the present-day reindeer nomads who live on the Chukchi Peninsula in the extreme northeast of Asia. Certain features of this are reminiscent of Basque, but it also seems to bear a relation to long extinct idioms of prehistoric and early historic peoples of the Mediterranean region, including Asia Minor. Von Natzmer propounds the very plausible suggestion that "the last remains of an Ice Age language of southern Europe have been preserved both in the remote valleys of the Pyrenees and in the far-distant peninsula of Siberia."

Von Natzmer bases this hypothesis on the wide-ranging migration of the hunting tribes of the Ice Age, which continued for thousands of years. They were obliged to change their hunting grounds as the periods of maxium glaciation alternated with the warmer interglacial periods. Some of these nomads, he argues, may have strayed as far as Siberia, while others may have found a temporary refuge in the Pyrenees. To this we may add, why not also in the valleys of the Caucasus, which are similar to the Pyrenees? Finck had a good reason for placing Basque with the Caucasian languages. "All these South Caucasian languages and dialects go back to the idiom of the old Iberians, which at the time of Herodotus was surely still much more uniform. The Mingrelians and Lasans, who also speak a South Caucasian language, are considered the descendants of the ancient Colchians and probably rightly so. This obviously does not rule out the possibility that they gave up their old language in favor of Iberian at an early stage. The great similarity of Mingrelian with Georgian, which has already been mentioned, and the recognized further development of ancient Iberian, supports this theory very strongly. If Herodotus's claim is correct that Colchian was a language related to Egyptian, the situation can hardly have been different from what we have assumed here. . . ."

These observations by an etymologist of high repute lend considerable weight to certain statements in Braghine's *Shadow of Atlantis*. Basque is said to include many linguistic roots, and many words that precisely match their Georgian equivalents. Braghine writes, "I was present when a former Russian officer of Georgian extraction discovered that he could speak to the inhabitants immediately on his arrival in northern Spain. He spoke Georgian, but the Basques understood him. . . ."

Braghine makes the interesting observation that the Basque language is said to bear a striking resemblance to Japanese. This is not altogether surprising, because the Mongolian stock from which the modern Japanese are descended is of Tungus origin, and the eastward migration of the Tungus is bound to have brought them into contact with the reindeer nomads. But the Turkomans and the Ugro-Finns were also relatives and neighbors of the Tungus. According to Finck, the lesser-known languages of the prehistoric inhabitants of the Mediterranean region are distantly related to ancient Basque, and we know that the oldest Italic aboriginal tribe was called Osci, identical with Ausci and Vascones. If we take these and all the foregoing facts into account, we begin to get a picture of a worldwide complex of linguistic relationships that transcend time and space. We can see Basque, an oddity among modern European languages, as the last relic of a prehistoric world language that was spoken on both sides of the Atlantic. Braghine, describing his experiences, writes, "During my stay in Guatemala I often heard about a tribe of Indios that inhabits the district of Petén in the northern part of the country. They speak a language similar to Basque, and I know of a Basque missionary who preached there in his native tongue with great success."

Finck claims that the idiom of the Lacandones is an ancient linguistic relic. It is still spoken, but only by a few hundred people. Here is another linguistic link with the remote past, and the theory is confirmed by a report quoted by C. W. Ceram in his book *Gods, Graves and Scholars:* "Most recently, in 1947, an expedition led by Giles Greville Healey went to Bonampac in Chiapas (Petén). They

very soon found eleven rich temples of the ancient empire, dating
from the time shortly before the emigration . . . but the most astonishing of Healey's finds in the jungle this time were the wall paintings. . . ."

Healey photographed a young Lacandone girl in front of one of the
paintings. Her face was like the profile of the Maya king in the picture. The racial features of this tribe, which is on the verge of extinction, have been preserved through many centuries. Both their language and their facial characteristics and bearing are very ancient
indeed. Can we tell, from these few remaining Lacandones, what the
Atlanteans looked like?

Petén is not far from Tula in Mexico, which is the home of the
equally interesting Indio tribe of the Otomi. Braghine has this observation to make on their language: "These Indios speak the old
Japanese dialect, and when the Japanese ambassador to Mexico visited this tribe some time ago, he conversed with them in it."

With this last connection the linguistic relationships come full circle. If Japanese is related to Georgian through its very ancient Tungus
component; and Georgian, via Basque, is related to Guatemaltec,
then it is not surprising that the Otomi, who are close relatives of the
Guatemaltecs, should understand ancient Japanese. So many related
idioms must surely have a common basis in a primeval world language.

In his book *Die Eiszeit war ganz anders (The Ice Age Was Quite Different,* 1973) Richard Fester investigated the archetypes of the human
protolanguage by examining six basic words. These were as follows:
ba, kall, tal, os, asq, and tag. He examined them for consonant and
vowel shifts and for their scale of semantic content, and correlated
innumerable languages with each other. This authoritative work
takes up von Humboldt's theory of the basic interrelation between the
world's 125 principal languages and classifies them according to the
degree of relationship.

In the opinion of Professor Liebermann, Neanderthal Man had no
pharynx and could not therefore master a complete language, but the
Cro-Magnon had and could. If we accept this view, then we must
accept the general and tactical superiority of Cro-Magnon Man, and
we may attribute the development of language to him.

Language is a record of prehistory. A standardized basic classification of languages has been established that is accepted by paleolin-
guists and that covers not only all modern, but also extinct languages.

To return to the Basque language, it was spoken by the ancient Iberians and it seems to be as closely related as any to the primeval world language. We can only get at this primeval language indirectly. But we can see clearly how all the striking linguistic relationships that we have been discussing can, in the last analysis, be traced back to the original Basque either as a root or as an intermediary.

The Basques still live in Spain and southwestern France, as they have probably lived from ancient times. Plato expressly states that their part of Europe belonged to the Atlantean kingdom. The Basques were the nearest mainland neighbors of Atlantis whose racial stock still survives. Can we find any solid reasons for believing that here, in the Basques, a relic of Atlantis has been preserved?

The Basques themselves provide one: they still have a clear memory of Atlantis.

Ernst von Salomon mentions this in his travel book *Boche in Frankreich (Boche in France)*. In about the year 1930, he met a Basque smuggler with aquiline features who talked to him about his people. They were, said the Basque, the finest, proudest, and most independent race on Earth, the same today as in the time described by Titus. They still wore the same costumes, used the same knives, employed the same methods of tilling their fields. Nobody ever betrayed his kith and kin; all still spoke their own language, the oldest language in the world.

Von Salomon continues, "The Basques, he said, are the last relics of a more beautiful, freer, prouder world, long ago sunk below the sea together with Atlantis, one of whose last remaining pillars was the Pyrenees, and the other the mountains of Morocco. . . ."

If what this Basque said is true, then we may look for similar relics at the other side of the Atlantic, in other words, the other end of the Atlantean empire. The aquiline appearance of the Basques is in fact echoed there in the profiles of the old Mayas (see Plates 9 and 10) and it survives among the pure descendants of the Mayas, the Lacandone Indios. There is a very ancient stone in the Vendée, which according to Baudion (cf. Braghine) is only visible at low tide, and which shows the same profile.

A second similar characteristic is the method of agriculture. The Basques still use a very ancient but efficient method of tilling their fields. This accords with von Salomon's story. They do not plough, but instead use "layas," two-pronged forks with which they loosen the ground, as market gardeners loosen the beds, before sowing. It is very strange that such a custom should persist in a country where the plough and other methods of agriculture have been known for thousands of years. It is perhaps even stranger that the Indios of Central America use the same method, and that this very method of cultivation was practiced by the ancient Mayas.

On this subject C. W. Ceram writes, "In the course of their entire history the Mayas employed the crudest known method of agriculture. It was dibble cultivation, which consisted of felling all the trees in a strip of jungle, and burning it as soon as the wood was dry just before the start of the rainy season. Shortly after the end of it, long pointed sticks were pushed into the ground and several grains of maize placed in each hole. . . ."

So in two quite different regions, separated by nearly 5,000 miles (8000 km) of Atlantic Ocean, exactly the same method of agriculture is employed. Surely this justifies assumption that this was the way that the Atlanteans tilled their fields on their island in the middle of the Atlantic, where the conditions were much more favorable than on the two continents, and that they taught the peoples of the continents either side of the ocean to use the same method. The method failed in the jungles of the Maya country, but it was eminently suited to the great, fertile plain of Atlantis. It was also successful in the Basque country, where there are also fertile plains that are easy to cultivate, and this ancient method of dibble cultivation still serves the Basques well in the present day. In the mountain jungles of Honduras, however, the Mayas could not produce enough food by this means. They were forced to abandon their splendid cities and continually move on to clear new tracts of land.

The third similarity is the game of pelota. "Pelote basque" is the Basque national game. As von Salomon describes it, "It is a game whose rules could not be simpler, although it demands the greatest possible skill. Even the children play pelota against any available wall and notices are put up on the walls of churches: *Peloter interdit.* The real games were competitive and extremely tough and men only mastered them after long training. Two teams of one man each, or preferably two men each, played each other. The first player hurls a ball the size of a tennis ball, but made of a dark, hard, yet extremely elastic material, against a large square wall with the utmost force. It bounces back sharply and must be returned by the opponent with his bare hand, either by the player who plays close to the wall or, if the man at the front misses it, by his teammate at the back. A square recess in the bottom right-hand corner of the wall provides surprising variants for the ball's trajectory. . . ."

In addition to the bare hand, a club-shaped bat fastened to the forearm may be used. This is probably the ancestor of the modern tennis racket. This account of the favorite game of the Mexican nobility is given in Eduard Stucken's historical novel *Die Weissen Götter (The White Gods):*

"The rules of the ball game were very grotesque indeed. The red, blue, and yellow caoutchouc balls, about the size of an apple, were bounced into the air with a bat strung with leather and ending in a horseshoe shape. Only competent players succeeded in sending the ball through the hole in the stone below the ceiling. When it had passed through the millstone hole the opponent had to catch it and bounce it back with his shoulder, head, hip, or buttocks without using his arms and hands. Sometimes the ball was bounced repeatedly from buttocks to buttocks, and the strange postures of the players resembled those of jumping frogs and monkeys. . . ."

One can see that more hazards had been introduced in Mexico. But apart from these, the game was the same on both sides of the Atlantic. Did the kings and nobles of the island of Atlantis play pelota as long as ten thousand years ago, as Montezuma played it in the time of Cortes, and as the Basques still play it today?

Pelota bats and laya, dibble cultivation, linguistic and racial characteristics: these three similarities form a bond between peoples on two sides of the Atlantic. But they only apply to those who had been at one time in cultural contact with the rulers of the sunken empire. Von Humboldt drew attention to some puzzling similarities between the ancient civilizations of the Old and the New Worlds. Our arguments have supplemented these. Combined, they all point to a common cause, a common center: Atlantis, heartland of this long-vanished maritime power. Only by working laboriously, and always using indirect methods, can we at last probe far enough into the twilight of the remote past to catch a glimmer of this ancient glory.

The heart of the culture has vanished long ago. The cultural relationships whose existence we suspect can be arrived at only by indirect analogy. These analogies do not by any means constitute a proof. But they can, and should, be taken seriously as pointers to the distinct probability that this great cultural center really did exist and spread its influence far and wide.

These are the best results we can hope to achieve unless the seabed yields up its secrets and provides us with incontrovertible evidence of the existence of Atlantis. Until that day we must be content with what we have. It is better than nothing. Atlantis and all its achievements have not completely disappeared from the face of the Earth.

PART FOUR

THE CATACLYSM

The Geological Evidence

IT WAS INEVITABLE that there should be doubts as to whether Atlantis had ever existed so long as there was no scientific evidence available. But evidence from the Quaternary period has proved conclusively that during this era the Gulf Stream was deflected westward by a barrier in the middle of the Atlantic. Paleoclimatological research has established that the land ice in northwestern Europe was able to advance as far south as the 52nd parallel because there was at that time no warm current flowing toward the European coast which would have melted it. The warm current was held back in mid-Atlantic by a large island that bore the same name as the ocean. Such a great mass of land cannot disintegrate or disappear entirely, and it remains for the most part under the sea, a submarine plateau. The depth chart of the Atlantic has revealed the secret. That island, with all its huge walls and broad canals, sank under the waters and became a unique submarine landmass. It no longer blocked the Gulf Stream, so that the warm current has flowed freely eastward ever since.

That the Barrier Island X of the Ice Age is no longer visible is obvious; where it disappeared is revealed by the relief map of the ocean floor. This is geological evidence that cannot be questioned. How did the large island become a land under the sea? Leaving aside Plato's account of Atlantis and all the folklore connected with it, how did the island disappear?

According to Wegener's theory, the two great continental platforms bordering the Atlantic fit so neatly into each other that there could have been no space between them for a large island. Hence Wegener's disbelief in the existence of an Atlantic barrier island. Figure 26 shows the outline of the continental platforms after they began to drift apart.

Wegener's theory can be seen to hold good for the South Atlantic. The west coast of Africa fits well into the east coast of the Brazilian platform. The projecting landmass that divides the equatorial current

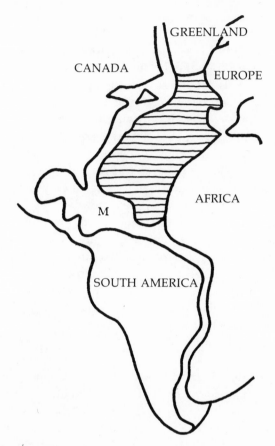

Fig. 26. The shelves do not match. Contrary to Wegener's drawings, the shelves match only in the South Atlantic—South America and Africa—but not in the North Atlantic, which plays a much more important role in the problem of Atlantis. Here a "black patch," a hole northeast of the structural basin of Mexico (M), is found between Africa and Europe on one side and Canada on the other. The shelves in the North Atlantic cannot be matched without due allowance for the Atlantic Ridge.

exactly fits the Gulf of Guinea. But the landmasses of the North Atlantic do not complement each other. A great gap opens up between the two continental shelves, a gap much too wide to be acceptable to the draftsman. In this region Wegener's reconstruction, admirable in its basic concept and very credible, calls for modification.

But first we must look more closely into the methods by which Wegener built up his theory.

The continental landmasses which now form the Old World and the New World were at one time in the Earth's history united in one great land system. This landmass split along a certain seam deep enough to cause the continental platforms to break apart. Where the seam was is now the vast trench of the Atlantic Ocean.

Wegener's reconstruction makes the arbitrary assumption that the seam itself disappeared completely. According to his theory, the separation of the continental landmasses was caused by a clean fracture between the platforms. When put together again they should, therefore, fit as neatly as the pieces of a jigsaw puzzle. This is the theory behind Wegener's reconstruction, though he did not formulate it in this precise manner. But as the "hole" in Figure 26 shows, the North Atlantic continents do not fit neatly into each other. If we think of it as a vast jigsaw puzzle, there is a piece missing in this area.

In fact the comparison is not very apt. Only a reasonably homogeneous body such as a sheet of metal can be cut up into sections with smooth edges that can be fitted together. Geological events are concerned with very different sorts of material and very different types of structure.

A comparison of Figures 26 and 27 will show that a modified reconstruction results in a much better fit of the continental shelves. This is very important. The western edge of Europe now matches the eastern edge of the Atlantic Ridge. The eastern edge of North America in turn matches the western edge of the Atlantic Ridge, apart from a section between Florida and Cape Hatteras. There is a gap here that will play a significant part in our continuing investigations, a gap that indicates that there was at one time land here.

In order to better understand the idea of continental drift, Wegener suggests the analogy of icebergs floating in the water. In the same way, he says, the continental platforms floated in a sea of sima. This is a useful analogy for a fundamentally correct theory, but it does not go quite far enough. The continental platforms do not, in fact, float as if in water. They are held by the viscous, gluey sima, which grips them with a strong adhesive force. When the platforms shift, great frictional power is generated wherever the harder sial adheres to the pitchlike sima. This friction is beneath the platforms and along their edges. The mechanism of the drifting is therefore more complex than it appears to be, and its effects are greater. The drifting platform is

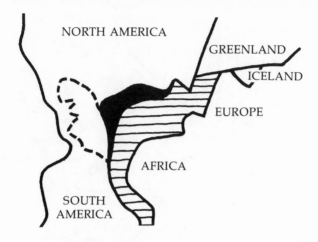

Fig. 27. The shelves match the Atlantic Ridge. In rectangular parallel projection, the map shows the Early Tertiary position of the shelves before the first continental drift began. The shelves are a perfect fit of the edges of the Atlantic Ridge. Only the black patch in the North American basin indicates a subsequent subsidence of the land.

exposed to abrasion. Here and there fragments of varying size will break off, and as they become lodged in the slipway of the sima, will mark the direction of the drift.

A striking example of this process is shown in Figure 28, which illustrates the U-shaped drift marks of Patagonia—a shape traceable in the South Sandwich Islands, the South Orkneys group, the South Shetlands, and the Palmer Archipelago in the direction of Graham Land in the Antarctic, while in the north the U-shape is completed by the Falklands and the tiny Slaten Island. The fragments of land that form this shape are not remains or bridge piers of a submerged land platform, but are the easily identifiable marks that indicate the course of a very ancient drag process. If we look at the geological evidence with this process in mind, we can almost see the process at work. The sima tears into the sole of a continent and chews at the edges of the platforms. It tears away fragments of these and holds them in its sticky grip, while the heavy sial block continues on its drift.

If we now look at Figure 29 with this interpretation in mind we see a diagram of the Atlantic plateau system. This has presented even

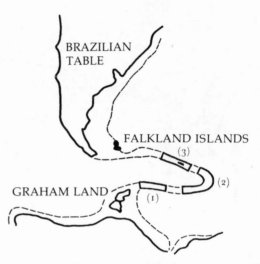

Fig. 28. The drift mark of Patagonia. The Brazilian table drifted from its original position in Graham Land, which is a peninsula of the Antarctic continent. It has left a typical arc of islands and shallows behind as a drift mark: the South Orkney Islands (1), the South Sandwich Islands (2), and South Georgia (3). The shallows merge into the shelf of the Brazilian table near the Falkland Islands. The loop form is typical; it shows that we must distinguish between two types of drift movement: an Early Tertiary, which pushed Patagonia eastward, and the postdiluvian, which caused an opposite westward drift.

more difficulties for geologists and oceanographers than has the question of the origin of the central Atlantic Ridge.

To the left and right of the central ridge, plateaus branch off like the branches of a tree. Most of them end in island fragments. These, too, are drift marks showing the paths taken by the individual sections of the platform as they moved from their original to their present position. Strong base and lateral friction occurred where the platforms were torn apart by the forces that originally produced the drift. The undersides of platforms drifting apart in such circumstances would hardly be smooth, but would be uneven and of varying thickness. The displacement they caused to the magma base would vary. Hence the drag marks of varying depth. Neither were the drifting platforms of equal consistency. Some parts would be more resistant to abrasion, others would break off more easily, and these broken-off fragments

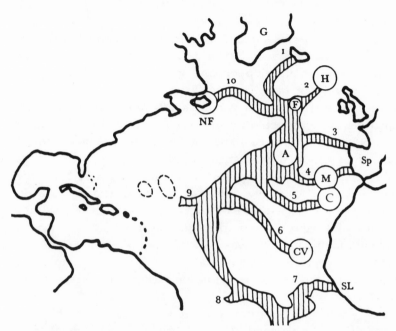

Fig. 29. The North Atlantic transverse plateau system. The map shows the present (Quinternary) position of the shelves surrounding the Atlantic Basin and of the Atlantic Ridge with its transverse plateaus.
1. Reykjanes Ridge toward Iceland.
2. Rockall Plateau to the Hebrides (H)
3. Biscay Plateau to Cape Finisterre, Spain (Sp.)
4. Azores Plateau from the Azores (A) through Madeira (M) to the Sierra Morena.
5. Canary Platform to the Canary Islands (C).
6. Cape Verde Plateau to the Cape Verde Islands (CV).
7. Sierra Leone to the Loma Mountains (SL).
8. Stump of the Para Plateau.
9. Stump of the Puerto-Rico Plateau.
10. Newfoundland Plateau (NF). G = Greenland.
    Broken lines: the two deep-sea holes near Puerto Rico; Hatched: Atlantic Ridge with transverse plateaus.

became lodged in the sima substrate and merged with the drag mark, the associated transverse plateau. This whole remarkable ground relief has neither existed from the very beginning nor is it the relic of a submerged Atlantic continent. The process that created it was set in motion during the Early Tertiary Age when the platforms began to drift; it developed with the drift and attained its present complexity and magnitude.

It must have been a stupendous force that dislodged the large platforms from their original anchorages. The "pole-flight force" postulated by Wegener and Köppen, and open to strong geophysical objections, would not have been sufficient. Moreover, it would have driven the platforms in a parallel southward direction toward the equatorial zone; it would not have caused them to drift away from each other toward the east and the west. There is no existing force that can be regarded as an adequate triggering agent. Lyell's type of interpretation cannot be applied to this Early Tertiary Earth revolution which led to a new order—or disorder. There was a drastic change in the whole surface of the Earth. Hundreds of thousands of square miles were covered with thick layers of lava and enormous folds of mountains. This was no leisurely process but a cataclysmic event. The geological evidence here is of the utmost importance. It provides incontrovertible proof of the existence of terrestrial revolutions.

Nor was this Early Tertiary catastrophe the only one. It must have been followed by a second. A glance at the U-shape of the Patagonian drift marks in Figure 28 reveals this. Continental platforms are tremendously inert. Once they have received the initial impetus they will move in a straight line. They will not describe loops and curves unless they receive a second impulse which causes them to change direction. The pointed Patagonian trail of the Brazilian platform provides the geological evidence for this. Here we see the effects of two clearly distinguishable drift impulses, and therefore of the two terrestrial revolutions that generated them.

The Brazilian platform was torn from its original site, Graham Land in the present Antarctica, during the Early Tertiary Age. It drifted eastward at first, leaving an eastward-pointing drift mark at around the South Orkneys. Had it received no further impulse it should, in its inertia, have continued to drift eastward. But the geological evidence shows that the eastward drift was slowed down by an opposite impulse. This resulted in the crumbling away of many island fragments, a sign that new georevolutionary forces had become active. Their effect is shown in Figure 28. The original eastward drift was reversed into a westward drift. Brazil moved farther and farther away from the west coast of Africa and tore open the trench of the South

Atlantic. In the North Atlantic, the westward drift of Canada probably started during the Early Tertiary Age, but was intensified and accelerated at the end of the Quaternary. At the end of the Diluvial Age the Atlantic was much narrower than it is today. Its widening was due to the second great terrestrial cataclysm, the force that set South America on its new westward drift.

For the purpose of our investigation only the second cataclysm at the end of the Diluvial Age is relevant. The Patagonian drift mark shows that this cannot have occurred until long after the Tertiary Age. However sudden the start of the drifting, it will soon be slowed down by the highly viscous sima. The long eastern portion of the Patagonian drift mark must therefore have taken a very long time to grow. From a geodynamic point of view, the middle and Late Tertiary Ages constitute, together with the Quaternary Age, a single epoch of declining activity and increasing new geological stability. The uniformity of this combined epoch is borne out by the great difficulty of distinguishing deposits of the late Tertiary Age—for example the Pliocene—from early Quaternary Pleistocene deposits. These resemble each other in name as well as in nature. In the opinion of most geologists and paleontologists, this combined epoch lasted many millions of years. It is fully explicable in terms of Lyell's gradualism. No second terrestrial revolution can have taken place during this time. A terrestrial disturbance on such a scale is consistent only with the transition from the Quaternary to the Quinternary Age. There is no doubt about the sudden switch from the diluvial to the postdiluvial climate. In the nineteenth century it was generally thought that this change came about spontaneously, of its own accord. But this cannot be so. Something must have happened that interrupted the normal course of events and brought about a profound change, something powerful enough to make a complete change in the existing pattern of climate. If we are looking for a time in which the Patagonian drift marks could have been made, then it is in this epoch of renewed geological activity that we must search.

But this is the very epoch into which we have placed the submergence in the Atlantic of Barrier Island X. This barrier island, Plato's Atlantis, became submerged at the end of the Quaternary Age in the course of a terrestrial revolution. This is what we want to prove. This second cataclysm did not affect the entire Earth, as did its predecessor during the Eocene period. It was concentrated in the vicinity of the Atlantic. Only these regions suffered directly from this catastrophe at the end of the Diluvial Age; outside this region we find only the evidence of secondary side effects.

Let us now look at these marginal regions.

In the southern part of the North Atlantic lies the oceanographic region of the Azores. At its northern end this ocean borders on the North Polar Sea. The Wyville Thomson Ridge between Iceland and the Orkney and Shetlands Islands forms the boundary. This part of the ocean was first systematically explored in 1883–1896 by a Norwegian Polar Expedition led by Fridtjof Nansen. Large quantities of shells and otoliths of animals inhabiting shallow waters were found on the seabed between Iceland and the small volcanic island of Jan Mayen in the latitude of about 72° north. These were found at depths of 3300 feet (1000 m) and, toward the south, of 8200 feet (2500 m). Nansen and his colleagues concluded that these areas must have dropped to 6560 feet (2000 m) very suddenly, and in the geologically most recent period, because otherwise the shallow sea animals would have had time to escape to the continental shelf. Their marine environment must have changed too abruptly to allow such an escape. They, together with countless other creatures, became victims of the Atlantic catastrophe.

Figure 30 shows a depth chart of this area. Iceland, the Jan Mayen Island, and the Faroe Islands are all embedded in remarkably wide deep-sea outcrops and connected by narrow transverse plateaus. There are similar drag marks, or drift marks, extending from Iceland to Greenland and to the Atlantic Ridge. Before the great change took place, the island of Iceland was about four times as large as it is today. Fjords, narrow trenches, or drowned valleys, are as much a characteristic of Iceland as they are of Norway. The Faroes and the Beerenberg volcano on Jan Mayen are all that remains above sea level of what were previously large landmasses. Farther south, the Azores are all that is left of a similar mass. The sinking of Atlantis, so often ridiculed as mere myth, was paralled by similar events on a smaller scale in the northern regions. In the northern area, however, Nansen's explorations have provided us with certain essential information. There is no doubt at all that an area of ocean the size of a continent—several million square miles—has sunk 3300–6560 feet (1000–2000 m) during the most recent geological era. For some reason that we can only try to reconstruct by means of geophysics, the sima level of the basin must have dropped. The little island fragments of sial that were lodged in it inevitably sank too. All these fragments of land became submerged except for the few remains that are still visible today.

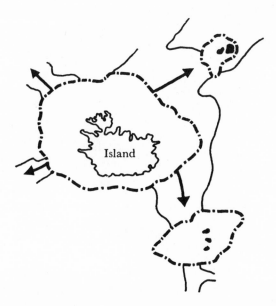

Fig. 30. Subsidences in the Arctic Ocean. The depth chart of the Arctic Ocean around Iceland illustrates the subsidence, noted by Fridtjof Nansen, of the entire basin north of the Atlantic. The dash-dot 3300 ft (1000 m) depth line shows the small island platforms previously above sea level; today only their highest regions are dry land. As a result of the subsidence of the magma level the small platforms that sank with it isostatically, were "drowned." The region of the Arctic Ocean reveals, although on a smaller scale, exactly the same phenomena as claimed by the Atlantis tradition for the Azores region.

The degree of subsidence is not uniform throughout the North Atlantic, but increases from north to south toward the Wyville Thomson Ridge. It is very likely, therefore, that the slope was imposed upon the polar fringe by the larger basin in the south. The center of the catastrophe that triggered this widespread lowering of the sima level was situated in the middle of the Atlantic.

We now come to the Rejkijanes Ridge, which points to the Telegraph Plateau. This derives its name from a dramatic event in the history of the laying of the transatlantic cable. The cable laid in 1898 suddenly snapped at 40° north and 29° west of Paris, and the ends disappeared into what appeared to be a bottomless sea. They were only retrieved with great difficulty, and during the course of these operations various other objects were dredged up from the seabed. Among these was a huge piece of rock which was deposited in a Paris museum. Fifteen years later it was examined by Paul Termier, director of the Oceanographic Institute at that time, and well-known as a scientist both in France and in other countries. The specimen was a tachylite of typically vitreous structure. Termier publicized his findings in a sensational lecture given in the Oceanographic Institute. He called his lecture "Atlantis" and these were his conclusions:

First, the specimen was of volcanic origin. Large tracts of the ocean floor were covered with lava. To produce the flow of lava of which the specimen formed a part, there must have been at some time very considerable volcanic eruptions in the region of the Telegraph Plateau.

Second, the specimen was amorphous, vitreous, and of noncrystalline structure. It must have solidified in free air, not in deep water, Termier believed. It could have been ejected only by an above-water volcano, not by a submarine one. The lava covering those vast areas of ocean floor must have come from former land volcanoes, he concluded. (In this respect he was mistaken; it has since been established that the vitreous quality is the result of gases present in lava, coming from the mantle. But the tachylites nevertheless were on the seabed as a result of a major eruption.)

Third, the whole region must have sunk through more than 6560 feet (2000 m) either at the same time as the eruption or very shortly afterward. The specimen was therefore evidence of a prehistoric catastrophe in the middle of the Atlantic—where according to Plato the island of Atlantis was said to have subsided.

Fourth, the specimen was a tachylite according to mineralogical classification. Tachylite dissolves in sea water within about 15,000 years. But the find had sharp contours and appeared intact. The catastrophe in the Atlantic must therefore have occurred less than 15,000 years previously. In other words, later than 13,000 B.C., and probably considerably later. This time limit agrees surprisingly well with Plato's statement of "9000 years before Solon," about 10,000 B.C., which also corresponds with the mean value of the geological estimates of the end of the Quaternary Age.

In opposition to Termier's arguments are those of a German geologist, Hartung, who described the Azores islands in about 1860. He mentioned curious beach blocks consisting of rock of a type that was not found elsewhere on the island. He argued that these blocks must, therefore, have been brought to the Azores from somewhere else and deposited along the shoreline. Most likely they had been carried by icebergs which had long since melted, leaving on the shores the rocks that had been embedded in them. It was, however, on the shores of the Azores islands as they were in modern times that these rocks were found. Therefore, Hartung concluded, no major postglacial change in level could have occurred in this region.

From this evidence, Högbom and others deduced that no catastrophe could have taken place in the Azores region, since the change in level associated with such an event was ruled out by Hartung's argument. But what does this argument really prove? It proves that no major postglacial changes in level occurred in the Azores region. It does not prove anything about what happened shortly before the postglacial period began, or that a change took place at the end of the Quaternary era, and was already completed by the gradual onset of the postglacial melting period. This was precisely what Paul Termier had established, that there had been a sudden and catastrophic subsidence of the seabed of more than 6560 feet (2000 m), associated with tremendous volcanic eruptions. By the time that the great ice sheet was breaking up and the icebergs were drifting southward, the island of Atlantis had already disappeared, leaving only the tiny Azores archipelago. It would have to be along the present-day shores of the islands that the melting icebergs deposited the rocks. No changes in sea level have taken place in this region since that time.

There is, therefore, no contradiction between Hartung's argument and Plato's account, or between Termier's conclusions, and the conclusions of this present investigation. On the contrary, Hartung's argument adds force to the opposite view.

For there to be no contradiction between the theory of Atlantis and Hartung's argument, the subsidence in the Azores region must have been sudden and catastrophic. Had the subsidence postulated by Termier been a gradual process over a considerable period, during the postglacial age, then the odd blocks transported by icebergs during this long period would have been deposited, not along the present shores of the Azores, but along the earlier shoreline, now submerged.

Further circumstantial evidence is provided by the part of the Azores region that borders directly on the Telegraph Plateau. Here the shallow seabed slopes sharply downward. In the narrow strip formed by this steep slope there is an unusual proliferation of steep rock pinnacles and sharp rocks. Their shape is well-preserved. There has been no rounding off of either the steep pinnacles or the deep hollows. This submarine landscape fits in very well with Plato's remark that all the soil had been washed away. The sharp, fine profiles would have been eroded, and the lava covering the ocean floor would have decayed if all this rocky terrain had been immersed in sea water for more than 15,000 years. Chemical forces are very destructive, but mechanical forces are equally so. Sharp edges and points can be ground down and blunted by abrasion, erosion, and the action of waves. But the entire seabed below the present surf zone has retained its sharpness of profile. Had the subsidence taken place gradually, chemical and other forces would have ground down this sharp profile within a few hundred years. The island whose highest peaks still stand above water must have sunk suddenly not more than 15,000 years ago. This underwater profile proves it.

From the geological evidence, then, we may conclude that a huge area between Jan Mayen Island and the Azores suddenly sank at the end of the Quaternary period. The nearer to the center of the catastrophe, the greater the degree of subsidence. This center was probably somewhere south of the Azores, and it has indeed been known since 1900 that this catastrophic subsidence extended far to the south of the Azores region. In that year the research vessel *Gauss* hauled up a sediment core measuring 1 foot, 6 inches (46 cm) from the Romanche Trench, which is 24,250 feet in depth (7300 m). This deep trench lies very close to the equator, to the west of the Liberian plateau on the boundary between the northern and southern basins of the Atlantic. It crosses the Atlantic Ridge, bisecting it as it were, at a distance of about 2800 miles (4500 km) from the Azores.

This sediment core picked up by the *Gauss* contained five strata. At the top was red clay, followed by three chalk-free continental sedimentary strata, and lastly, at the bottom, by globigerina ooze. This ooze, according to the life mode of these plankton organisms, is found only at depths of 6560–14,800 feet (2000–4500 m). The Romanche Trench cannot, therefore, have been deeper than 14,800 feet (4500 m) at the time when this layer of globigerina ooze was deposited. The depth today is 24,250 feet (7300 m), so the seabed must have subsided at least 9400 feet (2800 m). This is approximately the depth that Paul Termier had postulated for the Azores region and the Telegraph Plateau. So we now have a considerable southward extension of the area affected by the catastrophe at the end of the Quaternary Age.

This sudden collapse of an area covering many millions of square miles must have been accompanied by violent seismic and volcanic activity. The sima basin of the Atlantic could accommodate itself to very slow deformations in a viscously-elastic adjustment, but its raw material is too brittle and nonelastic to adapt to sudden change. It cracks and breaks into rifts and fractures, and the magma close to the surface is extruded and overflows. A large part of the Atlantic basin is covered by acid volcanic magma of recent origin. In contrast, the floor of the Pacific, though scarcely less active, consists of paleogenous basic magma. In this respect the evidence is not geological, but paleomineralogical.

A considerable contribution is also made by volcanology. The Atlantic contains a surprising number of volcanoes. There is a main chain of active craters running through the entire active region, a chain that coincides fairly closely with the Atlantic Ridge. Here is evidence that this is a very ancient fracture seam that ruptures more easily than a healthy portion of the platform (Figure 31).

The deadly chain of Atlantic volcanoes begins in the north with the Beerenberg on Jan Mayen Island, where the downward slope of the seabed is also noticeable. It continues to Iceland, that land of ice and fire where about five hundred active craters erupted during the dreadful year of 1783, and from there it proceeds to the nine islands of the Azores, of which five boast active volcanoes. This is the center of instability in which islands can appear and disappear as rapidly as in the neighborhood of Iceland. Fuego is an active volcano on the Cape Verde Islands, and Madeira is a seismic subcenter. The fracture line continues southward via St. Helena, Tristan da Cunha, and Diego Alvarez, as far as the South Orkneys. A branch line veers off to the Antilles, where the island of Martinique is notorious for the violent eruption of Mount Pelée. On the May 8, 1902, all of the more than thirty thousand inhabitants of the island's capital, St. Pierre, were suffocated by erupting gases. This branch line extends to the giant volcanoes of Central America. Figure 31 shows a survey map of this Atlantic volcanic region. Changes that take place in such a volcanic region are more likely to be sudden than gradual.

The evidence of geology, paleomineralogy, and volcanology all goes to support the assumption that the sinking of the Atlantic seabed did not take place gradually but was a cataclysmic event. The greater the subsidence, the nearer the center of this event, and we must, therefore, look for this center to the south of the Telegraph Plateau, because the extent of subsidence increases southward through the region of the Azores. The system of transverse plateaus, shown in Figure 29 (page 139), may help us in our search, because it may have preserved evidence of extreme destruction.

In the northern region this system is fully developed and is apparently intact. There are no gaps. This is not the case farther south. The Puerto Rico Plateau is broken and only a stump indicates its former existence. In the adjoining North American basin, there are no plateaus at all; everything has disappeared. It looks as if the southwestern part of the North Atlantic, which covers about a third of the total area, suffered a fate of its own. This fate involved the fragmentation of whatever transverse plateaus previously existed there, to-

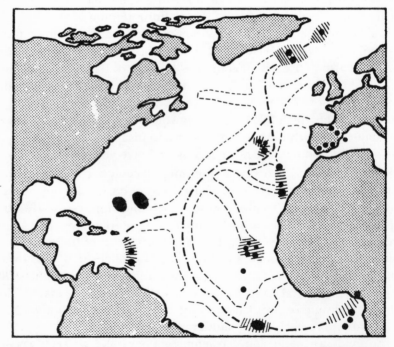

Fig. 31. Distribution of volcanoes in the North Atlantic. The Atlantic Ridge and its plateaus are shown on the map in dashed outline. Active volcanic centers are marked by dots, seismic regions by parallel lines. The bold, dash-dot line represents the fracture line which formed the original edge of the platform.

gether with the creation of the structural basin illustrated in Figure 27 (page 137) as the inexplicable gap between Florida and Cape Hatteras. This, too, has now become associated with similar features.

All this implies that there was a sudden cataclysmic subsidence all the way from the Polar Sea in the north right down to the region southwest of the Azores. The subsidence between Florida and Cape Hatteras would account for the fact that the city of Charleston became the center of a tectonic earthquake region. Figure 35 (page 182) shows how the lines of equal earthquake intensity were distributed in this region during the earthquake of August 31, 1896. It was no accident that their focus was in this area.

Here, then, are three areas that have suffered catastrophe: the North Polar Sea, the Azores region, and the North American basin. Can we postulate three different terrestrial revolutions at three different times? Such a proliferation of cataclysms seems unlikely in the extreme. The ordinary process of geological events is much too leisurely and undisturbed, much too "Lyellistic" for such an assumption. No. It must have been one and the same catastrophe that affected all these three regions. The geological evidence shows that the Atlantic cataclysm was a terrible reality in the Earth's history. It disrupted the normal geological development and brought the fourth age of the Earth to an abrupt conclusion.

This is no empty hypothesis. It is supported by the description of certain soil samples recently collected from the Atlantic by the American geophysicist Piggot. They consist of stratigraphic cores of 9 feet, 10 inches (almost 3 m) in length, and Piggot noted that they frequently included two zones very rich in volcanic ash. Professor Pettersson comments on them in his book, *Atlantis and Atlantic*. "This ash must have originated in enormous volcanic eruptions of the volcanoes either in the West Indies or, more likely, on the central ridge of the Atlantic. . . ."

This is followed by an even more important observation: "The topmost of the two volcanic strata is found above the topmost glacial stratum, which indicates that this volcanic catastrophe or catastrophes occurred in postglacial times."

This disposes of Högbom's criticism of Termier's conclusions. Pettersson's analysis of Piggot's record cores led him to the same conclusion as Termier. There is no doubt that a volcanic catastrophe did occur in the Atlantic, which brought the Quaternary Age to an end and initiated the postglacial age.

Similar cores collected from near Newfoundland also contained layers of volcanic ash, all of which date from the transition period from the Quaternary to the Quinternary Age. Pettersson was forced to the following conclusion: "This at any rate offers weighty reasons for the assumption that the period after the last great glaciation during which Plato's Atlantis is said to have perished was really one of volcanic-seismic catastrophes in the North Atlantic region. . . ."

But the ocean floor has yielded up even more of its secrets. One of the cores was taken from a spot in which we are particularly interested, the area of the Atlantic Ridge where we have established that the Gulf Stream barrier island was situated during the Quaternary Age.

What did this core show? As might have been expected, it differed considerably from those obtained from the two Atlantic basins on either side of the central ridge. It was unusually short, with a sediment no deeper than 3⅛ inches (8 cm). Professor Pettersson says, "Below it the pipe seems to have struck hard material, probably rock, of which no samples at all were obtained. . . . It can therefore not be entirely ruled out that the Midatlantic Ridge, where the sample originated, was above sea level up to about ten thousand years ago and did not subside to its present depth until later."

The Center of the Cataclysm

EVERY TRUE CATACLYSM has a center. The Atlantic catastrophe, for which we have established a historical date and a geographical location, can have been no exception to this rule.

The geological evidence that we have been using has been obtained from modern researches and therefore shows the modern aspects of the region we are concerned with. In order to reconstruct the prehistoric catastrophe we must deal with any obvious geographical changes that have occurred during the intermediate period.

The depth chart in Plate 11 provides an invaluable piece of information. A study of the ocean floor shows a great structural basin to the east of what is now the southeast coast of North America. It reveals a marked abnormality. Near the stump that remains of the fractured Puerto Rico Plateau, there are two great holes of nearly 23,000 feet (7000 m) in depth. These holes are in the center of the fragmented coastal area, not very far from the southern edge of the submarine landmass that acted as a barrier to the Gulf Stream before its submergence, and that we have identified as Plato's Atlantis. The Puerto Rico Trench, which has a depth of about 30,000 feet (9000 m) encircles the southern part of the central area of catastrophe. A study of the ocean bed in this region will enable us to forge a further link in our chain. From it we will be able to draw far-reaching conclusions, not only about the center of the catastrophe, but about its cause and its wider effects.

There is no doubt that the Atlantic catastrophe was centered on these two holes, and that its most violent effects were felt in their vicinity.

An American anthropologist, Alan H. Kelso de Montigny, has put forward a theory about the eastern part of the Caribbean Sea bordered by the arc of the Lesser Antilles. The depth chart here also

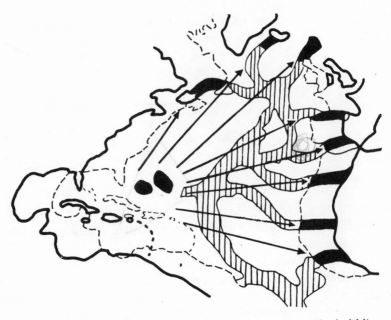

Fig. 32. Reconstruction of the center of the catastrophe. The bold lines on the map show today's, the thin ones the Quaternary coastline. The plateaus formed during the Tertiary and Quaternary Ages and the Atlantic Ridge are hatched, and the Postdiluvial end sections of the plateaus black. Shown in black in the center of the catastrophe are the two deep-sea holes in the neighborhood of Puerto Rico, directly next to the stub of the shattered Puerto Rico Plateau and the deep Puerto Rico trench.

reveals a deep sea hole, right in the middle of the Antilles arc, which surrounds it like the remains of the rim of a half-submerged giant crater. Kelso de Montigny thinks that an asteroid must have struck here not more than 10,000 years ago. This date agrees surprisingly well with the one in which we are interested. The site of this suspected strike is not very far from the two huge holes in the floor of the North American basin, and therefore, not very far from the center of the catastrophe. This deep sea hole in the Caribbean is smaller and shallower than the other two, and it may well be that it was caused by a fragment of the celestial body which unleashed the Atlantic catastrophe at the end of the Diluvial Age.

The two large holes occupy a vast area—about 77,000 square miles

(200,000 sq.km). It must have been an indescribably powerful force that drove these deep holes in the sima floor of the Atlantic basin—an ocean floor that may well have been deeper than it is today. In the age of the atom bomb one is tempted to think of it in terms of a colossal submarine nuclear explosion.

What could possibly have caused these two gigantic impact holes? Were they subsidence craters produced by tectonic earthquakes or enormous sinkholes, elutriation products of submarine vortices? Their immense size and depth rules out the second possibility.

Both these explanations are inadequate and we must look further for the primary cause. The most satisfactory explanation is that the propellant which triggered off a whole revolutionary event was ignited here, the center of the cataclysm. In that case we could regard the two deep sea holes as the unhealed scars left by two deep wounds inflicted on the Earth's crust by the impact of a celestial body of considerable size.

Earlier research workers, among them Wyston, Count Carli, de Lalande, and Braghine, have put forward theories of this type. The present investigation is aiming, with the help of many different scientific disciplines, to confirm these theories and give them a quantitative dimension. The conclusion that we shall come to was that the celestial body in question was not a comet, or the head of a comet, but a much larger heavenly rover, an asteroid.

The two impact craters are adjacent and are similar in size and shape. Both are roughly oval, and in both, the major axes of the ellipses run from northwest to southeast. This would suggest that the objects that struck like cosmic shells and gouged out these deep sea holes came either from the southeast or the northwest.

Nothing of relevance is to be found in the southeast, but in the northwest there is the subsided coastal strip, which we may regard as our first piece of evidence. The stupendous force of the impact fragmented the land so that it sank beneath the sea. These are two aspects of what was certainly one and the same catastrophe. We may safely deduce that the celestial body came from the northwest rather than from the southeast. But if it came from the west, out of the evening sky, then it must have been traveling at a speed greater than that of the Earth in its orbit round the sun, otherwise it would not have overtaken the Earth. The planet Earth travels in a nearly circular orbit at almost constant velocity. The orbit of the celestial body must have been very eccentric for it to travel faster at the perihelion than the Earth.

The main shock was no doubt absorbed in the two deep sea holes. But the secondary effects and the aftereffects were felt on the mainland. On the Puerto Rico Plateau, a million or so cubic miles of the tough viscous material of the sima cover have been displaced and fragmented. But the land in the northwest remained.

Taking these facts into account, we are drawn to the obvious conclusion that the deep sea holes situated in the center of the catastrophe were the entry points of the core of the asteroid, which had split in two. The points of impact which fragmented the coastal region to the northwest are those of pieces of the asteroid's solid crust. Heated in the denser layers of the atmosphere, it splintered into gigantic boulders and left its trail along the land.

A cosmic bombardment of such force must at least have grazed the remaining land in the northwest. But the points of impact were presumably less concentrated, so that the cohesion of Earth's crust was preserved. In searching for evidence on the strip of land that has remained, we would expect to find a field of craters, preserved through the thousands of years that have passed since the catastrophe. In fact we do not find the sort of rugged moonscape that we might have expected. The region is flat and marshy, and is traversed by troughs or bays. Superficially it looks very much like any other marshy, coastal strip and for a long while nobody ever suspected that evidence of a cosmic catastrophe could be hidden here. But such remains have been found, and since their discovery the region has been called the "Carolina crater field."

In 1931 the authorities in the two adjacent states of North Carolina and South Carolina decided to carry out a new photogrammetric survey and commissioned a company specializing in aerial photography to undertake this task. There was nothing unusual or sensational about this, and there was no intention to contribute to research into Atlantis. This aerial survey included, among other regions, the area that is of vital interest to us. The stretch between Florida and Cape Hatteras, and also its hinterland, was startlingly exposed by the eagle eye of the aerial camera. When these films, together with all the others, were enlarged and examined in the stereo-comparator they created an unexpected sensation. The pilots who saw the pictures were vividly reminded of the battlefields of the 1914–1918 War, of the hell of Flanders, Ypres, and Arras. All the pictures were characterized by huge circular or oval shapes, sometimes overlapping, that could be clearly identified as enlarged mud-filled craters caused by the impact of gigantic boulders. This was the only conclusion that could be drawn from the unbiased evidence of the aerial photographs. By a lucky chance, the survey camera had thrown a completely unexpected light upon a section of the Earth's history. Its keen and incorruptible eye had discovered the so-called Carolina Meteorite. Plate 12 shows a section of the aerial photographs.

These pictures caused a considerable stir and some lively scientific discussions. A report was unearthed that had been written thirty-six years previously by L. C. Glenn. In his opinion, the large number of oval or circular shallow troughs was a peculiar feature of the coastal strip. Nobody had taken very much notice of his observations, and his report had gathered dust in the archives. But the aerial photographs of 1931 were authentic and impressive documents that could not be so easily ignored. A lively and sometimes heated debate took place about what might have caused the crater field of Carolina.

The aerial survey revealed about three thousand such troughs. Half of them are longer than 1300 feet (400 m) and more than a hundred are longer than 5250 feet (1600 m). As Figure 33 shows, they are distributed over a very extensive area. But this area is only the marginal zone of an elongated ellipse which, when completed, represents a total area of impact of at least 63,500 square miles (165,000 sq. km). Only a small part of this is on the land that remained intact; much the greater part is on the fragmented coastal region and the sunken strip of land. From the 3000 troughs actually counted on land, we may estimate a total of 10,000 for the whole cosmic bomb.

Each fragment of this bomb produced a trough of unknown depth, circular or oval according to the angle at which the fragment struck the ground. All the longitudinal axes are parallel. The fragments must therefore have consisted of boulders traveling parallel to each other. Another feature is that most of the troughs still display remains of the thrust wall in the southeast, although they are almost 11,000 years old. This provides conclusive evidence that the boulders must have come from the northwest. The soil of the craters would only have been pressed into a thrust wall at the southeast if the driving force had come from the opposite direction. All the circumstantial evidence therefore agrees with the hypothesis that a large celestial body entered the atmosphere from the northwest and exploded at a consider-

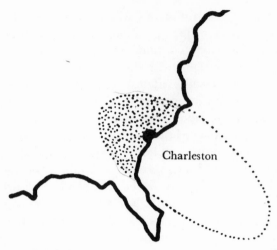

Fig. 33. Map of the Carolina crater field. An area, part-elliptical in shape, extends around the American city of Charleston (Carolina) and as far as the Atlantic coast, which is dotted with "bays," large, formerly deep, but now peat-filled troughs. They are the holes created by the impact of a meteorite (Carolina Meterorite) that had fallen from the sky about ten thousand years ago. The major part of the exploded fragments fell into the sea; the dotted line indicates the approximate outline of the area affected.

able height. Fragments of its solid crust dropped to the Earth before the heavy massive core. The core itself traveled farther to the southeast before it split and caused the two deep sea holes.

If a large meteorite had struck this area during historical times it could hardly have left traces any different from those revealed in the depth chart and the aerial photographs. Soon after the photographs were made public, the theory was put forward that the Carolina crater field was caused by a shower of meteorites, in short, the so-called Carolina Meteorite.

Dr. F. A. Melton and William Schriever, geologists in the University of Oklahoma, lost no time in investigating the origin of these giant holes. There was no mention of Atlantis in the theory that they put forward. In the opinion of these two scientists, the pattern of craters in the Carolina field showed that it had been caused by a huge shower of meteorites resembling a very large comet head. Fletcher Watson, Jr., was the only one to oppose this view. He pointed out that the holes made by all true meteorites were circular, similar to the famous Arizona Crater that had been identified as a hole made by a meteorite. The majority of the Carolina troughs, however, were not circular but oval in shape. He was unable to agree with the theory that these holes were caused by a meteorite shower produced by the disintegration of a comet head in the Earth's atmosphere. Such a comet head, he argued, was not nearly massive enough to provide the fragments necessary for such a bombardment. And in any case, the Earth had on several occasions passed through showers of comet heads and tails and meteorites without any catastrophic effects. Watson concluded that a cosmic origin of the Carolina troughs was quite out of the question. In his opinion they were not impact craters at all, but drifts similar to the shifting sand dunes in the deserts of Central Asia that are known by the name of bajirs.

This gradualist explanation is obviously inadequate. It does not account for the unique position of the crater field in relation to the center of the catastrophe, the deep sea holes, and the subsided coastal strip. Nor does it explain why the craters are concentrated in an elongated elliptical area, or why they occasionally overlap. It is, in fact, deficient in many respects.

But this critic was undoubtedly right on one point. The crater field could not have been formed by either a burst comet head or by a very large shower of meteorites. A comet head is much too small and too deficient in mass. Its explosion might have caused an impressive display of celestial fireworks in the marginal zone of the nitrogen envelope, but these illuminations high up in the atmosphere would have had no consequences on Earth. A shower of meteorites consists of small fragments traveling parallel to each other. Even had they been larger (although no such shower of supermeteorites has ever been observed), they would still have entered the atmosphere parallel to each other and would therefore have struck the ground from these parallel descents. All the craters that they produced would have been identical in shape. They might have been circular or they might have been elliptical, but not both. The random distribution of the shapes actually found in the crater field of Carolina shows that the descents and the angles of impact must have differed considerably. This randomness makes it very difficult to put forward a theory about their origin. Vertically descending bodies, such as the giant Arizona meteorite, carve circular, obliquely descending holes in the ground.

What sort of celestial body could produce this random occurrence of steep and flat descents throughout the dispersion zone? Surely such a pattern and variety of craters could only have been caused by the various fragments of a disintegrating celestial body. It would have to have been much larger than a meteor, as defined by astronomers, and it would have disintegrated into separate parts as a result of a number of partial explosions at various points along its path of descent. Each of the fragments thus created would become themselves independent bodies, descending along their own paths. These may have been steep or flat according to circumstances. The rate of acceleration they acquired from the explosions in the celestial body would have contributed even more to the kinetically random nature of the bombardment. According to this theory, the area we are concerned with may be regarded as a sort of explosion strip. It was attached by cosmic fragments of various sizes, directions, and velocities, and of completely random and irregular distribution. It is possible that they converged on the center of the strip, for here they apparently descended so densely that fragments hit the same spot as earlier ones already buried in the ground. Hence, the overlapping of craters. The aerial photograph shows a confusion of circular and oval impact craters of various sizes. Such a distribution could have resulted only from the process described.

One would expect a cosmic bomb of this nature to scatter its fragments before its core finally came to rest. This is the law of celestial mechanics, and in fact the distribution pattern shows that the core of the exploded celestial body forged ahead, while the tail of fragments produced their impact behind like a giant comet. The discovery of the Carolina Meteorite provided a full and unexpected confirmation of the hypothesis of cosmic catastrophe.

In order to reach a conclusion about the cause of the fate of Atlantis, we need to go more fully into the nature of comets, meteorites, showers of meteorites, and other celestial wanderers.

Astronomers make a distinction between fixed stars and planets. In our immediate stellar system there is only one fixed star; the sun. The planets illuminated by our sun travel around it in Kepler orbits. These lie in an almost common plane, the ecliptic. This in turn almost coincides with the equatorial plane of the rotating body of the sun. The whole forms a wonderfully simple and apparently very stable system of celestial mechanics. But meteorites, meteor showers, and comets refuse to fit into this system. The great majority of them originate within our solar system, but their orbits are rarely in the ecliptic. Their planes are at angles to it, and they nearly always move along extremely eccentric ellipses which intersect the almost circular orbits of the planets. As a result, they sometimes come very near to the Earth. These encounters are usually harmless because there is only a minute amount of substance in these "shooting stars." The core of a comet, sometimes called its "head," is very insubstantial and often breaks up into several parts. So does the "tail," which consists of the mass of gases following the comet's head and which is affected by the sun's radiation. Biela's Comet, for instance, which returned periodically, was seen to break up as it passed through it perihelion in May 1846. It probably disintegrated owing to the sun's gravitational force. It made one more appearance in the recognizable form of a comet and then disappeared completely. Possibly it was swallowed up by one of the large planets, or dissolved into a shower of meteorites. Most comets end up as showers, which continue in the original orbit of the comet. When the Earth passes through such a shower, shooting stars will rain from the sky. It is very rare for larger rocks, the so-called fireballs, to fall. If they do, it is not usually in association with these periodic showers. At one. time these "heavenly messengers" were regarded with great respect and even reverence. Nowadays we look on them in a more mundane fashion. They often consist of pure nickel iron, and this is useful.

Another question arises about the nature of meteorites: why are shooting stars and fireballs luminous?

The basic law is that every cosmic particle, large or small, circles its celestial mechanical center of movement in a Kepler orbit. In our solar system this center is the sun. Suppose a cosmic particle comes too close to a large planet such as Earth, whose orbital plane forms a straight line of intersection, the so-called nodal line, with that of the particle. The particle will be drawn even closer by the Earth's gravitational pull. Its orbit will become distorted, and the stronger the pull of gravity from the planet, the greater the rate of acceleration of the particle. This increases, as the square of its velocity, the centrifugal force that tries to counteract the planet's attraction. If the velocity of the particle is sufficiently high, it will escape and do no more than graze the marginal layer of the atmosphere. But it will become very hot, and the extremely rarefied gas around it will become luminous, as in a Geissler tube. All we see will be the luminous streak of a distant shooting star flash across the sky. The longer the streak, the farther into the atmosphere the visitor from outer space has descended.

But not all shooting stars are able to escape. In many cases, their orbits become strongly deflected toward the Earth, and they approach it more closely. Geocentrically, the orbit appears as an almost parabolic descent. The particle first passes through the layers of the ionosphere, then through the extremely rarefied hydrogen layer, usually without announcing its presence by luminosity. It is only at the edge of the nitrogen layer, at a height of about 37 miles (60 km), that the gas will become dense enough to offer increasing atmospheric resistance. These cosmic bodies have an extremely high entry velocity, traveling at the rate of several miles per second. Their front section therefore becomes extremely hot, reaching thousands of degrees Centigrade. The top layers are vaporized, and some of their molecules are ionized, and begin to emit radiation typical of their line spectra. The meteor can be seen as a dim, gaseous ball, its brightness increasing toward the center, which is usually reddish or greenish in color. Occasionally it trails a gaseous tail like that of a comet, and the very large specimens are sometimes brighter than the sun. The tremendous heat expansion sets up high tensile stresses in the body of the meteorite, usually strong enough to explode it, often with a thunderous bang like the firing of a grenade. In this case, and if the meteor is large enough, fireballs of various sizes may rain from the sky. But the vast majority of meteorites, for all their amazing brilliance, are minute in substance. Only a few weigh more than 3½ oz (100 gm). They become vaporized and are extinguished long before they reach the ground. Nothing remains but a memory in the mind of the observer of a sudden streak of light—white, red, or green—across the night sky. Not all meteorites are harmless, however, as the enormous hole of the Arizona Crater shows. There are similar craters, some of them made quite recently.

On February 12, 1947, a huge fall of meteorites occurred in the Sichota-Alin mountains northeast of Vladivostok in Siberia. An area of more than 5 square miles (13 sq km) was bombarded by at least a hundred large fragments. The craters produced were roughly circular, up to 82 feet (25 m) in diameter and 50 feet (15 m) in depth. The forests in the region were devastated. Many trees were torn out of the ground and hurled great distances. The whole area was strewn with lumps of iron of various sizes, some weighing as much as 220 lbs (100 kg). Attempts were made to estimate the size of the original meteorite, which had clearly exploded in midair. Judging from the remains that were found, it would have been about 33 feet (10 m) in diameter and weighed about 1000 tonnes. This is small for a celestial body, but large for a meteorite.

But even this was small in comparison with the meteorite that struck in 1908, also in the primeval forests of Siberia. There are detailed and well authenticated records of this event that give a full description of the impact and its after effects. An account was given by the Russian astronomer Kulik:

"On the thirtieth of June 1908, at 7:00 A.M., such a mass of cosmic material hurtled to the ground near the Podmanen Naya Tunguska River (61°north, 102°west of Pulkov) that the effect of the fall surpassed anything ever seen before. Although the day was bright and sunny, the incandescent masses of rock in the sky were seen from more than 360 miles away. A thundery roar could be heard up to 900 miles away and the report of the explosion could be heard within a circle of 4200 miles.

"The atmospheric shock wave was so strong that it flung people and horses to the ground at a distance of 400 miles. In addition, a powerful seismic shock wave was produced which traveled around the Earth at a speed of 317 miles per second. All the observatories recorded it as a catastrophic earthquake in Siberia. According to the records of the Potsdam seismological observatory, the wave took only thirty hours to circle our planet, and continued on its way.

"Enormous quantities of meteoric dust were introduced into the atmosphere, which produced the so-called silver clouds in the sky. All over western Siberia and Europe these clouds turned the light of day into a dim, reddish twilight as they quickly spread across the entire northern section of the Old World.

"The silver clouds were observed throughout Europe. The light they reflected was so intense that the Heidelberg astronomer Max Wolff was unable to take astronomical photographs during the following night. In the area of the Black Sea it was possible to read a newspaper without difficulty at midnight on June thirtieth. . . .

"Had the meteorite descended four hours earlier it would have hit St. Petersburg and completely destroyed the Russian capital. At the point of impact of the meteorite, where the entire kinetic energy was instantly converted into heat, a column of fire immediately rose 12 miles (20 km). A smaller meteorite fell near Kiev at the same time as the Siberian one.

"In 1927, an expedition investigated the scene of the Siberian catastrophe and found pieces of the meteorite that weighed 150 tonnes. The whole meteorite must therefore be estimated to weigh at least one million tonnes, and probably more.

"The expedition noted that the forest had been completely razed to the ground within a circle of 60 miles. The crowns of the huge Siberian larch and pine trees pointed outward and the soil was scorched within a circle of 12 miles. The greater part of the cosmic material penetrated so deeply into the ground that it can no longer be seen.

"Local people told various stories about the catastrophe in 1908, and described the colossal fire in the sky."

This instructive and vivid account of the Taiga meteorite, which has since become famous, supplements what we have said about the celestial mechanics of meteorites. It provides us with valuable points of comparison with the body from space that dug the two deep sea holes in the Atlantic basin about 12,000 years ago, and produced the crater field of Carolina.

Even a comparison between the two Siberian meteorites of 1908 and 1947 can be instructive. In mass, their proportion is about 1000:1, but the difference between the destruction wrought in the two cases is much greater than this. The fall of the smaller meteorite was unnoticed except in Siberia. The aftereffects of the Taiga meteorite, on the other hand, were seen in the whole of the northern hemisphere in the form of a reddish glow and silver clouds. This is a very important point.

Presumably the bolide that scooped out a crater in hard rock in Arizona was even larger than the Taiga meteorite. Great efforts have been made to dig it out with the most modern equipment, but so far without success. Meanwhile, much of the crater has been filled by landslides and by pressure from the surrounding rocks. The Arizona meteorite fell in prehistoric times. Was it perhaps a smaller satellite, a weaker twin of the giant of the Atlantic?

The Fall of the
Asteroid

HOW CAN WE ESTIMATE the size of the celestial body that produced the crater field of Carolina, the two deep sea holes in the southwestern part of the North Atlantic, and the shallower trough in the eastern Caribbean?

We have only the effects of the impact to work from. The core gouged out the deep sea holes, and fragments of the solid crust dug the craters around Charleston. We cannot measure the holes and estimate the size of the cores from them, because the echo soundings do not provide sufficiently accurate details about the seabed, but we can try to reconstruct the event.

When a large meteorite explodes and disintegrates into two cores and innumerable fragments of solid crust, we can assume with a fair degree of confidence that the greater part of its total mass was contained in the heavier nickel iron core. The weight of this can be estimated to be at least equal to that of the solid crust. We can make an estimate of this value from the tangible relics available in the form of the Carolina bays.

From the available data, it was estimated that there would be about ten thousand holes scattered within the distribution area, that is, the "explosion strip" of the bursting bolide. Of these, the vast majority are beneath the sea. The size of the holes varies considerably, we can only use an average value for our calculations. About one half of the three thousand holes above sea level are said to have diameters exceeding 1300–1640 feet (400–500 m). Of these, a fair proportion, more than 100 or 3 percent, measure 5000–6560 feet (1500–2000 m) across. Allowing for this proportion of larger holes, an assumption that the average diameter of a medium-sized crater is 1640 feet (500 m) will probably not be too wide of the mark.

Each boulder must have gouged out a clean cylindrical hole. We know this because several of the holes intersect. Each boulder dug its own hole, in its own size and shape, like a die stamp. The speed of impact was so great that the ground was sharply pierced; it did not give way toward the periphery. The "mean" crater size therefore represents the "mean" diameter of the boulders. We cannot, of course, reconstruct the shapes of the boulders, but we may regard them as being approximately spherical. We now have the means of calculating the volume of the solid crust; it consists of the sum of the constituent volumina of all fragments of spherical shape that have left 10,000 holes of an average diameter of 546 yards (0.5 km).

Calculation is now straightforward. Each individual boulder must have had an average volume of at least 0.01 cubic miles (0.05 cu.km). Ten thousand such fragments have a total volume of at least 120 cubic miles (500 cu.km). If we assume a specific gravity of at least 2 tonnes per cu. km (or .24 cubic miles), then the weight of the solid core of the exploded celestial body will be in excess of 10^{12} tonnes. The nickel iron core must have weighed at least as much. We therefore arrive at a total weight of 2×10^{12} tonnes and a total volume of about 144–168 cubic miles (600–700 cu.km), which corresponds to a sphere about 6¼ miles (10 km) in diameter. Even allowing for an error in one direction or the other of up to one degree of magnitude, it is still fair to assume that this celestial body had a diameter of several miles before it exploded.

At any rate, even if the body was only one tenth that size it was a giant, compared not only with the Siberian meteorite of 1947 whose diameter was apparently no more than 33 feet (10 m), but also with the Taiga meteorite. According to our calculation above, it must have weighed at least a million times more than the greater of the two Siberian meteorites. If the latter was regarded as a particularly large example of a meteorite shower, then the Carolina Meteorite—to use the accepted term for the time being—must in fact have been something greater than a meteorite or a comet. It was much too big to be included in this category of small, or very small, celestial vagrants. It must have been an asteroid. These miniplanets are almost as old as the meteorites; their orbits lie in the so-called asteroid zone but occasionally extend beyond it.

Asteroids are interesting phenomena in our solar system, worth examining in some detail.

Earth's nearest neighbor, measured by distance from the sun, is the red planet Mars. Between Mars and the giant planet Jupiter orbiting beyond, there is an unusually large gap. Jupiter is characterized by the very bright and slightly yellowish light that it emits, but the intermediary gap appears to be devoid of planets. Johannes Kepler placed an imaginary planet in this gap that had never been seen. A simple but not entirely satisfactory formula for measuring the solar distances of the planets is contained in the Law of Titius and Bode. This Law also assumes the existence of such an invisible planet. On New Year's Day 1801, Piazzi saw through his telescope a light patch of the eighth magnitude in the constellation of Taurus. He identified this as a planet because of its proper motion. It was, however, of abnormally small size for a planet, and a new category was therefore established into which this and similar bodies were placed: the category of asteroids or minor planets. The first to be discovered was named Ceres, one of the largest of these miniplanets.

In the same year, 1801, Gauss solved the problem of calculating the orbit of a planet from a few closely-spaced elements of observation on the basis of Kepler's Laws. Ceres, which Piazzi had been able to observe for only a short time until its conjunction with the sun, was thus rediscovered in 1802.

Piazzi's discovery let loose a large-scale asteroid hunt among astronomers. Olbers found Pallas in 1802, and in 1804 Harding discovered Juno. Three years later, in 1807, Olbers had another success and discovered Vesta, the largest asteroid, with the not inconsiderable diameter of 518 miles (834 km.). These were the easiest of the catches. In 1845, using an improved instrument for his search, Hencke found Astraea. Since that date, varying numbers of asteroids have been discovered every year. There were more than 500 known in 1905. By 1950 this figure had risen to over 2000.

Most of these smallest of small celestial bodies move within the asteroid zone, the space between Mars and Jupiter. Some of them travel in most unlikely orbits. There is the so-called Trojan group, for instance, consisting of three tiny spheres sharing the same orbit and traveling at precisely equal distances, so that at any one moment they look like the three apexes of an equilateral triangle. But there is another group, also with a classical name, which is of much greater interest, characterized as it is by extremely eccentric, elongated elliptical orbits. Their aphelion positions are beyond the orbits of Jupiter and Saturn. At the perihelion they come very close to the sun inside the orbits of Mars, of Earth, and even of Venus (Figure 34). The only other bodies that have such extreme orbital conditions are periodical comets and meteor showers. The minor planets differ from these equally eccentric celestial travelers only in their much greater mass. In fact, the two categories are very similar, and it was understandable

THE CATACLYSM

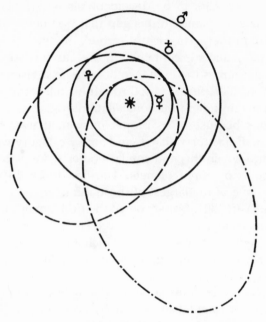

Fig. 34. Orbits of the Adonis Group. The Adonis Group consists of a
few small asteroids circling the sun in eccentric orbits. On the diagram,
that of Adonis is dot-dashed, that of Amor dashed. For comparison:
The orbits of the inner Planets Mars, Earth, Venus, and Mercury are
intersected by the eccentric elliptical orbits of the asteroids, so that the
possibility exists of a close encounter between planets and asteroids.

that Melton and Schriever should attribute the Carolina findings to a
shower of meteorites that originated in an exploded comet head. This
view was quite justifiable, but it did not conform to astronomical
nomenclature; it did not have the correct label on the file.

The second group of asteroids was discovered in record time. Eros
(Witt, 1898); Alinda (Wolf, 1918); Ganymede (Berge, 1924); Amor
(Delporte, 1932); Apollo (Reinmuth, 1934); Adonis (Delporte, 1936);
and Hermes (Reinmuth, 1937). Major planets seem to have a special
attraction for this group of asteroids. In February 1936, a member of
the group, Adonis, came so close to Earth—about 186,000 miles
(300,000 km)—that it was almost captured by Earth. Had it fallen, the
effect would certainly have been worse than a nuclear explosion. But
it traveled a little too fast and was therefore able to escape on a

slightly distorted orbit along a geocentric hyperbolic path. Eleven thousand years ago, however, things turned out otherwise, and those living on Earth at the time suffered badly.

It is perfectly reasonable to assume that the celestial body that fell into the Atlantic at that time was a member of this group of eccentric asteroids. We have calculated that it was about 6¼ miles (10 km) in diameter. Eros, Amor, and Adonis are all about this size. In 1936, Adonis almost fell to Earth. When we calculate the effects of the impact of a body of this size, and assess the destruction it can cause, we can only feel immense gratitude for our lucky escape from a danger as unforeseen as it was horrible.

We will call the celestial body that fell into the Atlantic 11,000 years ago "Asteroid A." The evidence of its impact has already enabled us to make some assumptions about its orbit.

It approached from the northwest, that is, from the direction of sunset. It traveled much faster than Earth and overtook our planet in its rotation and in its orbit round the sun. The orbit of Asteroid A must therefore have been very flat and elongated. This is a characteristic of all the asteroids of the Adonis group. The smaller body may have approached the larger near a nodal point, that is, a point in which both orbits intersect. Asteroid A would thus have come even closer to Earth than Adonis did in 1936. It was attracted by the Earth's gravitational pull, which bent its orbit into a progressively steeper parabolic trajectory and progressively accelerated it. The asteroid must have entered the hydrogen layer of the atmosphere at a speed of at least 9–12 miles per second (15–20 km per second) (velocity referred to the Earth) in an orbit that intersected that of Earth at an angle of 30°. At a height of about 248 miles (400 km), it began to be surrounded by the red glow of the hydrogen light. The hotter the asteroid became, the whiter and more brilliant was the light that it emitted. Its gaseous tail became immense. This lethal thunderbolt must have struck more violently than any comet could possibly have done, and in a blaze of light that made the sun pale. Eyes that saw it would have been permanently blinded. The temperature of its front surface, where it was exposed to the greatest atmospheric resistance and therefore heated most intensely, would exceed 36,032° F (20,000° C). Its luminosity would be 20–100 times that of the sun's disk. The gases hurled backward would have increased the fantastic appearance of this flaming giant. After entering the nitrogen layer and speeding through the lowest and densest part of the atmosphere, the heat and tensile stress became so great that it burst. As a result of several explosions, the brittle, solid crust shattered into innumerable lethal fragments, gouging a trench of deadly devastation across the southeastern part of North America. The core broke in two immediately above the ground, with a thunderclap that ruptured every eardrum. Two giant boulders, each weighing about 10^{12} tonnes, plunged into the sea, which surged to mountainous heights. This stupendous tidal wave rushed in all directions from the vortex around the impact holes. At a height of 2000 ft. (600 m.) it caused appalling devastation in coastal regions and extinguished all traces of antediluvian civilizations there.

The trajectory and impact of the asteroid can be reconstructed with a fair degree of accuracy on the basis of its orbital data. It must have appeared as a parabola rising into the sky in the northwest from the horizon and spanning about 500–620 miles (800–1000 km). Brilliant fragments would have dropped from this silently approaching mass, which would give the appearance of disintegrating in the sky. Barely two minutes can have elapsed between the moment when it first flared up on the horizon and the thunder of the impact of the core. It was no doubt heard in every part of the Earth except by those who lived in the explosion strip. They would be dead before the sound could reach them.

The light in the sky could be seen from more than 1250 miles (2000 km) away. Could this have been the dreadful fiery sign described by St. Augustine in his book *De Civitate Dei?* This light, according to lost accounts by Adrastus and Dion, appeared in the evening sky at the time of the mythical King Phoroneus's deluge and was so powerful that it changed the orbit of Hesperus, the evening star.

A catastrophic event so overwhelming in extent, so disastrous in its effect on human civilization, must have left a terrible and indelible mark on those who survived. They told their descendants of their experience; what they said was handed down from one generation to the next, and became preserved in the form of myth. The imagery of the myth is typical of a visual experience that has been handed on. On the one hand we have these mythical residual recollections of mankind. On the other we have an objective reconstruction based on as much evidence as we can muster. It is interesting to compare the myth and the reconstructed picture to see to what extent they agree.

Little remains of the accounts of this event that were handed down by ancient peoples to later generations. In the West Indies, the

Spanish conquest destroyed virtually all existing evidence. Among this were irreplaceable Maya law books, going back to mythical early periods, that had never been deciphered. Of the few surviving descriptions of this celestial catastrophe, two are particularly worthy of mention. They are mythical, poetic accounts—not in the least resembling a scientific report.

In the *Popol Vuh*, sacred book of the Quiché Indians, Huracan, the god of terror, flooded the Earth at the same time that a huge conflagration was seen in the sky. Setting aside the vengeful and punishing god Huracan, this account agrees with our reconstruction. The Arawakens of Guyana likewise remember that the Great Spirit first punished them with fires and then with a terrible flood. Here again, is first the fall of meteorites and then the tidal wave which swept Guyana. But to the east of the Atlantic, there is also a myth that deals with similar events. This myth dates far back beyond the prehellenic times. It describes Phaëthon who wanted to drive the chariot of the sun but lost control of the fiery steeds. He came too close to Earth, scorched half of it, and struck by lightning, fell into the sea near the mouth of the Eridanus.

A particularly poignant account is contained in Chapter 5 of the strange book of *Chilam Balams*, which was written in the Maya language but in Roman script. If we ignore irrelevant or obscure mythical images and allusions, we can extract the following account: "This happened when the Earth began to awake. Nobody knew what was to come. A fiery rain fell, ashes fell, rocks and trees crashed to the ground. He smashed trees and rocks asunder . . . And the Great Snake was torn from the sky . . . and skin and pieces of its bones fell onto the Earth . . . and arrows struck orphans and old men, widowers and widows who were alive, yet did not have the strength to live. And they were buried on the sandy seashore. Then the waters rose in a terrible flood. And with the Great Snake the sky fell in and the dry land sank into the sea. . . ."

This description is particularly important because it is very detailed and originates in a country not far from the coast that was struck by the Carolina Meteorite. The fall of the celestial body must have been clearly visible there. The imagery of the Great Snake torn from the sky is very vivid. The asteroid with the luminous trail of gases flooding from its head must, indeed, have looked like a snake composed of suns and stars, and brighter than the sun. It was as if the great snakelike constellation of the Milky Way was coming down to destroy the Earth. And the terrible apparition in the sky did indeed appear to have a mouth that was breathing fire, and it did suddenly explode into fragments. As the account says; ". . . its skin and pieces of its bones fell onto the Earth." It is difficult to think of any other image that could so vividly and accurately describe this event, the nature of which was almost beyond the power of words to portray.

Asteroid A was only one of many similar members of the Adonis group of asteroids. They all move in eccentric orbits; they all approach the Earth closely at some time or another. Good luck saved our Earth from disaster in February 1936. Can we hope that it will always do so?

The Great Bang

IN THE PRECEDING CHAPTER, we described the fall of the celestial body in the southwest area of the North Atlantic. This unleashed the greatest and most terrible catastrophe recollected in the myths of mankind. Asteroid A penetrated deep into the bed of the Atlantic basin and ceased to exist; it was swallowed up by Earth. But in its disintegration it left appalling scars upon the face of the Earth.

The astronomer Kulik tells us that a column of fire 12 miles (20 km) high rose from the crater left by the Taiga meteorite. Yet this body was almost negligible in comparison with Asteroid A. It had only two-millionths of its mass, and it struck the earth at a speed that could not have exceeded one mile per second (1–1.5 km per second). We can deduce this from the area of impact, which is almost circular and therefore suggests an almost vertical trajectory. On such a highly curved trajectory the velocity cannot have been so very excessive.

The speed of Asteroid A must have been ten times as great. In this case there was a flat elliptical approach path. It arrived from the west and the elliptical shape of the two deep sea holes shows a grazing angle of impact. Also, unlike the Taiga meteorite, which was a much smaller body, it lost only a fraction of its velocity in the Earth's atmosphere. Taking all these factors into account, we can estimate the force of impact of Asteroid A as at least 200,000,000 times that of the Taiga meteorite. The devastation caused would conform to this degree of force. The primeval forests on the banks of the Yenisei certainly suffered an extremely severe local cataclysm in 1908, but it was nothing compared to the catastrophe in the Atlantic 11,000 years before. The Taiga explosion would need to be multiplied 200,000,000 times to be comparable. In 1908, the column of fire was 12 miles (20 km) high; its equivalent in that far-off time must have risen from the Atlantic beyond the limit of the atmosphere, up into the ionosphere—a gigantic pillar flaming up from the surface of planet Earth.

Total force, or impulse, as it is called, is measured by multiplying mass and velocity. The relationship of weight and mass is: a weight of about 2×10^{12} (weight) has a corresponding mass of about 2×10^{11} (mass). Multiply by the velocity of about 12 miles (20 km) per second, and the result is an impulse, or total force, of 4×10^{15} tonnes per second—a truly astronomical figure. But we are dealing here with astronomical values.

An impulse of this magnitude even softened by water, must have had a dynamic effect on that slowly rotating gyroscope, our planet Earth. Admittedly, the spin of the Earth's crust would be about 10^{12} times greater than this figure. If the impulse of the impact had any accelerating or decelerating effect on the Earth's rotation, it can only have been infinitesimal. But the gyroscopic movement of the Earth would be affected. Imagine the Earth as a slowly rotating, spinning top and the asteroid as a small pebble that suddenly hits the top obliquely from above.

What happens to the top when it is hit in this manner? It will react in the same way as a stabilizer. It will begin to wobble; in scientific terms, to precess. As its axis begins to wobble, it no longer remains in a vertical position on its base but executes a gyratory movement. It is an established fact that the Earth, or more precisely, the Earth's crust, has wobbled at least since the end of the Quaternary period. The Earth's axis executes one gyratory movement within about 25,000 years. The Earth rotates about nine million times around its axis during the time that the axis is completing a single gyroscopic movement. The ratio provides an interesting prognosis. The rotating Earth's crust has impulses to the order of about 1×10^{24} kg per second, two hundred and fifty thousand times more powerful than the impulse of the falling asteroid, which we estimated at 4×10^{15} tonnes per second (4×10^{18} kg per second). According to gyroscopic theory, the Earth must initially have completed a full gyroscopic circle within 250,000 days or about 700 years. But the time for completing a gyroscopic circle has increased to 25,000 years, which means that the gyroscopic motion has been largely absorbed. It has been slowed down by the internal friction between the Earth's crust and its magma, which acts as a friction bearing. The Earth ceases to wobble; the angle of aperture of the gyratory movement progressively narrows, because the frictional force keeps the axis of rotation erect. The whole process is also influenced by the sun and the moon, whose gravitational forces generate a tilting momentum, and therefore precession impulses on the

Earth, which as we all know is not an exact sphere but bulges at the equator. This precession motion is the cause of the solar periodicity of the seasons. It was certainly stronger at the beginning of the Quinternary Age than it is today.

During the first 700 years after the catastrophe, the wobbling motion resulted in a "fluttering" of the Van Allen Belt, which consists of two cup-shaped zones of increased radiation intensity that surround the Earth. Their cause is the Earth's magnetic field.

The Van Allen Belt absorbs energy-rich protons from the solar flares. This takes place primarily in the first of the "cups," which begins at a height of 1990 miles (3200 km) above the Earth's surface. The second, outer cup is larger. It forms an elliptic bulge toward the sun and extends from a distance of 9900 miles (16,000 km) away from the Earth up to 31,000 miles (50,000 km) into space. Only above the Earth's magnetic poles do the cusps of the Van Allen Belt penetrate the ionosphere down to a distance of 200 miles (320 km).

The result of this fluttering or breakdown in the Van Allen Belt is to expose the Earth to the effects of solar storms and their associated hard radiation. In other words, more nitrogen atoms are transformed into carbon isotopes, which leads to an enrichment of radioactive carbon in the atmosphere. This can, after a certain lapse of time, restabilize the Earth's magnetic field externally.

The more the gyratory motion decreased, the more effectively the Van Allen Belt was able to resume its protective function. The problem is no longer of significance today, with the gyratory motion slowed down to 25,000 years for a single gyration. We do not yet know much about its effects during the 1000 years following the catastrophe. The solar periodicity of the seasons was related to a radiation intensity and transmission different from today, and almost certainly more dangerous.

We do not know whether this periodicity existed during the Quaternary period. On the basis of Laplace's hypothesis, which is unconfirmed and quite improbable, it is assumed that the solar system is stable and that it permits only minor fluctuations of the orbital elements around certain mean values. The 32° F (0° C) isotherm is made up of mean annual temperatures. For it to mark the edge of a permanent ice sheet there would have to be no great variation from this mean throughout the year. The ice could not survive periods of summer heat. We can therefore assume that in the Quaternary Age the seasonal fluctuations of temperature might have been considerably narrower than they are today. This would have happened if the Earth's axis had been fairly vertical to the ecliptic at that time, if it included only a very narrow angle of obliquity. It is possible that the angle was indeed much smaller in the Quaternary Age than it is today.

The size of this angle today is 23° 27' and it is currently decreasing at the rate of about 47" (or 0.785') per century. This corresponds to 0.013° every 100 years or 1° in 7630 years. This steady decrease also corresponds to gyroscopic theory. Every wobbling, spinning top, including the Earth, will right itself if frictional forces act in its support point. In the case of a child's spinning top, these forces originate in the friction between its point and its support. In the case of Earth, it is only the solid crust, and not the molten sphere or the gaseous center, that wobbles. The forces are generated by the friction between the solid crust, or lithosphere, and the underlying magma. We may therefore assume that the decrease from maximum obliquity of the ecliptic, rapid at the beginning of the Quinternary Age, became progressively slower because of frictional retardation. If we take the line representing the obliquity of the ecliptic as a function of the time elapsed since the onset of the Quinternary Age and extrapolate it backward, then it will not be straight, but will be a curve, rising gently at first and more steeply later.

The great bang that heralded the end of the Quaternary Age made the Earth tremble and wobble, but, we do not know through how many degrees. The event was engraved on the memory of mankind. It became enshrined in the myths and legends through which primeval man handed down his knowledge from one generation to the next, myths and legends that are often descriptions of cosmic experiences.

The best place to look for the evidence of myth is not among the red-skinned people who lived near the center of the catastrophe, since in these regions the overwhelming effects of conflagration and tidal wave would blot out any other impression. But on people more remote from the center the effects, though bad enough, were not so overwhelming. But these effects also became part of the folk-memory and were passed on in myths. In these more distant regions the Earth trembled and the heavens were in disarray.

The story of Phaëthon that was mentioned earlier forms an important part of this collective memory. It is only in the later versions that

Phaëthon is actually called the son of Helios, the sun god. In Homer and the earlier poets "Phaëthon the Radiant" is another name for Helios himself. In the myth, the sun-chariot leaves its prescribed track across the sky, comes too close to the Earth, and scorches half of it. The charioteer, struck by Zeus's thunderbolt, glowed like the meteor that is implicit in his name as he plunged into the waters of the Eridanus, the mythical river in the west. Suppose we regard this not as a mythical description, but as a poetic view of a real cosmic event.

It is not too difficult to reconstruct the cosmic disturbance that could be illustrated by the imagery of the myth. Man lives close to nature; his senses are always geocentrically oriented; the Earth is the rock-steady disk upon which the heavens rest. The world's axis, which ends in the Pole Star, is the pivot around which the heavens revolve. This crystal sphere supports the cycles and epicycles of the planetary orbits, including that of the sun. At a very small ecliptic obliquity it remains fairly constant year in year out: a large circle which includes an angle with the horizon equal to the degree of latitude. If we should feel this stable Earth of ours receive a tremendous shock—much greater than an earthquake—we will not, oriented as we are, have the impression that the Earth is wobbling and tumbling. The disturbance will seem to us to be in the sky, that great dome above us with its innumerable flickering stars. If it seems to the observer that the sun is tumbling across the sky this is, in fact, the course of the terrestrial disturbance. The observer sees it as a shift in the sun's orbit, and correctly describes what he sees. It requires a different sort of knowledge from the subjective visual impression to know what has really happened. The tumbling of the sun's chariot, which had actually been observed, became merged in popular memory with the fall of the meteorite, which was not directly visible in the east, but became known only from hearsay. The two images combined result in the myth of Phaëthon struck by a thunderbolt and tumbling from the sun's chariot.

Turning now to the *Völuspa*, that strange epic of the gods which dates back far beyond pre-Germanic times, and was still sung in Iceland in the Middle Ages, we can draw testimony that is much more matter-of-fact and to the point. The introductory verse states that it contains the most ancient history of man. We must, of course, regard this not as the whole of mankind, but only that part of it to which the mythical sibyl, to whom the epic is ascribed, belonged.

Verse 2:

First was the time when Ymir raged,
Sand was not yet, nor sea, nor salty wave,
I found no earth beneath nor sky above,
All was a gaping void—and grass nowhere . . .

Verse 3:

Until the sons of Bur raised the ground
Created her, Midgarth, the myth.
The sun shone on stone battlements from the south,
The ground turned green with verdant leek.

Verse 4:

From the south the sun, the moon's companion,
Touched the edge of the heavens.
The sun did not know his halls.
The moon did not know her might.
The stars did not know their places. . . .

Verse 2 describes the Quaternary period, the Ice Age. All that can be seen is a glittering emptiness of ice that covers land and sea; the sky is overcast and laden with snow clouds, and it merges into the gray-white ground so that there appears to be no horizon. The next two verses tell of the terrestrial and cosmic revolutions which ended the Ice Age and ushered in the new era. The gods of this new eon are the sons of Bur. In another epic they slay the snow giant Ymir, and drown the world of the frost giants in his blood. As the verse says, they "raise the ground"—a recollection of the Earth trembling. They lift it out of the cover of ice, which is now melting and retreating to Scandinavia. In the warm light of the sun, which rises in the south, the ground that has been freed from ice becomes covered with green growing things. Midgarth the myth is created.

In Verse 4 the wobbling, rising, and trembling of the Earth has been transposed to the sky. The sun, moon, and stars wander aimlessly, not knowing their places. Apparently they have left their geocentric orbits and entered new ones. When the Earth trembles, it is for those who live on Earth as if the universe with all its stars is trembling.

A glance at the night sky, particularly in the polar regions, will show that the fixed stars move around the celestial pole in recognizably circular orbits. When they leave their fixed places, their crystal seats, this means that they follow orbits that always appear circular to us, around a different celestial pole. Verse 4 describes the phenomenon of the celestial pole shift.

But the celestial pole exists only in our imagination. It is the point of junction between an infinitely extended Earth's axis of rotation and the imaginary dome of the sky. If this celestial pole, this imaginary point, seems to be displaced, it is really the Earth's pole of rotation that has shifted. It is not the celestial axis that wobbles until it has established a new equilibrium; it is the Earth's axis.

These strange verses are the unique and invaluable account by a naive eyewitness of the displacement of the Earth's axis and of the beginning of an increased precession. Line 2 of Verse 4 illustrates this quite clearly. The sun is suddenly hurled from his position high in the sky to the "edge of the heavens"—in other words, the horizon. It looks as if he is clinging to this fixed margin in his fall. He is called "the moon's companion," which may suggest the constellation of the new moon, in which the sun and the moon, the latter as a thin crescent, are close together.

Biblical accounts of metaphysical happenings also make frequent use of mythical images which may well have come from actual cosmic events. The Fall of the Angels is a well-known example. Lucifer, the strongest and most beautiful of the first-created angels, rebelled against the Lord Creator and tried to remove Him from the throne of the universe in a heavenly coup. The attempt ended in the fall of Lucifer and his followers and their damnation to the depths of hell. The Old Testament contains only the one reference to this, in a passage of Chapter 14 of *Isaiah*. The context is a prophecy that Babylon and her kings will suffer the same fate as the former "princes of the Earth."

"How art thou fallen from heaven, O Lucifer, son of the morning! how art thou cut down to the ground, which didst weaken the nations!

"For thou hast said in thine heart, I will ascend into heaven, I will exalt my throne above the stars of God: I will sit also upon the mount of the congregation, in the sides of the north:

"I will ascend above the heights of the clouds: I will be like the most High.

"Yet thou shalt be brought down to hell, to the sides of the pit."

This uprising of Lucifer and his rebel angels vividly recalls similar Greek myths—the uprising of the giants, the rebellion of the Aloades, and the battles between the gods and the titans. In these cases it is a thunderbolt from the god of the heavens that decides the issue. The rebels in each case—Typhon, the giants, and the Aloades—are hurled to the ground and buried under volcanoes.

Between these mythical, poetic accounts on the one hand and the factual reconstruction of the fall of Asteroid A on the other, there is a connection which is impossible to overlook.

The story of the Fall of the Angels can be interpreted as a recollection of the Atlantic catastrophe, of which Atlantis was the victim, recorded in vivid images and handed down from one generation to another.

If we take the myths into account when we survey the problem as a whole, and keep an open mind, we will find that the lore of these ancient peoples describes an event that can be clearly reconstructed. Their language is poetic and colorful, but their description is faithful and factually correct. Their manner of narration, 11,000 years ago, differs from ours. But we must not reject their stories just because they are expressed in an unfamiliar terminology.

The Cosmic Explosion

FLAMES SHOT UP to a height of 12 miles (20 km) from the impact point of the Taiga meteorite. Kulik, a down-to-earth Russian scientist, described the aftereffects of the fall of this meteorite and called it a catastrophe. But if we look at his account objectively, and note the calculations that he makes, those who are familiar with the effects of atomic bombs are not likely to be greatly impressed.

Kulik put the weight of the Taiga meteorite at about 1 million tonnes. Its impact velocity may have been about $5/8$ miles (1 km) per second. Its force of impact was therefore about 500,000 tonne kilometers or 5×10^{10} kilogrameters, which is the equivalent of a little more than 100,000,000 thermal units. To produce the same local effect, about 75 tonnes of nitroglycerin would be required. This is less than a hundredth of the force of an A type atomic bomb.

In comparing the Taiga meteorite with Asteroid A, we have calculated that the latter consisted of at least 2×10^{11} (mass) tonnes; its entry velocity relative to the Earth was 12 miles (20 km) per second, and its resultant force of impact was 2×10^{19} mkg. The thermal value was therefore more than 4×10^{16} calories. To produce the same explosive force we would have to detonate 3×10^{10} tonnes of nitroglycerin. If we regard 1 million tonnes of this explosive as the equivalent of a modern hydrogen bomb, this would mean 30,000 of the most closely packed hydrogen bombs.

We can therefore express the total force of impact of Asteroid A in terms of 2×10^{19} mkg or 4×10^{16} calories. Imagine that this quantity of energy was represented by an explosive charge that arrived from space, buried itself deep in the ground, and was detonated there. Half of the charge resided in the solid crust, and the other half in the core. Each of the two cores into which it split therefore contained a quarter of the total; each of the 10,000 boulders into which the solid crust disintegrated contained 1/20,000 of it.

Let us deal first with the boulders that cut the monstrous swath of devastation called the crater field of Carolina, and that has been attributed to the Carolina Meteorite.

We shall have to base our reconstruction on the medium-sized boulders, since we are dealing in averages. Each one of these hit an average area of 24,000 square yards (20,000 sq.m) with an impact force of about 1×10^{15} mkg per square meter. In the case of the Taiga meteorite the area scorched by the impact measured 12 miles or 20 km across, representing about 116 square miles (300 sq.km). Even if we assume that only one-third of this area was directly bombarded by the meteorite, it remains a sizable figure. The impact force in the Taiga case was 50,000 tonne kilometers or 5×10^{10} mkg, that is 500 mkg per unit area (square meter) which is only 1/5,000,000 of the comparable value of Asteroid A. This calculation of impact force is of great interest because it explains why the catastrophe in western Siberia was not as grave as it might have been. The energy density of the Taiga meteorite was only about 1/5,000 of that of a grenade fired at a target from a field gun at point-blank range. But in the case of Asteroid A it was about 2000 times greater even in the boulders that came from the solid crust.

Energy density, which may also be called the ballistic coefficient, is a decisive factor in the penetrating power of a celestial or terrestrial missile. The boulders must have scooped enormous holes out of the ground and only come to rest after penetrating to depths that could be measured in miles. This all happened in a few seconds. In this short time virtually none of the frictional heat that had been generated and built up at the front of the celestial projectile could be dissipated. The energy accumulated here would have been enough to heat the entire boulder to a temperature of about 7232° F (4000° C). But the heat was not spread evenly throughout the boulder. Because of the extremely short impact time it was almost entirely concentrated on a narrow marginal area in the front. Temperatures of 18,032° F (10,000° C) and more must have been reached there. We may gain some idea of the light emitted by this missile in the depths of the Earth if we compare it with the sun. The light of the sun is radiated at a surface temperature of about 10,832° F (6000° C). This is at most only one-tenth, and probably only one-hundredth, of the brightness of this invisible light source.

No substance can resist a thermal attack like this. Its structure will disintegrate, it will instantly vaporize. At the opening of the crater, the gases released found their escape route blocked by the closely-packed fragments crowding in behind the missile. The destructive force of the gas cloud, which was incredibly hot and subjected to enormous pressures, must have been exerted downward and sideways. Even the granitic and dunite shells gave way before these forces and became deformed like pitch. Huge cavities were created far down in the depths of the Earth by the expanding gas. The substratum was perforated and became spongelike.

But the land that remained above sea level also suffered severely. The points of impact appear to be farther apart in this region, possibly because the boulders were lighter. At any rate, the substratum retained its cohesion. But here, too, the hot gases would have worked on the walls of the huge subterranean cavities and weakened the forces that were exerting a counterpressure from below. The surface layer probably healed comparatively quickly, through mud-silting and peat formation, and acquired the typical appearance of the Carolina bays. But it would continue to weigh heavily on the badly damaged substratum.

The geological healing process of transformation and stabilization then began. Even now, after 11,000 years, it is not yet complete, so severe was the damage to this ground. Tectonic earthquakes have shaken the areas that are not yet healed. The walls of cavities deep down in the earth become brittle and collapse; the unstable equilibrium of the damaged Earth's crust is disturbed once more.

The city of Charleston is situated in the center of the crater field (Figure 33) on what is now the coast; in other words, on the edge of the land that survived the catastrophe. It has therefore been the center of tectonic earthquakes. Figure 35 illustrates the intensity gradient of the ground movements during the tectonic earthquake of August 31, 1896. A comparison of these two drawings reveals that the area of the earthquake is the same as the crater field, the explosion strip of the solid crust of the asteroid.

But the impact of the core of the asteroid had very much greater and more widespread effects. It split into two halves, each weighing about 5×10^{11} tonnes. Each of these crashed with a force of about 25×10^{12} tonne kilometers on an area of about 10 million square meters (12 million square yards). That is an energy density of about 250,000 tonne kilometers per square meter, corresponding to 2.5×10^{11} mkg per square meter. This is 100,000 times higher than the comparable factor of a field gun, and 100 times higher than that of a fragment of the solid crust.

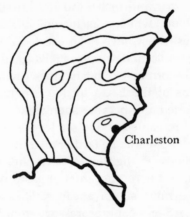

Fig. 35. Isoseismal lines around Charleston. The U.S. city of Charleston, South Carolina, is situated in the center of a tectonic earthquake region. The isoseismic lines (lines of equal earthquake intensity) are almost concentric around the seismic focus; a comparison with Fig. 33 shows how accurately the position of the focus coincides with the crater field of Carolina.

We can obtain from this quantitative relation a rough estimate of the depth of penetration. The Earth's crust is not very strong below the Atlantic. It is never thicker than 25 miles (40 km) in this region. It was bound to be punctured by such force, and the big bang ruptured it completely at the point of impact. After 11,000 years of retransformation and superficial silting up, the two holes are still about 4 miles (over 7 km) deep.

We do not know at what depth the core of the meteorite came to rest. Probably it consisted of nickel iron, like most of its kind. If that is the case, then the Earth's largest metal deposits, many thousands of millions of tonnes of nickel iron, will be concentrated down there, beyond the reach of man. Or perhaps the core was partly vaporized as were the smaller bodies formed by fragments of the solid crust. It would then have produced incredibly hot gases which under intense pressure and with gigantic force would dig out huge holes and cavities in the deepest layers of the Earth's crust. The gases would cool after some decades or centuries and would precipitate on the walls of the cavities, where they would probably form thick deposits of nickel, treasure almost beyond the imagination of man. Their recovery is also barely imaginable. It would be excessively difficult even to detect them. A gravimeter would refuse to function because of the indefinable perforation of the ground, and even a magnetic needle would not be much help. Nickel alloys tend to be antimagnetic, and this normally very sensitive instrument would fail to respond.

The effect of those inconceivably hot gases blowing out of the impact holes defies description. The first tidal wave, which immediately followed the impact, cannot have been anything like as high as the second. The tidal wave caused by the Krakatoa explosion in the Sunda Archipelago claimed the lives of 40,000 people, a negligible figure in comparison with this prehistoric catastrophe.

How many became its victims?

We cannot answer this question by reconstructing this catastrophe, but only through the recollections of mankind. The Troano manuscript states: "In the sixth year of Can, on the eleventh Muluc of the month of Zar, terrible earthquakes occurred and lasted until the thirteenth Chuen. Mur, the land of the clay hills, and the land of Mound were its victims. They were rocked twice and suddenly disappeared in the night. The Earth's crust was continuously raised and lowered in several places by the subterranean forces until they could no longer withstand the pressure, and many countries were separated from each other by deep rifts. In the end, both countries sank into the ocean with 64,000,000 inhabitants. It happened 8060 years ago."

This translation by Brasseur de Bourbourg of part of the text is not accepted as reliable. Many experts have strong reservations about it. But its description of the fate of the hapless inhabitants of this doomed region agrees surprisingly well with our objective reconstruction. This evidence from remote prehistory should not be disregarded, even if the text is apocryphal. We will discuss in another context the dating given by the Codex Troanus.

The quoted passage may or may not be an accurate description of the devastation that followed the impact and subterranean explosions of the cosmic charge. But in any case this was not the Atlantic catastrophe proper; it only triggered it.

"In the Course of a Single Dreadful Day and a Single Dreadful Night"

THERE WERE TWO MAIN REASONS why the Taiga meteorite described by Kulik did not cause major damage. First, the rather low energy density of its impact; second—and very important—it crashed in an uninhabited region and struck a huge, healthy, rock-steady sial platform. Yet Kulik calculated that it was powerful enough, had it fallen four hours later, to destroy St. Petersburg. Four hours difference in time and this almost ignored event would have entered the annals of history as a terrible catastrophe. And yet the infinitely greater, well-attested catastrophe of the Atlantic that we have been reconstructing step by step is ignored by the history of mankind.

Not only was Asteroid A incomparably speedier and more massive than its tiny Siberian brother, but its energy density in the area of impact was 5,000,000 times greater, and it fell in the worst possible place. The Taiga meteorite crashed onto a healthy sial platform; Asteroid A crashed into one of the thinnest and most sensitive regions of the Earth's crust. It fell on a fracture zone dotted with volcanoes, the zone that we call the Atlantic Ridge.

This fracture zone is divisive rather than connective. It is a crack in the entire area of seismic activity that extends from Jan Mayen Island in the north to Tristan da Cunha in the south. The solidified part of the crust of sialitic texture below such an ancient fracture seam is considerably weaker and thinner than it is elsewhere. The magma-bearing molten layer is therefore much closer to the top layer, usually not more than 9–12 miles (15–20 km) below. Hence the large number of volcanoes in this region. Their vents extend into isolated pockets of magma and lava-bearing zones. This glowing substance is everywhere under high pressure because of its water vapor and carbon dioxide content; there is power enough to hurl the lava from a volcanic vent up to a height exceeding that of Mount Everest. Pressure from the magma pushes the red-hot liquid substrate against the dividing top layer of the crust. Only this thin crust, this weak plug, holds the subterranean fire back and prevents the waters of the ocean from coming into violent contact with it. At this critical spot, it is only this fragile safeguard that protects the environment of mankind from all the forces of hell. If this safeguard is pierced, then the powers of those red/hot zones beneath will be unleashed.

The armor was in fact pierced by the two halves of the core of Asteroid A. Two holes were forged by the impact which acted like two volcanic vents. They extended far into those red-hot depths, and the great bang triggered off a cosmic explosive charge equal in force to 30,000 hydrogen bombs. What this implied can be better understood by a simple comparison.

The Earth is encased in a crust 25–30 miles (40–50 km) thick. We can imagine it as an industrial high-pressure vessel covered by very thin pieces of sheet steel. These steel sections are joined, not by strengthening welded seams, but by rows of rivets which have a weakening effect. These rivets correspond to the fracture lines and zones of the Earth's crust. With this comparison we can see the impact of the Taiga meteorite as a light hammer blow on the center of a sheet of steel. It rumbled, but it held. The armor remained intact. But in the case of Asteroid A it was as if an armor-piercing rifle had fired at the vessel and damaged the row of rivets at this weak point. What would happen to a high-pressure vessel that had been treated so roughly: the internal pressure would remain unchanged, but the damaged row of rivets would no longer be able to hold it back; it would burst open, causing the high-pressure vessel to explode.

This is precisely how the "vessel" below the Atlantic basin exploded when the core parts of Asteroid A punched the first decisive hole in the fracture zone on the Atlantic Ridge.

And the forces of hell were let loose. Through these two newly formed vents the glowing, red-hot magma shot up at terrific speed and mixed with the waters of the Atlantic. This created all the conditions for a submarine volcanic eruption of the greatest possible violence. The fracture seam was torn apart. The bottom of the sea burst open to the north and to the south. All existing volcanoes were activated and new vents were formed. Terrestrial fire and ocean water became embroiled in ever-increasing volume. Magma mixed with steam. The chain of fire ran all the way between the two continents, from the Beerenberg volcano on Jan Mayen in the north to Tristan da Cunha in the south.

And it must have all happened at fantastic speed. For two minutes the trajectory of the descending asteroid flashed across the sky. Its impact caused a tidal wave, but before this reached the coasts the gates of the underworld had burst open and the fire erupted before the deluge could drown everything. The volcanic eruptions ran along the entire fracture in a huge chain reaction, and fresh masses of magma and water were continually thrown into the all-destroying battle of the elements.

We can make a fair estimate of the duration of this inferno. Let us take a very conservative estimate, the rate at which minor and medium-strength earthquakes open up fissures in the ground, and assume that the event propagated itself along the fracture line at a speed no greater than this. This gives us a value of about 50 feet (15 m) per second. The fracture seam running northward from the point of impact was about 1860 miles (3000 km) long. It can have taken only two or three days at the most for the seam to open up from Puerto Rico to Iceland.

At a point south of the small Atlantic land platform of Atlantis, the single fracture seam splits into two. It must have taken less than twenty-four hours for the explosion to reach this point. Northward, there were two fracture seams, passing on either side of Atlantis, each about 745 miles (1200 km) in length. It would have taken at most a day and a night for these rifts to open up. The entire island platform was caught in a fire trap. Along its entire periphery, the bottom of the sea burst open and the Earth's crust beneath it was shattered. Red-hot magma welled up from the depths into the waters of the Atlantic producing superheated steam, whose magma content cooled and rapidly solidified into fly ash. The heat content of these magma droplets was transferred to the steam. Overheated, it rose at an incredible speed, taking with it infinite quantities of red-hot matter. Tornado spouts topped by mushroom clouds shot up far beyond the troposphere into the region of the luminous silver clouds and the ionosphere. Clouds of steam and ash the size of whole continents formed above the entire zone of the catastrophe. Large quantities of magma in the form of ash, lapilli, and pumice stone were thrown up into the highest zones of the atmosphere. We know exactly what happens when a submarine volcano explodes from the comparatively recent example of Krakatoa in the Sunda Strait on August 26–27, 1883. This was only a tiny disaster in comparison with the Atlantic catastrophe, but it is well documented and provides valuable information.

This island volcano, together with two-thirds of the island itself, was blown sky-high by the entry of sea water. Of the island's total area of 13 square miles (33 sq.km), the active volcanic area that burst open comprised about 8 square miles (20 sq.km). The quantity of lava ejected is estimated to have had a volume of 12–24 cubic miles (50–100 cu. km), roughly 1.5–3 cubic miles to every square mile of active area (3–4 cu.km to every sq. km). This corresponds to a mean height of roughly 2–2½ miles (3–4 km) of the eruption above the active area.

The Atlantic catastrophe was a submarine volcanic explosion similar in character but on an incomparably larger scale. Applying the specific values obtained from the Krakatoa explosion, we can arrive at what is probably a very conservative estimate of the damage.

We can put the total length of the North Atlantic fracture line, including the bifurcation around Atlantis, at 2480 miles (4000 km). If we take the width of the reactivated volcanic area as 63–93 miles (100–150 km), this will give a mean of 78 miles (125) km), and a total volcanic area of about 190,000 square miles (500,000 sq. km). If the mean eruption was no larger than that of Krakatoa the volume of magma ejected would still have been in the region of 360,000–480,000 cubic miles (1½–2 million cu.km), weighing at least 5×10^{15} tonnes.

As long as the fracture seam continued to burst open, magma, water vapor, and gases continued to increase. Fresh magma continually welled up from the depths and the Atlantic waves crashed ceaselessly into the fire zone, producing more and more vapor and ash. Everything that erupted from the depths of the Earth was hurled into the uppermost layers of the atmosphere by the evaporating water of the ocean and the water vapor dissociating itself from the magma that had absorbed it. But the magma blown high into the sky did not fall back. It was widely dispersed by the storms that were a by-product of the eruption. There was therefore a considerable drop in the level of magma in the Atlantic, since so much was blown away and not replaced. A magma depression was created below the center of the Atlantic basin. It varied in depth, but was deepest where the fracture line bifurcated and surrounded Atlantis with its two branching seams. Even assuming that in the very center of the catas-

trophe the eruption quantities were no greater than those for the
much weaker Krakatoa eruption, we can estimate that in this region
the magma level must have dropped by 2–2½ miles (3–4 km). This
must have been the depth of the depression created by the total
dispersion of the magma.

Along the whole periphery of the small island platform, the magma
forming its sima bed was blown high into the atmosphere in the form
of ash. This began the last act of the drama for the sial platform
embedded in the sima substrate. Relatively small and mobile, it followed isostatically the drop in the level of its magma bed. It did not
sink quickly. It took about 24 hours, which corresponds to a rate of
about 1½–2 inches (4–5 cm) per second. But by the time it began to
sink all life on the island had doubtless been extinguished. The har-
bingers of the final catastrope—asphyxiating gases, storms, and tidal
waves—would have caused this. Figure 36 illustrates the progress of
this drama in three stages. As the sea water was carried away, the
supply of water vapor and lava diminished, and the streams of lava
ceased to flow. The thunder of eruptions and explosions gradually
died away and the red-hot surface closed. But while it was still glowing it was flooded by the Atlantic. The ocean waves rushed in, hissing
and emitting clouds of steam, to their newly created bed. The previous day, that bed had been a large island with high mountains and
splendid buildings. Today Atlantis lies some 2 miles (3 km) lower, in
the center of the depression, right on the ancient fracture seam.
Cemented by extruded magma, Atlantis maintains its new position
with the viscosity of pitch. There it lies, a submarine landmass, a
mysterious broadening of the Atlantic Ridge, which is no longer so
mysterious now that its origin has become clear. All that remains
visible of Atlantis is nine small islands rising above the sea, display-
ing their bare lava slopes to those who pass in ships. The Azores. No
hindrance to the Gulf Stream on its way to Europe.

The island that had blocked the Gulf Stream, and turned it back to
America, had sunk on its magma bed and become submerged. The
depression of the magma level was enough to sink the island, but
compared with the width of the Atlantic Ocean it was shallow. We
must not think of it in terms of the formation of a marginal trench. In
this region there is at least 930 (1500 km) of Atlantic either side of the
Atlantic Ridge. The ratio between the width of half the ocean and the
greatest depth of the depression is roughly 500:1. This is a negligible
gradient. From the edges of the continental platforms to the center of

the basin, the magma level becomes imperceptibly lower. The depression is so shallow that appreciable retransformation forces cannot be expected—certainly not forces capable of raising the sunken island above the level of the sea again.

In Plato's account of the sinking of Atlantis that has met with so much criticism and ridicule he wrote, "But later, when violent earthquakes and floods occurred, the entire populous valiant generation of your people was swallowed up by the Earth and the island of Atlantis was similarly swallowed by the sea and vanished in a single dreadful day and in a single dreadful night."

How do we react to Plato's description now? Earthquakes, floods, fissures in the ground, sinking of land, and subsidence of the bottom of the sea: our objective reconstruction of the Atlantic catastrophe has included all these important phenomena. Plato had said it all, and it is this part of the text that has aroused least criticism among the experts. He would appear to be describing here the general characteristics of Cuvier's "revolution of the Earth's surface." But Plato's contention that it all happened "in a single dreadful day and in a single dreadful night" is what the critics have found so hard to accept.

But Plato's statement agrees very well with our reconstruction of the catastrophe. The subsidence of the barrier island was bound to reach noticeable proportions at the moment when the chain of explosions arrived at the bifurcation of the fracture seam to the south of the island. And the chain of explosions then proceeded along both sides of the island and lowered the magma level as a blown-out fissure. The two branches of the explosive chain rejoined north of the island and proceeded toward Iceland and Jan Mayen. They would not, by this time, be causing any further subsidence in the Azores region. The island platform would have ceased to sink by the time the explosion had reached the second fork. The subsidence would therefore last for as long as it took the explosion of the fracture line to travel from the first to the second junction, a distance of about 750 miles (1200 km). If we assume a velocity of about 50 feet (15 meters) per second, it would have lasted 24 hours. The island would indeed have disappeared "in a single dreadful day and a single dreadful night."

PART FIVE

AFTERMATH

The Eruptions

IF WE LOOK on the catastrophe of Atlantis purely as a volcanic event, then we can call it a submarine eruption of the most monstrous dimensions. The immediate partial effects have been described in detail.

Even the very much smaller Taiga meteorite demonstrated the aftereffects to a considerable extent. They are caused by the masses of volcanic or meteorite dust and rock introduced into the upper reaches of the atmosphere by a volcanic eruption or a fall of meteorites. The dust or rock produces falls of ash, rains of blood, silver clouds, and the "red glow." The Krakatoa explosion was more powerful than the Taiga meteorite. It produced a devastating tidal wave which traveled clear across the ocean from the Cape of Good Hope to Cape Horn, halfway around the globe. The atmospheric pressure was such that a very loud bang was heard 2240 miles (3600 km) away at Alice Springs in Central Australia, and on the island of Rodriquez nearly 3000 miles (4800 km) away. The shock wave must have circled the Earth three times. Who would have heard the thunderous roar of the Atlantic catastrophe? Certainly all mankind alive at that time. And some survived to pass on the tale from one generation to another, but later, people refused to accept the accounts as describing a real event and laughed them away as fairy stories. But we can say with confidence that throughout the entire history of mankind there has been no other fall of meteorites or volcanic eruption comparable in extent to the catastrophe of Atlantis.

According to our calculations, 5×10^{15} tonnes of magma erupted into the atmosphere during this cataclysm. This value is not difficult to establish. There can be no doubt that during the most recent geological period the seabed between Jan Mayen Island and the South Atlantic suddenly subsided a mile or more. Nansen noted a drop in level in the North Polar Sea of ⅝–1¼ miles (1–2 km). In the region of the Azores the drop is as much as 2–2½ miles (3–4 km). The depression in the sima basin of the Atlantic can be reliably measured by means of echo soundings. Magma in its raw state, however, is a liquid and it tends to assume an equipotential surface. In other words, it forms a surface without depressions, of a sphere or an ellipsoid of revolution. Kinetic microforces work in the opposite direction, and their effect would be to fill in the depression and retransform the depressed surface into the equipotential one.

It cannot have been these forces that formed the depression. It was not formed by the gradual draining away of the deficient magma, but by erupted magma dispersing elsewhere. The 5×10^{15} tonnes of our calculation correspond to a volume of 360,000–480,000 cubic miles (1.5–2 million cu.km). If we look at this volume as if it were a parallelepiped based on the area of the North Atlantic, about 19,250,000 square miles (50,000,000 square km), then its mean height will be about 130 feet (40 m). The North Atlantic measures 3100 × 6200 miles

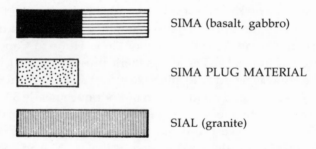

SIMA (basalt, gabbro)

SIMA PLUG MATERIAL

SIAL (granite)

Fig. 36. How the island of Atlantis was destroyed. Top: Before the catastrophe. The island platform is situated between the continental platforms, presenting a broad expanse above sea level. To the right and left of it are fracture lines closed by plugs of extruded magma. Center: During the catastrophe. Substrate magma welling up from the opened fracture lines is violently hurled into the air by the evaporating sea water and dispersed by the wind. The magma level begins to sink. Asphyxiating gases and sea floods invade the continents. Bottom: After the catastrophe. The surface of the magma suffered its maximum depression below the island platform and has subsided considerably. The island platform subsided and has become a submarine landmass; two mountain peaks have become rock islands. The inner edges of the continental platforms subsided and are slightly sloping, which caused coastal subsidence.

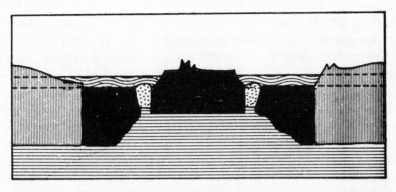

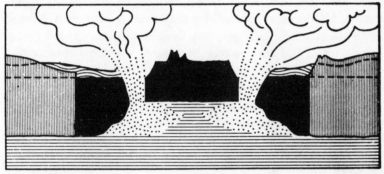

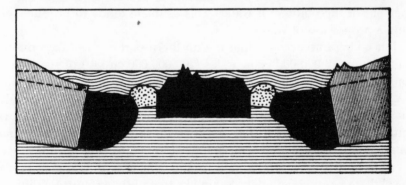

(5,000 × 10,000 km). If we compare the mean height of the erupted volume with the smaller of the dimensions of width, then the ratio between the two values will be as 1:125,000. This is a negligible dimension. It is well within the realm of possibility that in this, the most catastrophic eruption in history, enough of the immeasurable store of magma below the Earth's crust erupted to cause a mean subsidence of about 130 feet (40 m).

If we accept these calculations, we have sufficient information to estimate the extent to which these eruptions disturbed life on Earth. A catastrophe like this one of 11,000 years ago produces gases, water, and lava in its eruptions.

We already have quantitative data about the lava. There were 360,000–480,000 cubic miles (1.5–2 million cu.km) of it, weighing about 5×10^{15} tonnes. This solid material was transported in the form of large boulders, fly ash, and very fine dust. It was carried up to the high reaches of the atmosphere by means of water vapor, which is always the main product of volcanic activity, especially when it takes place under water. To hurl 5×10^{15} tonnes of lava to such heights, a quantity of water weighing four times as much would be required, or 2×10^{16} tonnes of water, a volume of 4,800,000 cubic miles (20,000,000 cu.km). 1¼ cubic yard (1 cu.m), weighing 1 tonne, would have added to it about 250 kg of lava in the form of ash. This would have taken up a partial volume of about 100 liters, comprising 10 percent of the volume of water. This estimate tends to produce too low a proportion of water.

But taking into account that the northern part of the Atlantic contains about 48,000,000 cubic miles (200,000,000 cu.km) of sea water, only about 10 percent of its volume would have been involved in this catastrophic eruption. But distributed over its area, it would certainly have led to an appreciable drop in the sea level. Water, however, is much more mobile than lava and therefore regains its equipotential shape more quickly after temporary deformation. Water would rush in from north and south to make up the deficiency in volume. At sea level there would be no depression like that of the rapidly solidifying substrate magma. We have calculated that about 4,800,000 cubic miles (20 million cu.km) of water erupted in the form of steam and carried with it about 480,000 cubic miles (2 million cu.km) of magma. Compare with the total qualtity of sea water on Earth—about $.58 \times 10^{12}$ cubic miles 2.4 × 10^{12} cu. km) we see that only a small fraction, 1 in 120 parts, of the total volume of water took part in this catastrophe.

Before this water was able to return to the oceans, the sea level dropped by up to 130 feet (40 meters). This may have lasted only for a few weeks, and later it may have risen somewhat above normal, because the water of absorption released from the magma would have slightly increased the global circulation.

The process of readjustment after the catastrophe may have been tremendously impressive, but it is easy to understand that they were not reflected in the myths of the flood because of the more overwhelming reactions experienced by those who survived.

The erupting gases included, in addition to water vapor, carbon dioxide (CO_2) and other asphyxiating gases such as sulphurous vapors and hydrogen sulphide, hydrogen chloride, ammonium chloride, chlorides of iron and copper, boric acid, and cyanides. Carbon dioxide, hydrogen sulphide, chloride, and the other highly volatile compounds are particularly dangerous because they spread over great distances and their heat and poisonous constitution are then lethal to men and animals.

The incombustible gases of the freon type, liquefied under pressure in the magma, adversely affected the ozone layer at a height of 20–30 miles (32–48 km).

Functioning as a filter, this layer protects the Earth by absorbing the harmful shortwave ultraviolet radiation of the sun by absorbing it. The temperature of the ozone belt is therefore always higher than that of the belts immediately above and below.

The effect of the damage to the ozone belt, which surrounds the entire Earth, was not felt until several hundred years after the catastrophe. Ultraviolet radiation changed the hereditary factors of surviving generations.[47]

The gases analyzed by Day and others at the crater of Halemaumau of Kilauea on Hawaii in December 1919 are fairly typical of the composition of volcanic gases, and it is fair to assume, of the gaseous components of the Atlantic eruptions. Their analysis was:

	Percent weight
Carbon dioxide	42.9
Nitrogen	25.8
Water	27.5
Sulphur dioxide	3.7

The gases contain about half again as much carbon dioxide as water vapor. Estimating the proportion of the water of absorption set free from the ejected magma at about 0.1 percent of sea water vapor, we can deduce a carbon dioxide proportion of 0.15 percent by weight of the total water circulation, which was about 2×10^{16} tonnes. The carbon dioxide production was therefore about 3×10^{13} tonnes, or about three times as much as the quantity of atmospheric carbon dioxide today.

Very large quantities of asphyxiating gases must have been released during the Atlantic catastrophe. A standard cubic meter of carbon dioxide weighs about 2 kilograms (about 1¼ cubic yards weighs about 4⅜ lbs). About 1.5×10^{16} standard cubic meters (roughly 1.9×10^{16} cubic yards) of this gas alone must have been freed. This is scarcely more than 0.1 percent of the entire atmosphere, which is not much, but it erupted from a closely confined space within a few days, and it could travel a great distance on its wave of dispersion and have a catastrophic effect on life. The eruption of Mount Pelée on the island of Martinique in 1902 killed more than 30,000 inhabitants. In the well-known destruction of Pompeii, most of the victims suffocated. These are minor examples in comparison with the Atlantic catastrophe.

The total involvement was about 5×10^{15} tonnes of solid substances; about 4,800,000 cubic miles (20,000,000 cu. km) of water; and 2.5–3.7 $\times 10^{16}$ cubic yards (2–3 $\times 10^{16}$ standard cubic meters) of asphyxiating gases. This was quite enough to produce terrible and long-lasting disturbances in the whole of the life on Earth. One of the effects was the deluge, so familiar in myth. This did not, as might have been supposed, destroy the island of Atlantis by flood. Rather the reverse. The flood was itself a direct consequence of the Atlantic catastrophe, and followed the sinking of the island of Atlantis, as Plato relates.

The Sea of Mud

THE MATERIAL EJECTED during a volcanic eruption does not remain indefinitely in the upper atmosphere. It will eventually return to the ground, though seldom to the place from which it rose. The finer and more delicate it is, the longer it will take to return to Earth, and the greater distance it will be carried on the prevailing winds. If we think of the atmosphere as an industrial air-separator, the largest and coarsest particles ejected during the eruptions came down fairly close to their original positions, while the finer particles were carried considerably farther away. But the finest of all had a very special and notorious result.

Using the data obtained from historic volcanic eruptions, we can arrive at a rough estimate of the proportions of these three different types of substance produced in the Atlantic catastrophe. The coarse particles would have formed about one-third of the total; the fine dust barely more than a twentieth. The greater part of it, roughly 62 percent, would have consisted of fly ash. From these proportions we arrive at these rough estimates of weight:

1.5×10^{15} tonnes of coarse matter
3.25×10^{15} tonnes of fly ash
2.5×10^{14} tonnes of fine dust.

Let us take first the coarse matter.

The products of submarine volcanic eruptions differ from flowing lava. They are not compact and vitreous-amorphous or crystalline. They originate from the interaction between water vapor and red-hot matter and this makes them porous. When surface lava, rich in absorbed water, is extruded from a bursting fold it enters a region of normal pressure, which is less than the pressure to which it had previously been subjected. The water it contains bubbles up as steam, and together with carbon dioxide escapes from the intramolecular

199

spaces. The expanding gases loosen the structure into a spongelike consistency. When the red-hot substance solidifies it becomes a loose, light mass interspersed with innumerable bubbles called pumice stone.

The toughest, firmest, and most coherent particles of the eruption turn into pumice stone. Fly ash is pumice stone disintegrated into its component parts and fly ash will form a greater proportion of the whole, the stronger the disruptive forces exerted during its formation.

A very large part of the total erupted material usually consists of pumice stone. If it falls back into the nearby sea, it remains floating on the surface for a fairly long time because of the air trapped in its bubbles. This happened in the eruptions of Mount Etna, Vesuvius, and Krakatoa. If it is not ground to powder by the action of the waves, it will eventually soak up the water and slowly sink. After a major eruption it can form such a widespread and long-lasting surface layer that it can interfere with shipping. Svante Arrhenius, in *Erde und Weltall* (*The Earth and the Universe*, Leipzig, 1926), writes, "Large stones containing innumerable bubbles, pumice stones, float on the sea and are slowly ground to sand by the waves. Volcanic sand and mud cover large areas of the seabed. The amount of the floating pumice stone is such that it often endangers or interferes with ships. This was a disturbing consequence of the eruption of Krakatoa in 1883."

No one who has read this book by the Swedish Nobel Prize winner has ever accused the scholarly author of talking nonsense in this passage. But Plato, quoting his ancient Egyptian authority, has been accused of making up stories when he wrote, "This is why the sea is no longer navigable there and cannot be crossed in ships because this is prevented by the very deep mud, the remains of the island when it sank."

In the eruption of Krakatoa, the ejected material amounted to barely 24 cubic miles (100 cubic km). This was enough to cause considerable interference with the running of modern steam ships. How much greater must have been the disturbance caused by the Atlantic catastrophe, which was twenty-thousand times greater and produced 1.5×10^{15} tonnes of pumice stone, occupying a volume of about 720,000 cubic miles (3,000,000 cu.km). If we imagine this volume spread out to cover the entire 19,250,000 square miles (3,000,000 sq.km) of the North Atlantic, it would be about 200 feet (60 meters) thick. Pumice stone is unlikely to be densely packed and would therefore form an unbroken layer over the sea to a thickness of up to 330 feet (100 meters). Its strong damping effect would prevent the formation of swell or high waves throughout the affected areas. It would be less susceptible to destructive wave motions than would a thinner cover of smaller dimensions. Such a layer could persist for a fairly long time.

In the comparatively small Krakatoa catastrophe, there was about 24 cubic miles (100 cu.km) of erupted material, weighing about 2.5×10^{11} tonnes. Pumice stone accounted for about a third of this total, 38½ cubic miles (160 cu.km) weighing 8×10^{10} tonnes. Pumice stone, with a specific gravity of about 0.5, is rather light. Imagine this volume of pumice stone spread out to a radius of about 310 miles (500 km), which probably corresponds to the actual conditions. It would cover a total area of about 290,000 square miles (750,000 sq.km) at a thickness of about 9⅞ inches (25 cm). This does not sound very thick, but it was a nuisance to shipping and probably interfered with regular sea traffic for weeks and possibly months.

On the mud sea around Atlantis the cover was about 330 feet (100 meters) thick, 400 times thicker than in the Sunda Strait in 1883. It would take, proportionately, far longer to break up than the smaller and thinner cover, and it must have been a much longer lasting obstacle to the less powerful ships of that time.

A reasonable assumption about its duration is that the cover of pumice stone increases in persistence in proportion to its volume. In that case it would have persisted around the island of Atlantis twenty thousand times longer than around the exploded half of Krakatoa. If this persisted, at a rough guess, for two months, the former would then have lasted 40,000 months, or about 3000 years. This is a very long time, certainly long enough for the rumor to get around that the sea beyond the strait, which was in fact opened up by the Atlantic catastrophe and later called "Pillars of Melkart" or "Pillars of Hercules," was so choked with mud that it was unnavigable. How many ships over those centuries must have tried in vain to sail through this sea of mud!

Plato's account is thereby confirmed. But we must remember that those estimated 3000 years would have long been over by Solon's time, and the waters in the Azores region were probably navigable again. Perhaps by then the floating mud had settled on the seabed, to be covered later by a layer of globigerina, foraminifera, and diatom shells. This could be the answer to the vital question of what became of the vast quantities of erupted coarse material. We cannot expect to find accumulations of pumice stone in the coastal regions of the Atlantic. After this loose, spongy stone is subjected to wave and chemical action by the sea it takes a few thousand years at most for it to decompose and turn into mud, which will gradually sink to the seabed or be carried away by currents.

After the disappearance of Atlantis, the Gulf Stream was free to continue its eastward flow. This surface current would have carried with it huge quantities of the erupted material from the area of catastrophe, ranging in size from pumice stones to dust grains. As mud, it would gradually sink into the zone of cold water currents close to the seabed. These currents, hugging the irregularities of the basin, would leave deposits everywhere, so that the entire coastal region became liberally covered with mud. This had an interesting result, which can be seen on the map. In the whole of the Bay of Biscay as far north as La Rochelle, the coast is level, rises gently, has few distinguishing features, and is without a single river delta. The Garonne ends in a characteristic funnel-shaped estuary, but not in a true delta. In the opinion of the Swiss scholar E. F. Schlaepfer, this special feature is connected with the silting-up of the remains of the Atlantic catastrophe.

Naturally this process had been completed long before Plato's time. The sea of mud that had existed to the west of the Pillars of Hercules several thousand years earlier persisted into Plato's time only as a folk memory.

The Deluge

IN ADDITION TO the sea of mud produced by the coarse fragments, the other two constituents of the erupted material also had far-reaching and sometimes catastrophic effects. Again, we will make quantitative comparisons with the data that have been collected about the aftereffects of historic volcanic eruptions.

The medium-sized erupted fragments vary in size from a pea to a walnut and are called lapilli. They are produced in large quantities in all major eruptions; sometimes in astonishingly large quantities. The material ejected in the localized but fairly violent eruption of Vesuvius in 1906 consisted mainly of clouds of ash. So dense and so heavy was the rain of ash in the immediate neighborhood of the volcano, that roofs in Naples collapsed under it. In A.D. 79 the city of Pompeii suffered a much worse fate. In *The Earth and the Universe,* Arrhenius says, "A layer of ash 69 feet (7 m) deep provided Pompeii with a protective cover, which preserved it up to the excavations in our own time. The fine ash and the mud deposited by the rain formed around bodies like plaster casts and hardened like cement, and when the rotted and decomposed remains were flushed out of these casts it was possible to mould most detailed positive casts of the objects they had enclosed. A kind of tufa in which sea animals and algae were embedded congealed from the ash that had fallen into the sea. This tufa makes up the soil of the Campagna Felice region near Naples. . . ."

This classic eruption was certainly catastrophic for the cities in the immediate vicinity of Vesuvius, Pompeii and Herculaneum. It was, however, by no means one of the great volcanic eruptions. And these, too, do not stand comparison with the prehistoric super-catastrophe in the Atlantic. It is impossible to estimate the quantity of ash that fell into the sea when Atlantis sank. The likelihood is that the major part of the fine particles that were hurled high into the troposphere and the ionosphere did not return to the Atlantic at all, but were blown very great distances and settled in those regions to which they were carried by the prevailing winds.

In the equatorial belt the prevailing winds are the easterly trades. At the higher latitudes, beyond about 40°, the westerlies predominate. Ash ejected near the equator would therefore be blown toward the west; ash from the main area of eruption, the Azores region, would be blown toward the east across the Old World.

But this stupendous wall of black cloud drifting eastward contained not only the 3×10^{16} tonnes of volcanic ash ejected in the North Atlantic, it also contained no less than 2×10^{16} tonnes of moisture in the form of wet, rainbearing steam that had been ejected together with the fragmented particles of magma. These innumerable minute particles, together with the sea salt crystals that always form when sea water evaporates, were ideal nuclei of condensation for raindrops. The gradually cooling water vapor condensed on them. The cloud of ash, enriched by the salinity of the sea water it was carrying, became a rain cloud of unique dimensions. These lowering, ominous, inky-black clouds were blown eastward across the landmass of the Old World at the higher latitudes, and westward across the tropical regions of the New World by the easterly trades farther south. So it was in these two great regions that the rains came. Those who lived there and survived this torrential downpour handed on their experiences to their descendants, and the myths of the flood came into being.

The deluge is a subject over which there has been a great deal of lengthy controversy. It is also of particular interest because of the biblical account. Let us first look eastward, to the countries that produced the classical myths about the Deluge.

If we take a total of 2×10^{16} tonnes of water mixed with 3×10^{15} tonnes of ash and spread it evenly across the whole of northern Eurasia this will yield a mean depth of rainfall of about 100 feet (30 m). This was the immense reservoir out of which the downpour burst on the Old World. The floodgates of heaven were truly opened. Springs, small streams, great rivers—all swelled under the tremendous cloudbursts. They mingled with the tidal waves to produce overwhelming floods. On vast tracts of the Earth's surface, all life was destroyed.

Asteroid A hit the Earth at a certain time and at a certain spot as a result of celestial mechanics. The most sensitive fracture seam in the middle of the Atlantic was ruptured. The ensuing clash between fire and water produced, among other phenomena, gigantic rainclouds which were carried both east and west of the Atlantic. These clouds unleashed their burden and produced the result that has become known to us under the collective term of the Deluge or the Flood. This was the causal chain. We must make it clear that we are not concerned here with the religious interpretations or the metaphysical significance of this violent natural event, because it has been the religious or mythical element in the story of the flood that has led many scientists to reject it. For them, this aspect went against the grain.

It has sometimes been assumed, in order to explain the biblical myth of the Flood, that the region in Mesopotamia between the Euphrates and the Tigris was inundated by the sea or by the rivers themselves. But this is not so. It was flooded by extraordinary rains of mud, preceded by equally extraordinary tidal waves. The epic of *Gilgamesh* describes the approach of the catastrophe and its subsequent course very vividly and without exaggeration:

"There came the time when the rulers of darkness sent down a terrible rain. I looked at the weather; it was frightful to look at . . .

"At daybreak clouds as black as the night appeared in the sky. All the evil spirits raged and all light was transformed into darkness.

"The southerly gale roared, the waters roared, the waters reached the mountains, the waters buried all the people . . .

"For six days and six nights the rains roared like torrents. On the seventh day the tide relented. It was like the calm after a battle. The sea became calm, and the storm of disaster abated. I looked out at the weather, and the air was very still.

"All the people had turned into mud. The ground of the Earth was a bleak desert . . ."

The story is being told by Ut-napishtim, who is an ancestor of Gilgamesh and the Sumerian equivalent of Noah. He is the only man warned in time by the god Ea. He survived the deluge in his ark and was thereafter transported with his wife to the western sea, to the mouth of the rivers on a blessed island.

The details in the story seem to be authentic enough: the torrential rain, the dreadful weather, the clouds black as night, the turning of the day into dark night, the roaring of the gales and waters, the mountainous rise of the floods. Finally we have the enormous mass of mud formed by the mixture of ash and inky rain. It buried the people and left the Earth a "bleak desert."

For a long time this story was regarded as a mere myth or fable. If admitted to have an element of truth in it, the story was still played down as an exaggerated tale of a minor local catastrophe. And then in 1928 Leonard Woolley carried out his famous excavations at Ur (the modern Warka). He and his team found here what was undoubtedly a relic of the allegedly mythical flood. Far below the tombs of the early Sumerian kings, and about 40 feet (12 meters) below the present surface, they found a layer of alluvial clay about 8 feet, 2 inches (2.5 m) thick which was completely devoid of finds.

Nor even Woolley could have had any doubt that this was evidence of a genuine, enormous inundation. Perhaps Woolley least of all, because he was in possession of the lists of the Sumerian royal dynasties up to the deluge. Woolley dated this blank layer in the fourth millennium B. C. How did he come to this conclusion? If a layer devoid of finds is uncovered beneath a layer that is rich in finds, even the most astute archaeologist can say no more than that it is older than the one above. He cannot say how old it is.

Woolley suggested that the barren alluvial layer originated in one of the particularly heavy floods that are said to occur from time to time in the flood plain of the Euphrates and the Tigris. But this is not tenable. Events like this never leave layers that are completely without finds. If the sea invades the land or the rivers burst their banks, then the raging waters carry everything with them—people, cattle, huts, utensils. Everything carried away by the water settles in the ground where it is deposited, mixing with the mud and the fertile soil that has been stirred up. Alluvial layers left by sea or river floods are bound to contain occasional finds of human or animal bones, fossilized pieces of wood, or artifacts of various kinds.

The layer discovered by Woolley could not therefore have been formed by a flood of this nature. It could be produced only by a rain of ash and mud such as occurred 11,000 years before; a rain that washed away everything and left as its final and most thoroughly sifted deposit this layer of fine-grained clay; and this layer could never contain any archaeological object because everything had been carried away into the sea by the rain floods before it could become fossilized.

This layer of clay 8 feet, 2 inches (2.5 m) deep is geological evidence of the reality of the monstrous Flood described in the Bible. ". . . the same day were all the fountains of the great deep broken up, and the windows of heaven were opened. And the rain was upon the earth forty days and forty nights . . . and the waters prevailed exceedingly upon the earth; and all the high hills, that were under the whole heaven, were covered. Fifteen cubits upwards did the waters prevail; and the mountains were covered . . . and the waters prevailed upon the earth a hundred and fifty days." (*Genesis*, Chapter 7.)

Is this an exaggerated account? Were the mountains in and along the edge of the plain of Mesopotamia really covered by water? The layer uncovered by Woolley can be used as a basis for an estimate of the extent of the flood. Most of the mud from the sky would have been carried to the sea in the torrential rains. This alluvial layer consists of the residual quantity of mud that was left behind as a substrate deposited on the flooded continent.

Only a very small proportion of the total quantity of mud can have been thus deposited: hardly more than 5–10 percent. If all the mud had been deposited, then the barren zone would have been 80–160 feet (25–50 m) deep, not 8 feet, 2 inches (2.5 m). We can calculate the volume of water that would be associated with such a depth. We have assumed an average of 3 parts by weight of mud and ash to 20 parts by weight of water. This is equivalent to 1 part by volume of mud to 20 parts by volume of water, because the specific gravity of the mud and ash is about 3.0. This brings the associated layer of water to 20 times the depth of the layer of mud: that is, 1600–3000 feet (500–1000 m) deep, which does not allow for any loss over the intervening period, so it is a conservative estimate. Flood levels like this are obviously high enough to cover the tops of hills and mountains and to rise another 15 cubits above them. In the whole of Mesopotamia, which at the time was probably inhabited mainly by herdsmen and nomads, there is hardly any ground high enough to give protection against such floods. The Bible story does not exaggerate.

It may be objected that we have previously calculated the mean depth of rainfall at only 100 feet (30 m). How then could the floods in Mesopotamia have been so very much deeper?

It is not the mean depth that is decisive, but the actual inrush of water in a particular area. This inrush of water will be determined by the geographical structure of the catchment area. The normal rainfall in Mesopotamia is insufficient to sustain two rivers as large as the Tigris and the Euphrates. The water of these great rivers comes from a very large catchment area extending far beyond the region of

Mesopotamia. Conditions during the deluge were unusual only because of the amount of water involved. Then, as at other times, the
waters from the entire catchment area to the north collected in these
rivers. But there was so much water that not only the rivers, but the
valley between them, and in fact the entire region, acted as a drainage
trench. The floods in this area were therefore many times deeper than
the average rainfall calculated at 100 feet (30 m) for the whole of
Eurasia. We can fairly say that Woolley's discovery of the barren layer
confirms the texts of both the biblical and the Sumerian account of the
deluge. It tells us that the dimensions stated in these ancient accounts
are no exaggeration.

Other quantitative investigations also bear out the biblical tradition.
The combined catchment area of the two great rivers of Mesopotamia
covers about 308,000 square miles (800,000 sq.km). At a mean depth
of rainfall of 100 feet (30 m) and reinforced by the masses of sea water
invading from the south, a total of about 6.5×10^{12} cubic yards
(5×10^{13} cu.m) of water collected in the rain trench of Mesopotamia.
The mean length of the drainage trench is 435 miles (700 km). Hence
the discharge section is 65,000,000,000,000:765,000 = 85 million
square yards. (50,000,000,000,000:700,000 = 70 million sq. meters.)
The outlet of the rain trench is about 100 miles (160 km) wide. The
mass of water covering the entire length of the lower reaches of the
two rivers, and being slowly discharged, must therefore have been
about 1600 feet (500 m) deep. This agrees with the value produced by
the estimate of the quantity of deposited clay. A study of the geography of Mesopotamia removes any doubts about the accuracy of the
biblical account of the Flood. Its language is poetic; the facts it contains are not exaggerated.

"And all flesh died that moved upon the earth, both of fowl, and of
cattle, and of beast, and of every creeping thing that creepeth upon
the earth, and every man:

"All in whose nostrils was the breath of life, of all that was in the
dry land, died.

"And every living substance was destroyed which was upon the
face of the ground, both man, and cattle, and the creeping things, and
the fowl of the heaven; and they were destroyed from the earth: and
Noah only remained alive, and they that were with him in the ark."
(*Genesis*, Chapter 7.)

The Sumerian story also claims that people were turned into mud.
But why should the birds be destroyed too? If this was nothing more

than a particularly extensive normal flood, as Woolley and others have maintained, why couldn't these winged creatures simply fly away from the flooded area near the river mouths? They were unable to escape because the torrential rain sucked them into the maelstrom in which all life was destroyed. The death of the birds shows how different this catastrophe was from a normal marine inundation. The water that fell from the sky was far more lethal than even the most prolonged downpour could be. So saturated was the air with condensation centers that a cubic meter of air could have contained up to one kilogram of water mixed with mud (1¼ cubic yards contained up to 2¼ lbs). This would be an extreme value. The mass of cloud which could produce a mean rainfall of 100 feet (30 m) must have had a mean height of 18½ miles (30 km)—three times higher than Mount Everest. The crests and cumuli of these mountainous clouds reached high into the stratosphere. They were black because of their ash content—a detail that is mentioned in the Sumerian story. Such particles rapidly acquire high electrostatic charges. So the black clouds were rent by lightning and thunder, and at the same time torn by thermal funnels, whirlwinds, and tornadoes of unimaginable violence.

The story goes that only one man escaped the catastrophe. The Bible calls him Noah; in the *Gilgamesh* epic he is called Ut-napishtim. His ark is said to have drifted on the storm-tossed waters and to have landed on the mountain of Nisir when the Flood subsided.

American explorers, taking this information literally, have claimed that they could see the outline of Noah's ark in the summit ice of Mount Ararat through their binoculars. This mountain is about 17,000 feet (5188 m) high. Can it be the Nisir of the Bible? Dr. Bender, a geologist and oil prospector who knows the country well, doubts it. Even a flood of the dimensions we have been considering could not, he argues, have carried floating objects, let along whole ships, across mountain ranges 6560 feet and sometimes 13,000 feet high (2000 m or 4000 m), and a distance of 680 miles (1100 km). Any relics of the deluge would have been deposited on the first high barrier, the mountain range of Cudi, a chain of limestone and dolomite formations running in an east–west direction. It rises 5260 feet (1600 m) above the lowland plain on which the river Tigris deposited its gravel banks. This plain gradually reaches a height of 1300 feet (400 m) above sea level.

This assumption has been confirmed. An Islamic scholar proved in an ancient Arabic record that the ark of Nug, which is the Mohammedan form of Noah, landed on the Al Judhi mountains. According to a Kurd sheik, this site has been a place of pilgrimage from ages past; if you dug deep enough into the sand you would find pieces of caulked timber—relics of Nug's ark that would protect you against black magic and disease.

Dr. Bender cleared away the snow from this area and found sand underneath covering a layer of decomposed humus that contained pieces of pitch-black material, organic relics impregnated with asphalt. Were they remains of wood, of the timber of Noah's ark? The Bible says, "Make thee an ark of gopher wood; rooms shalt thou make in the ark and shalt pitch it within and without with pitch. . . ." (*Genesis*, Chapter 6.)

Can we prove these finds are relics of something that floated above the deluge? The fragments of wood are minute and badly decomposed. It is difficult to date them. But there are other serious arguments in favor of this assumption. The sand covering the humus is like sea sand; it contains quartzite grains. How did sea sand find its way to 3900 feet (1200 m) above the banks of the Tigris? In this region there is nothing but limestone and dolomite in every direction. There are no primitive rocks whose weathering could have yielded the quartzite component. The sand must have come from the sea. And the only way it could have been carried up, with the organic floating matter, into the Cudi mountains is by water. It was found where the man who discovered it predicted that it would be found—in an unmistakable alluvial basin open to the south. In the language of the Bible, it was found where the patriarch established a new covenant with his God under the sevenfold light of the rainbow.

One problem, however, remains. The rains of the deluge came from the northwest and anything carried away in the flood would have been taken southeastward, toward the Persian Gulf. The Cudi mountains are to the northeast and the site of the finds is 5260 feet (1600 meters) above the lowland plain. How could anything have floated in this direction, and been lifted so high? We have assessed the depth of water at 1600–3000 feet (500–1000 m), considerably lower than the mountain.

But even this discrepancy can be explained. In Mongolia in the heart of Asia there was at one time a high inland sea surrounded by a wall of mountains. This sea burst its banks in the deluge. Tradition calls it the "deluge of Phoroneus." It poured through the Dardanelles and added its salty waters to the tidal waves which were radiating from the center of the catastrophe and repeatedly circling the globe. So the sea waters were flooding Mesopotamia even before the swollen rivers could do their work. It was the sea that destroyed the settlements and carried any floating objects to the northeast, which is why the flood in Mesopotamia rose to 6560 feet (2000 m) above sea level and 5260 feet (1600 m) above the base of the Cudi mountains. The sea waters and the dammed-up river waters combined to produce this height. Localized eddies formed from the current and the countercurrent. One of them was in the basin south of the Cudi ridge. It left on top of the ridge sea sand mixed with the substrate deposited by the diluvial rains. The mud basin dried out; the wood rotted below the sand. There remained only lumps rich in asphalt, fragments much sought after as charms against disasters, silent witnesses that the Bible story was true. Not only true, confounding all the skeptics, but also chronologically datable. Thanks to the causal relationship between the biblical deluge and the sinking of the island of Atlantis, we have enough scientific evidence to give a date to this early Bible story of about 9000 B.C.

As in Mesopotamia, rains of blood and mud wrought destruction and caused terrible floods in other eastern countries.

The Dardanelles straits are said to have been opened up by an earthquake. The waters of the high sea in Mongolia rushed through the depression of the Caspian and Black Seas and devastated the pre-Hellenic settlements. This is associated with the names of the Pelasgian king Phoroneus and of Deucalion, son of Prometheus. Phoroneus is the Greek Adam, the first man created. Deucalion, son of the titan Prometheus, was married to Pyrrha, daughter of Epimetheus and Pandora, whose box contained suffering, misfortune, and grief for mankind. Deucalion is the Noah figure who was advised by Prometheus to build a large ark, and like Noah and Utnapishtim, he followed the advice. The myths of the deluge in Mesopotamia and Greece are very similar. It is evident that they are all based on a common source, and that they describe the same fearful events in the imagery typical of myths.

Noah lands on the mountain of Nisir, and Deucalion lands on Mount Parnassus. Like the biblical patriarch he leaves the ark that saved him and offers sacrifices to his god. Zeus graciously accepts

the sacrifice, as does El in the Bible. And in both cases the plea of
the supplicant is granted: to become the patriarch of a new postdiluvian mankind.

In the Greek version, Deucalion and Pyrrha picked up stones from
the muddy grounds. Averting their eyes, they threw the stones
backward over their shoulders. The stones turned into men and
women who replaced the generation that had perished in the deluge.

The inanimate is magically turned into the animate with a backward throw—a throwback to the past. What were these strange
stones that were turned into human beings? In the Sumerian epic of
the deluge people were turned into mud. These strange stones must
have been the mud corpses. By being thrown back into the past they
were turned back into what they had been before: living people.
Mankind, almost entirely eradicated by the deluge, later began to
multiply again. The childlike mentality of these ancient peoples explained the renewal in this myth of the stones. If we do not take them
too literally, but look for the true image behind the symbol, we can
learn from this complex of myths.

In Egypt rains of blood also fell. According to Solon, the tradition of
Atlantis comes from Egypt, and we also have an Egyptian account of
the deluge that has been handed down to posterity and that is
significant in more than one respect. Dr. Trofimovich, in his essay
"Das linke Auge des Re" (The left eye of Ra), quotes from the
epitaphs of Seti I and Rameses III:

"It is the time when Ra, the god that gave birth to himself . . . the
King of mankind and of the gods became old. And men spoke against
him when His Majesty had become old. . . . and this Majesty heard
the tales of men. And he said to those who were members of his
retinue: 'Go and call my eye, and Shu, Tafnet, Geb, and Nut' . . . The
gods were called . . . they spoke to His Majesty: 'Speak to us, so that
we can listen.' Ra said to Nunu: 'Oh oldest of the gods, of whom I am
created, oh Divine forebears. See these men . . . they hatched plans
against me. Tell me what you would do to stop them. You see, I wish
to avoid killing them before I have heard your views.' The majesty of
Nunu said: 'Ra, my son, god who is greater than his progenitor and
more powerful than his creator! Sit upon your throne. Great is the
fear of you when your eye is fixed upon those that rebelled against
you.' The Majesty of Ra replied: 'See, they are fleeing into the desert,
because their hearts are full of fear on account of what they said.' The
gods spoke to His Majesty: 'Let your eye fasten upon the rebels and

smite them. The eye should not remain in the forehead. Let is descend as Hathor . . .'

Dr. Trofimovich points out that the Egyptian myth follows the *Critias* dialogues very closely. It may be regarded almost as a supplement to the dialogues in that it supplies the missing theological motive. Man had become too clever and too powerful and had rebelled against the gods, against Ra, who had "become old." According to the myth, the masters of the prehistoric era were due a terrible punishment. They had rebelled against the dwellers in the heavens, as the giants and the titans had done, and they destroyed their own world. The prominence of this motif in the Egyptian myth is perhaps due to the subjection of ancient Egypt by Atlantis. It is of less importance in the myths of the more remote Sumeria, and it was the Sumerian version of the deluge that was the basis of the later Babylonian-Assyrian myths from which the biblical story derives.

Both on the banks of the Nile and in Hellas, the hubris of mankind was punished by the gods. According to the hieroglyphs the hubris of the Atlanteans was directly responsible for the deluge. It was to punish them that the "eye of Ra" descended from its heavenly forehead to the Earth and smote it with disaster. What was this eye? In the text, the well-known hieroglyph for eye is placed next to the symbol for goddess, which is the rearing serpent Uraeus. This means that Ra's left eye is regarded in this context as a specifically divine force, numinous and effective; as Sekhet, the Powerful.

It was not the sun that was the left eye of Ra. It was the asteroid that fell from the sky as a destructive bolide, whose fearful glare dimmed the sun and darkened the sky. Egypt, too, was overwhelmed by the catastrophe that it unleashed. In the story, Ra was afraid that Sekhet-Hathor would destroy all mankind. He brewed beer and poured it over the country of the Nile. In the more modern version this is the rain of blood. When the lioness rose again in the morning to wreak further destruction, her image was reflected in the red flood. She was tempted by it and bent down. She drank the delicious beer, became intoxicated, and completely forgot about man. So the Egyptian version of the deluge story ends in something like burlesque. The intention was probably to explain the strange rain of blood.

The lands of the far north also perished in the sea of blood of the diluvian rains. Because they were situated very near to the center of the catastrophe, they suffered incomparably more than remote Egypt. The myths of these regions are a marked variation on the main theme.

The primeval god is slain by the young gods of the new era. In the verses quoted earlier from the *Völuspa* the young gods are called Bur's sons. They kill and disembowel Ymir, the ice god, and his whole tribe drowns in his red blood except one, the Nordic Noah. Sitting on a grinding box, he escapes across the floods. From the dismembered body of Ymir, the old world, the young gods create Midgarth, the verdant new world. They make the mountains from his bones, the fertile soil from his flesh, the sky from his skull. In this mythical picture we can see a strong suggestion of the blossoming forth of the postglacial landscape from the broken and melting sheet of ice. But why was the water that flowed from the glaciers and poured from the sky dark red like blood? Because it was not ordinary rain, but the rain of mud and blood of the deluge, colored black and red by the volcanic ash of the Atlantic catastrophe.

Let us compare these myths of the east with those of the western world. The Maya people who lived in the region where the west winds prevailed did not experience the deluge. But their country was devastated by the volcanic catastrophe, by earthquakes, fire, and the tidal wave caused by the crash of the asteroid. We have already quoted from the book of *Chilam Balams*, which is typical of the myths of this region. But the tribes living farther south, beyond the region of the west winds, passed on their memories of a great flood. The Tarascans have a myth about a priest called Tespi who built himself a large boat and escaped in it with his family. In Guatemala, a similar theme is associated with the names of Nala and Nata. The Toltec giant Shelua escaped the flood by climbing the mountain of the god of water. Later, he built the famous pyramid of Cholula, which was burned to the ground by Cortes.

The Algonquin tribe of North America have an interesting variant of the story. They lived in the zone where the westerly winds prevailed and did not experience the deluge. In their version the god and hero Minabozho threw himself into the sea, causing it to overflow and flood the Earth. This may be a residual memory of the fall of Asteroid A into the Atlantic; its visible trajectory traversed the Algonquin country.

We would expect the South American peoples in the tropical belt where the easterly winds prevail to have experienced the deluge and to remember it in their myths. This expectation is confirmed as regards the Arawakans in Guyana, Northern Brazil, and Columbia. The benevolent god Sigoo took all the animals and birds to a high mountain where they survived the terrible time of darkness and storms, while the fearful flood inundated the lowlands. The Arawak tribe of the Macushi have a myth similar to that of Deucalion and Pyrrha in pre-Hellas. It concerns the first human couple after the deluge who turned stones back into human beings and thereby re-populated the Earth. The Arawakans of Guyana remember both the fire and the deluge that followed it, which accords with their geographical location.

The Great Death
of the Mammoths

WE DO NOT FIND MANY MYTHS of the deluge in the vast regions of northern Asia that are covered by the eastern rain belt. But this by no means proves that no diluvial rains reached this area. On the contrary, these regions belong to the zone exposed to the prevailing west winds. They must also have suffered the torrential rains, blackened by the volcanic ash of the Atlantic catastrophe.

In the extreme northern tip of Asia, however, we find not only myths of the deluge but evidence of another sort. Here we have priceless and unique paleontological evidence of the huge flood that swept the country and drowned the gigantic animals living there.

The whole of this strange region is an enormous icebox, filled with well-preserved mammoth carcasses. (Plate 16.)

How did these huge representatives of the diluvian fauna come to be entombed? As herbivores, they would have avoided the inland ice.

These mammoth bodies, as well-preserved as if they had died only yesterday, have presented an apparently insoluble puzzle to scientists. These animals lived during the Quaternary Age and became extinct in the Quinternary Age. It is clear that they were destroyed by the epochal catastrophe. These remote areas would have suffered only the side effects of the Atlantic cataclysm; they would have experienced the devastating floods from the diluvial rains. The mammoths must have either suffocated in the wave of asphyxiating gases or drowned in the floods. But why they should be buried in the center of a glaciated region, when as herbivores they would have retreated from the ice, remains to be explained.

We may find a clue to the mystery from Figure 37, which shows where the frozen mammoths were discovered. As we have stated, the 32° F (0° C) isotherm of today runs an entirely different course from that of the Quaternary 32° F (0° C) isotherm, whose position has been

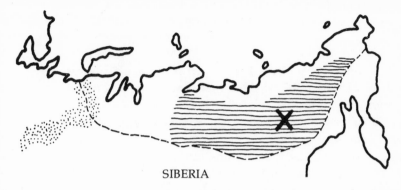

SIBERIA

Fig. 37. The mystery of the ice box of Siberia. In the horizontally hatched area, which includes the present cold pole (X) and extends southward as far as the dot-dashed limit of permafrost, thousands of mammoth cadavers lie frozen in ice and mud.

ascertained by the southern edge of the inland ice sheet. This accounts for the very great difference between the climates then and now. Northern Siberia today, including the "mammoth ice box," is all part of the arctic region of permanent ice, where the soil never thaws completely even during the brief northern summer. The corpses of mammoths buried in the ice are kept as fresh as in modern cold storage.

But during the Quaternary Age this area was completely ice-free. Its mean annual temperature was probably between 39.2° and 41° F (4° and 5° C). This is not particularly warm. In such conditions putrefaction would occur more slowly than at room termperature. Nevertheless, fresh meat would have decayed if exposed for longer than four days. The mammoth cadavers now being recovered from the ice are in a very good state of preservation and show no trace of decomposition. In the Quaternary Age the temperature in these regions cannot have been low enough to preserve them completely when they were destroyed by the catastrophe.

Yet they were preserved, and remain preserved to this day in the arctic climate of modern Siberia. So the mammoths must have entered the cold storage conditions very soon after their death. This means that the critical transition from one pattern of climate to another took place within a very short period.

This cannot be explained by the theory of continental drift. The giant Siberian platform could not conceivably have drifted 2100 miles (3500 km) within four days. It could only have been the North Pole that shifted so suddenly. The great platforms did not drift away from the stationary pole of rotation. Apart from secular movements, they remained in place. It was the center of rotation, and with it the axis of rotation, that moved.

This inescapable conclusion will become more intelligible if we once again use the analogy of the Earth as a spinning top. External influences will cause the spinning top to wobble, and the giant spinning top of Earth instantly reacted to the impact of Asteroid A and the eruption of huge quantities of material. The dynamic stabilization mechanism came into action. The Earth began to wobble, or precess. The mammoth carcasses in northeast Siberia show how quickly this took place.

The Earth's axis became oblique, or at any rate a great deal more oblique than it had been before. At the same time, the pole of rotation was displaced along a straight line pointing toward the point of impact of Asteroid A. The axis of rotation of Earth's solid crust, not of the entire Earth, passes through this pole of rotation. The line of displacement links the Quinternary and Quaternary positions of the pole of rotation. This proves that the impact of the celestial body did indeed cause a shift of the pole of rotation as the effect of the tilt of the Earth's axis through an angle of about 2°. Dynamically, this means that the angular motion produced by the impact of Asteroid A was superimposed on the terrestrial gyroscopic motion.

This polar displacement must not be regarded solely in terms of a displacement of the axis of rotation. In fact it was the entire crust of the Earth, closely supported by its spherical "friction bearing" of thin magma, that executed this tilt through about 2°. The oblique impact of the asteroid forced it to carry out this compensating movement. But the movement was quickly braked by the frictional resistance of the magma substrate. Looking at the event in greater detail, and assuming plausible viscosity values for the top layer of the magma, we find that the movement must have been slowed within the few hundred meters of the top layer of magma. This means that it was a strictly limited surface phenomenon. It had no effect on the dynamic equilibrium of the molten sphere containing the mass of the Earth proper. The Earth's axis of rotation, represented by the molten sphere unaffected by the dynamic disturbance, has maintained its position. In the sky it is reflected by the "pole of the ecliptic." Around this true pole, because of the frictional resistance of the substrate, the axis of the wobbling solid-crust spinning top describes a spiral. Slowly it becomes erect and the "obliquity of the ecliptic" decreases slowly and steadily at a known rate.

This is a result that can be scientifically verified. Linking it again with the myths, we can now understand the story of Helios-Phaëthon who lost control of the sun's chariot and careered across the sky. And we can see how Hercules, who visited the giant Atlas on his way to obtain the apples of the Hesperides, ripped open the Strait of Gibraltar and stopped the sun's chariot in its tracks; also the brief verse in the Edda which states that the sun lost his place along with the stars.

As for the mammoths, who have helped so much in our investigations, the Tungus have been digging the prehistoric mountains of mammoth flesh out of the ground for at least 1600 years. To the astonished diggers they look just as they did when they were alive, with their red, shaggy wool coats. The mammoth, the largest species of the Eurasian mammals, is as well known as any other antediluvian animal.

It is difficult to estimate how many mammoths have been uncovered over the centuries. Bears and snow wolves have always been strong rivals of primitive man in the hunt for food. This accounts for the fact that often partly eaten pieces, cleanly picked skeletons, or isolated bones of these giant animals are found.

The only marketable commodity obtained from these great cadavers is the ivory of the huge tusks, although the Tungus themselves, and their dogs, do not turn up their noses at the surprisingly tender meat of the mammoths. China is the main importer of the tusks. In the traditional home of the art of ivory carving there is a great demand for these strange products of the frozen soil. The elephant has been almost wiped out for the sake of its ivory, and nowadays there are very satisfactory plastic substitutes for natural ivory, but nevertheless mammoth tusks still supply about two-thirds of world demand. Hundreds of carcasses are dug up every year, and yet the Tungus cold store does not seem to diminish very much.

There must have been immense herds pasturing here, well-fed animals of all ages. Bulls, cows and calves alike were overtaken by sudden death, frozen so suddenly that they look as if they were still alive to us today. It is as if the moment of catastrophe was also frozen and time stood still, preserving for us today this monstrous lifelike image of these huge peaceful creatures in their Antediluvian paradise. It is impossible to imagine more convincing evidence of the terrible suddenness of the animal catastrophe than the presence of these thousands and thousands of mammoth carcasses preserved in ice and mud.

Many of the specimens have been carefully examined by anatomists and physiologists. None of them had suffered any external injuries. In every case the same diagnosis was made: the animal had died of asphyxiation. Scientific analysis of the stomach contents has shown how quickly they were struck down. Often these included undigested and even preserved fodder. Sometimes as much as 60 pounds (27 kg) of freshly torn off larch, pine, and fir needles were found. So recent does the feeding appear that one is tempted to look around to see where the animals have been breaking bits off the trees with their long trunks. But of course there is nothing but ice and mud, or at most the meager flora of the tundra. To find trees like those that supplied food for mammoths in the Ice Age one would have to go further south, to the region of Lake Baikal, to travel the same distance as the North Pole possibly shifted in the Atlantic catastrophe. The primeval forest receded southward as the North Pole shifted north.

Northeastern Siberia was a green and wooded country all those thousands of years ago. Where today there is only ice, snow, mud, and tundra, the primeval forest flourished. The tall, slender trunks of larch and pine and fir rose to 66 or even 164 feet (20 or 50 m). It was a landscape of huge rivers. The air was cool and fresh—ideal for the great shaggy animals in their thick, red woolly coats. Forests on a vast scale could sustain countless herds of these largest of land animals. Who knows how many thousands of years these prehistoric creatures had lived in their paradise when the whole Earth shuddered and trembled with the shock. The sun seemed to leave its orbit and to wander aimlessly across the sky. A rumbling sound grew louder, then a blast of thunder as the core of the asteroid exploded. As the shock waves raced across the Earth, it merged with the roar of the submarine catastrophe triggered by the explosion. This was the last sound that these herds of mammoths heard. These sound waves brought with them the asphyxiating gases that covered the land in a suffocating blanket. The animals died so suddenly that no signs of choking spasms have been found.

It may well be that not one in all those hundreds of thousands escaped the great death. And probably none of them saw the bank of inky-black cloud rising higher and higher in the west and northwest toward the zenith. It grew at phenomenal speed and blanked out the stars. It brought the diluvial rains in torrents from the sky. The storms whipped the sea far inland, reaching mountainous heights where it was funneled into the glens and valleys. It flooded the forests on the sides of the mountains and uprooted the largest of trees. All the land was covered in mud and water.

And then came the cold.

As the waters calmed down they froze. The layer of ice and mud became thicker and thicker, sometimes white, sometimes gray and brown, and sometimes tinted red and black by the volcanic ash of the Atlantic eruptions. It froze over the carcasses of the animals that still remain encased in their coffins of ice. For many thousands of years arctic animals have made use of this vast store of meat. Man has been using it for 1600 years, and he seems a long way from exhausting it.

In Alaska, the diluvial mammoth herds of this region apparently perished at the same time, and as suddenly. The asphyxiating gases crossed the Bering Straits to be followed, as in Siberia, by mud rains, tidal waves, floods, and arctic cold.

This explains the mystery of the mammoths—why the largest and most voracious herbivores of the subarctic region were suddenly and completely wiped out. The theory of gigantism—that outsize organisms, such as mammoths, suffered from physiological defects and could only survive under certain favorable conditions—does not account for it. Mammoths in all age groups were found in perfect physical condition. There were no physiological defects that might have imperiled their survival as a species. Indeed they must have been in excellent condition in order to keep their habitat free from predatory enemies. Had the species been fighting for its survival in an unfriendly environment, there would have been no herds of mammoths there at all.

The theory that it was man who killed off the mammoths is also quite untenable. If man had hunted and killed the mammoths he would have made use of his catch. But man was far too weak. He was weak in numbers and he lacked proper hunting equipment. In western Europe large pits were used to trap the animals, but these were apparently unknown in Siberia. The mammoths were huge, suspicious, and fleet of foot. Their skin was thick and their shaggy coats even thicker. Trapping them in pits was the only way to catch them. So it was not man who accounted for the death of mammoths in

Siberia. And had the change of climate come about gradually, nothing would have stopped them from retreating from the ice. They
would certainly have migrated to a warmer southern zone if they had
had the chance. There were a number of changes of climate during
the Quaternary Age, varying from Glacial to Interglacial. The mammoth herds must certainly have moved about to find the climate they
preferred. On this occasion the change of climate was too sudden for
them to move in time.

There is one more puzzling feature in this dramatic event in the
prehistory of northeast Siberia. The only carcasses that have been
found in the ice are those of mammoths and an occasional woolly
rhinoceros. But there must have been innumerable smaller animals
living in the clearings of the forests of this region, in addition to the large
beasts. Why then are there no remains in the postdiluvial ice? It
seems that the fate of the mammoths and the woolly rhinoceroses,
whose life habits were similar, was due to their enormous size.

There must have been powerful water currents during the deluge
in Siberia. Water from the sky flooded the whole country to a depth of
many yards. It collected in trenches and valleys and flowed in torrents and whirlpools. It carried with it uprooted trees, loose stones,
boulders, and everything else in the area, including the corpses of
asphyxiated or drowned animals. These flood waters dropped the
floating matter they carried according to size and weight. The biggest
and heaviest objects would be deposited first, among them the carcasses of the great beasts. These were very likely deposited near their
original habitat, where they were quickly frozen in the mud. But the
bodies of smaller animals, such as bison and red deer, were carried
considerably farther. The diluvial rains came mainly from the west
and northwest. The flow of the raging torrents would therefore be
toward the southeast. As the water carried the smaller animals away
from the northern zones, which quickly froze over, toward the more
southerly ice-free areas, they decayed. All that remains are the occasional parts of skeletons that happened to become fossilized.

The forest trees on which the mammoths had fed were also carried
along more easily on the flood waters than the giant beasts. Trees of
all sizes were carried to the south and southeast, there to rot and
disintegrate. Only the huge, heavy mammoths remained in their
icy graves.

Loess and
Carbon Dioxide

NOW WE MUST MOVE FORWARD in our reconstruction. The diluvial rains have long since ceased. The floods which covered half the Earth have subsided and returned to the oceans, and the waters have circled the Earth countless times.

The main mass of the diluvial mud, which consisted of a mixture of rainwater and volcanic ash, was deposited on the ocean bed, all 3×10^{15} tonnes of it. If only a tiny fraction of it remained it would still be enough to find and to recognize.

Let us assume that 90 percent of the diluvial mud was carried into the sea and 10 percent remained on land. In Mesopotamia we put this residual land deposit at 5 percent because the Mesopotamian drain covered only a small area. The main volume of the deluge inundated much larger stretches of land than this limited region. In general, therefore, there would have been a much greater proportion of the mud left on land. We can roughly estimate the mud left behind in the Old World at about 3.3×10^{14} tonnes in weight, with a volume of about 240,000–480,000 cubic miles (1–2 million cu.km). This is a considerable amount, even on a global scale, much too large a quantity to disappear without trace. Had it been deposited in the form of a mountain table with an average height of 330 feet (100 m), it would cover an area of 3,850,000–7,700,000 square miles (10–20 million square km), or as much as 5–10 percent of the entire land area.

This is no idle speculation. There really is a structure of roughly this height and extent in the parts of the Eurasian twin continent that were devastated by the rain of mud. It extends from the Atlantic coast of France right across Germany along the Rhine and Danube, the Elbe and the Oder, as far as Bohemia, Moravia, Hungary, and Galicia to southern Russia. In central and east Asia it broadens out to take in the

Fig. 38. Distribution of bank loess. The loess zone extends as an alluvial band which gradually broadens toward the east as far as the northern edge of the great chains of folded mountains: The Alps, Caucasus, Pamir, Himalayas. The alluvial zone ends in the Yellow sea. *Hatched:* main area of loess. *Black:* centers. *Dotted:* diluvian permanent ice sheets.

Tarim Basin, Turkestan, and part of northern China. Figure 38 shows how this area of loess extends across the two continents.

The loess belt is a geological mystery. "Loess" is the name given to clayey glacial deposits rich in quartz and chalk, and ocher or light gray in color. The interspersion with quartz granules, mica scales, and stone splinters is typical. Occasionally it contains mammoth bones, relics of Ice Age steppe animals, and typical land snail shells. Rare relics of Ice Age man have also been found. The skeletons are mainly of the Aurignac type and the artifacts are of rather poor quality.

The two types of loess, classified according to their origin, are the stratified loess and the unstratified, or mountain loess. The unstratified or true loess is usually the substrate and it is covered by the stratified loess. One can tell at a glance that the stratified loess took this form because it was rearranged by water. It rises in banks of sometimes imposing dimensions, particularly along the larger rivers, and adds considerable interest to the landscape.

According to the so-called Aeolian theory, loess is a deposit of the cold winds blowing from the steppes. These winds are said to have blown it on to the adjacent grasslands, where it was held and accumulated. There is no doubt that the loess substrate was already formed when the ice was repeatedly advancing and retreating during the Glacial period. But the substrate is of interest only because it forms a base for the huge banks of loess that were formed later, and contain by far the greater quantity of loess. Some examples of loess banks are shown in Plate 14. There is no alluvial evidence in the substrate, but the bizarre terraces of the stratified banks display all the characteristics associated with an aquatic origin. Their whole appearance is alluvial, and their concentration along big river beds and glacial spillways is additional confirmation.

But where did these vast quantities of stratified aquatic loess come from?

The chemical composition and physical structure show that unstratified or true loess is an unmistakable product of advanced weathering. Before this process began, the original material must have been rich in quartz and limestone in the form of calcium oxide that was converted by weathering into calcium carbonate. In theory, all loess, stratified as well as unstratified, could have been formed by the weathering of mountain ranges rich in chalk and quartz. But there are no mountain ranges large enough that contain not only quartz, but also calcium oxide (quicklime), which requires heat for its production. Nor are there any folded mountains accompanying the band of loess that extends across Europe and Asia into which the winds blowing down from the steppes could introduce their weathering products. There is scarcely a mountain range on Earth large enough to supply such masses of detritus. Its area, 480,000 cubic miles (2 million cu. km), is roughly equivalent to the area of the Tibetan highlands. We may therefore conclude that the stratified loess banks could not have been formed gradually by the same process as the loess substrate.

When the fiery molten magma erupted from the interior of the Earth during the Atlantic catastrophe it produced far more volcanic ash than is found today in the form of bank loess. This ash was first ejected into the higher atmosphere and then carried by the prevailing west wind to the area of diluvial rains in Europe and Asia and deposited there. The bank loess is the sediment of these masses of mud. It has exactly the same origin as the famous barren layer of alluvial clay below the shaft graves of the early Sumerian kings that proved the myth of the Flood to be true. The bank loess on a large scale and the alluvial layer on a small scale were both deposits of mud carried across the continents by the deluge.

According to this theory, the stratified loess is not a gradually accumulated weathering product of neighboring limestone and quartz mountains. It is magma atomized into droplets and turned into volcanic ash, ejected together with the calcareous marine ooze from the Atlantic seabed high into the stratosphere. At these great heights it was mixed with the marine ooze by the tornadoes and whirlwinds. That is the geological formula for the production of loess. Its chalk component comes from the marine sediments, and its quartz from the surface magma silicate. It is weathered magma mixed with marine ooze in which the weathering has reached microscopic proportions. The volcanic origin is evident from the chemical constitution but not from the structure.

A clear picture now emerges of the origin of the stratified loess. When the torrential downpours ceased, some of the volcanic ash remained in the flooded lands when the waters receded. We have estimated this residue as 10 percent of the total. If thick muddy water is allowed to drain off a slightly inclined board, minute runnels will appear which gradually swell into proper channels. They become deeper and deeper and cut out steep-sided canyons. As these ravines become deeper and narrower, a model of a loess landscape is produced. Plate 14 shows an example of this landscape in the Chinese province of Shansi. The terrace cultivation is the work of man.

Loess is the yellow earth of China. It provided the Middle Kingdom with its sacred color and with the basis for its sophisticated peasant civilization. Its volcanic and marine origins ensure an abundance of mineral salts and trace elements, which make it an ideal mineral fertilizer and probably the most fertile agricultural soil in the world. In the loess provinces of China, it forms layers many hundreds of feet deep and the peasants have planted, sowed, and reaped for at least four hundred years without using fertilizer.

Weathered volcanic ash is as fertile as loess. Lanzarote, the volcanic "Island of the Moon" in the Canaries is a living example. In 1730 and 1736, it was devastated by disastrous volcanic eruptions and covered with thick layers of ash. This ash was rich in nitrates and phosphates and soon turned into excellent humus. Its yields are phenomenal. Potatoes and cabbages, onions, pumpkins, melons and figs, tobacco, and wine are among its products. Like the yellow earth of China, it needs no fertilizers.

Loess is not always yellow. In the Ukraine, it takes the form of the famous black earth. In the Hegyala region of Hungary, it is reddish yellow, and on the Magdeburg Plain it is buff colored. But its fertility never varies and its products have a quality all of their own. Anyone who has ever drunk the wine of Tokay will recognize this. The Atlantic catastrophe that nearly destroyed all life on earth left behind it the great gift of loess, which helped the survivors to rebuild civilization.

The Atlantic catastrophe left a second great legacy to the Earth. The poisonous gases that preceded the clouds of ash and rain consisted largely of carbon dioxide. This odorless, transparent, and comparatively heavy gas is not in itself toxic but it cannot be breathed, so it spells death for animals and aerobic bacteria, but life for plants. Carbon dioxide is the life element of plants, which build up their carbohydrate content by the assimilation of water and carbon dioxide. The vitality and the rate of growth of a plant depends on the carbon dioxide content of its ambient air. Today this content is low, with a mean of 0.03 percent by volume. Directly above the mould it rises to 1 percent. The total weight of carbon dioxide in the atmosphere may amount to a few billion (10^{12}) tonnes. At least three times this volume of carbon dioxide is estimated to have been produced during the Atlantic volcanic eruptions, and the diluvial storms distributed it over the entire Earth. Some of it may have been absorbed by the sea and some may have been lost in weathering, but in general the average carbon dioxide content of the atmosphere must have increased suddenly and considerably.

It has been pointed out by geologists that periods of increased volcanic activity, such as those of the Tertiary period, have been accompanied by a great proliferation of plant life. All else being equal, we might have expected to see a great flourishing of plants in northern Europe after the disaster. The climate of the Ice Age was favorably transformed by the Gulf Stream and carbon dioxide was present in abundance. But all else was not equal, and northern Europe was very far from being a paradise of plants during this time.

Two Thousand
Years of Darkness

THE VOLCANIC ERUPTIONS produced three types of fragments: the pumice stone that blocked Atlantic shipping, the volcanic ash that mixed with water vapor and brought the diluvial rains, and a fine volcanic dust. This dust had a profound effect on the life and history of Earth. We have made an estimate of 2.5×10^{14} tonnes for the total volume of this dust. It was carried with the mushroom clouds up to the highest layers of the atmosphere, and being fine and light, it remained there for a long time.

In the Krakatoa eruption these finest particles were carried up to a height of 18½ miles (30 km). They remained suspended in the stratosphere for over two years and caused exceptionally picturesque sunrises and sunsets. A similar red glow was seen all over Europe after the eruption of Mount Pelée on Martinique, and the same phenomenon was observed after the fall of the Taiga meteorite. These effects were even more impressive following the enormous eruption in 1912 of the giant Mount Katmai in Alaska. It not only ejected an incredibly large amount of dust which caused the typical red glow, but it also resulted in an appreciable drop in temperature.

The dust from Krakatoa was observed to rise higher and higher, presumably borne up by stratospheric currents. The main portion eventually remained suspended at a height of 50 miles (80 km). At this height the atmospheric pressure is no more than 0.02 Torr, and the air consists of equal parts of hydrogen and nitrogen. In the diffuse white light of the rising and setting sun this free-floating ring of dust shone like a silver cloud. The phenomenon persisted for nine years, decaying as it gradually spread over larger and larger areas.

The Atlantic eruptions were twenty-thousand times as powerful as that of Krakatoa. Assuming that the fine dust that came from this eruption gradually spread across an area the size of Asia, about

19,250,000 square miles (50 million sq.km), on every square kilometer, a quantity of about 5,000,000 tonnes of dust would have settled. This is 5 kg per square meter (or 11 lbs per 1¼ square yard). How high an atmospheric layer would be needed to support such a quantity of dust?

We have a notorious example of dust-laden atmosphere, or smog, in some of our big industrial cities. In Los Angeles every cubic centimeter (about .06 of a cubic inch) is said to contain about 100,000 dust particles. This works out at 10^{11} dust particles per cubic meter (rather over 1¼ cubic yards). If the dust content of the cloud resulting from the Atlantic catastrophe approximated the atmosphere of an industrial center, then it would need to have a height of about 100 km (62 miles).

A dust cloud of such dimensions containing about 20,000 times as much dust as in the Krakatoa eruption, floating at an altitude of 125–185 miles (200–300 km), must have been a tremendous sight and its climatic effects are not too difficult to trace. This cloud was fifty times higher than a thundercloud. Its dust particles were ideal centers of condensation, enriched with water droplets and ice crystals. Its water content would be many times greater than its dust content.

The historic volcanic eruptions that we have been considering produced a partial turbidity in the high atmosphere which resulted in the phenomenon of the red glow. The Atlantic catastrophe resulted in complete turbidity. The color was not a delicate red, it was almost black. Any creature living in this area after the catastrophe would have been living in a permanent Los Angeles smog. For twenty-four hours there was a brown-black sky, with no moon or stars. Even the radiant power of the sun could not penetrate the gloom. A dim red glow was all that could be seen. In the lands blanketed by the dust cloud, this time of darkness was very real. It is recorded in the early European myths and in the ancient Indian and Japanese myths. Evil spirits had carried off the sun; they had bewitched him or captured him, and the mythical heroes set out to liberate him.

The cloud was by no means evenly distributed around the Earth. It was thickest in the north where the main part of the volcanic dust had accumulated. The prevailing winds carried it eastward and upward. But in the stratosphere the wind directions are reversed. So the cloud that had been blown by the westerlies over northern Europe was caught in the easterly current of the stratosphere and driven westward again. Sinking, it met the clouds being blown from the west and so was forced into a circular movement, piling higher and higher, becoming more and more dense. It must have been at its most concentrated to the east of the Atlantic, above Europe with its slowly receding ice sheet. Here the downpour of mud was at its heaviest. Here was the center of the smog cloud that followed the deluge. And it is from this region that the myth originates of the slain primeval god in whose blood the whole world was drowned.

The cloud was reinforced from the warm waters of the Gulf Stream, flowing all the way to Europe for the first time. The mild current bathed the ice sheet and evaporated in the cold air under the blanket of cloud. There was no sun to bring warmth to the air. Water vapor from the steaming sea rose high into the stratosphere and ionosphere and constantly swelled the volume of the cloud.

What did this sinister darkness do to the lands beneath? Both men and animals need plants in order to live. And plants need sunlight for their photosynthetic activity. Lack of sunlight is crippling to nearly all forms of plant life. A few plants, such as mosses, white dryas, and stunted arctic willows can adapt themselves to a deficiency of light and survive dark periods. The postglacial period in the north, and particularly in Europe, was a very long dark period indeed. Most of the plants died and with them most of the animal and human creatures that could not escape. Very few can have remained alive in these desolate lands. Perhaps there were some reindeer and musk oxen that feed on moss; perhaps there were even a few reindeer hunters, herdsmen, and fishermen. Their life must have been hard and poor almost beyond belief in this world of endless night, lighted only by a dim glow.

Like everything else that followed the Atlantic catastrophe, this strange shadowed landscape has also found its way into the myths. It is the prototype of the mythical abode of the dead. Here we have Tartarus and Erebus, Persephone's realm of shades, Hades and the hell of swirling mists of the Nordic Hel. The similarity between the words Erebus and Europe shows how closely the dark worlds were associated with this area. The suggestion that the very name Europe originally meant "world of darkness" is not very plausible, however, because it was more likely that the Europeans and not the Asians gave the continent its name. And for the Europeans their country was not the land of the sunset. For them the sun set even farther west.

The kingdom of the dead in the myths and the stories does not lie in the geographical west, which does not exist on a globe, but to the mythical west, which is the region into which all that is past and gone sinks with the departing day. The myths of the European peoples show that they imagined this land of forgetfulness as a dark, fog-shrouded realm of shadows. Here is evidence that there really was a long phase in the history of Europe in which the continent was as dark and misty as Erebus.

The memory of the realms of darkness lingered for a long time. It is still being referred to as late as Homer. In the *Odyssey*, there is mention of the "Cimmerian night" in the farthest west and northwest of the world. This seems to be inexplicable in geographical terms but looking behind it for the concrete cause that gave rise to the myth, we find that there was a time when the lands of the northwest were under such permanent darkness that they could easily become the mythical shores of the dead that had never been touched by the rays of the sun.

But the collective memory of the peoples of northwest Europe can provide much stronger evidence of the time when the land was blanketed with darkness. There were those who actually experienced it and passed on their experience to their descendants in the saga of Niflheim, which forms part of the prose Edda. At the beginning of time, says this saga, there was nothing; a huge gaping void like an abyss. At the end of this nothing there were two worlds, Muspelheim and Niflheim. The former world was in the south and was light, sunny, and warm. The latter was in the north and was dark, misty, damp, and cold. Ice advanced from Niflheim toward Muspelheim, where it melted into gigantic shapes.

There can be no doubt that Niflheim is the misty world of northwestern Europe, the shadowy underworld beneath the dark dome, buried under the land glaciers that slowly retreated from the sunny world of Muspelheim. Apart from the reference to the darkness this brief mythical description of the climatic conditions conforms with paleoclimatological evidence.

Geologists estimate that the Quinternary epoch, which is the epoch in which we are now living, began at about 10,000 B.C. In theory, an enormous expulsion into the atmosphere of volcanic carbon dioxide should have brought a rapid and favorable climatic change. Carbon dioxide raises the mean annual temperature. The Gulf Stream brought warm waters to Europe. Plant life flourishes in the highly fertile loess soil. But the optimum climate did not arrive until very late and it was greatly weakened. About five thousand years passed before the glacial climate of the last Quaternary phase gave way to the optimum climate of the Litorina epoch. There were two cold periods during this time of delay: subarctic Yoldia and the postglacial Ancylus period.

The first of these two periods is of considerable interest. Pollen analysis has enabled us to reconstruct its vegetation. This consisted of poor dryas flora, which are arctic plants capable of living with very little light; mosses, white dryas, and later on arctic willows. What was this arctic vegetation doing in such a southerly region? The Gulf Stream was by now bringing its warm currents to the shores of northwest Europe, so it cannot have been entirely for lack of warmth. It must have been the lack of light that set such strict limits on the plant life in this area. The postdiluvial screen of high altitude mist was blocking the rays of the sun. The Yoldia epoch represents the climatic situation during the darkest period of northwestern Europe.

Gradually the layer of mist dispersed and a few thousand years later Europe had become a lighter place with a better climate. Birches, pines, and aspen are characteristic of the Ancylus period. Nevertheless, these cold intermediate periods did not come to an end until five thousand years later, when the long overdue optimum climate arrived at last. This might have been expected immediately after the end of the Diluvial Age, but in fact it arrived only with the Litorina period.

From the optimum climate the warmth gradually decreased again, and even the Bronze Age was warmer than the present. The first relapse into a colder climate came with the Iron Age. Later, the rapidly growing human population brought the first signs of the transformation of woodland into steppes with its specific pattern of climate.

The negative factors that caused the deterioration in the climate were the dark blanket of mist and the gradual loss of carbon dioxide. The mist that cast its menacing shadow over the epiglacial period, blocking the sun's rays, resulted in a loss incomparably greater than the climatic gain from the Gulf Stream and the carbon dioxide enrichment. For this reason, the epiglacial climate was raw and bleak instead of mild and favorable.

The soil weathered little because the ice sheet retreated so gradually and vegetation was slow to develop. The consumption of carbon dioxide therefore remained low and the air above the ground remained rich in this valuable substance. When at last the darkness began to lift, and the sunlight warmed the thawing ground, this concentration of carbon dioxide and water vapor in the air had a hothouse effect on vegetation. It acted as a barrier to the infrared reflected from the ground that caused a sudden rise in the air temperature during the Ancylus period, and the first forests began to grow. When the blanket of fog had almost gone, they covered the sunlit landscape with the green and gold of trees and plants. These were the halcyon days of the Litorina period.

But in these changed conditions the consumption of carbon dioxide greatly increased. Much of it was absorbed by the vegetation that now covered the ground, but the sea, freed from the shackles of the ice, claimed the greater share. The inland ice retreated as far as Gotland and large areas of virgin soil became saturated with weathering carbon dioxide. The favorable climatic factor, carbon dioxide, decreased at a greater rate than the remnants of the unfavorable blanket of fog. The result was that the overall quality of climate no longer rose, as it had done before the Litorina period, but took a downward turn. The deterioration in climate was as inexorable as the previous improvement.

This explains the postglacial climatic variations. But the dark, cold, intermediate phase did have one very great advantage. By delaying the melting of the sheet of inland ice it saved the northern countries on both sides of the Atlantic from another great disturbance.

The thickness of the Würm ice sheet is generally estimated at 2600–4900 feet (800–1500 m). According to de Geer the sheet took about 5000 years to melt and to retreat to Gotland, the center of the ice cap. This estimate would give a mean annual melting depth of 6–12 inches (15–30 cm), which would produce a sheet of water 5–10 inches (12–24 cm) deep. In an area that probably had an annual precipitation of 5–6½ feet (150–200 cm) this added proportion of melted ice would not be very significant. In this respect the blanket of fog was an advantage. It slowed down the melting of the ice to a rate that rendered it harmless. The soil exposed by the retreat of the glaciers was able to absorb this additional water, and there was no noticeable upset of the water economy. This continued to be determined by the annual rainfall and not by the comparatively insignificant addition of melted ice. Surplus water was able to drain away without prolonged floods, large-scale water stagnation, or the formation of swamps.

Had there been no dark blanket of fog the melting process would have been much more rapid. During the critical periods, and above all during the Yoldia phase, the fog absorbed 90–95 percent of the sunlight and thereby reduced the rate of melting to a tenth or a twentieth of what it would otherwise have been. Without the slowing process of the fog, the melting would have occurred in 250–500 years instead of in 5000 years. The mean annual depth of the melted ice could have been as much as 15 feet (480 cm), given certain conditions, and this would have more than doubled the mean annual precipitation. The melted ice would have dominated the water economy. The damp tundra soil exposed by the retreating ice sheet would never have been able to absorb the additional water and the excess would have covered the low-lying regions, mixed with the sea water and become brackish. Neither North America nor northwest Europe could have become centers of advanced civilizations. Where there are now prairies and forests, there would have been salt marshes and swamps breeding myriads of midges and flies. But owing to the dark blanket, the immense ice sheet retreated on both sides of the Atlantic without catastrophic consequences to the land. The inland glaciers slowly decreased in size and the melted water gradually drained away into the soil. The sea level and the level of the water table gradually rose by about 330 feet (100 m) to reach their present values. This is not much over a period of 5000 years, nor when compared with a mean ocean depth of 13,000 feet (4000 m).

The epoch when the blanket of darkness hung over the north had the effect of a breathing space after the great catastrophe. The archaeological finds confirm that the march of civilization was halted during this period. Man as a culturally creative being is dependent on his natural environment. The bleak intermediate phase of the Glacial period corresponds to an equally arid phase in man's cultural development. The climate was poor and human achievement was at a standstill. This was the Mesolithic Age.

The fog converted the glacier landscape of northwest Europe into Niflheim. Most of its life, human, animal, and vegetable would have been destroyed by the deluge. But a sort of life managed to survive here during these dark ages.

A prolonged lack of light on plants causes them to lose the chlorophyll they need for photosynthesis and their leaves and stalks fade. This can be seen in the pallid, whitish shoots of potatoes sprouting in the dark, and in the white dryas, mosses, and arctic willows that are able to grow with very little light and are characteristically pale.

The chlorophyll of the photosynthetizing plants corresponds both
in structure and in function to the hemoglobin of the breathing animals and humans. Deficiencies of light and vitamins reduce the
hemoglobin content of the red blood corpuscles and result is an
anemic pallor. People kept in darkness for a prolonged period lose
their color and become pallid. This applies to people of all races. Even
the six months of the arctic night can have this effect. How much
greater, then, must it have been during the thousands of years when
Europe lay under the dark mist.

The Nibelungs who inhabited the land of Niflheim were presumably no exception to this rule. They must have looked anemic and
pale. Their bodies had to adjust to the prolonged darkness. The dark
period could be regarded as the incubation period for the development of the postglacial race with its characteristic pale—or more accurately, pigment-deficient—skin.

The bank of cloud that shrouded the north was about 62 miles (100
km) high and was drifting at an altitude of 124–186 miles (200–300
km). It could be seen as far away as 1250 miles (2000 km). This is the
distance from the present Arctic Circle to the range of the Alps, or to
the northern border of the United States. But we must assume that
the dark cloud probably extended as far south as 50° north, and could
be seen from the more southerly countries.

When the dust clouds of the Krakatoa eruption ascended to the
high atmosphere, they were seen as silver clouds, particularly luminous at night when they were still lit by the sun that had sunk below
the horizon. If we imagine this phenomenon increased twenty
thousand times we will get an idea of the luminous shimmering cloud
cap above the North Polar region. To the southerner it would appear
to be permanently hovering near the horizon. It would look to him
like a gigantic mountain range, forty times higher than the
Himalayas, brilliantly reflecting the light of the sun, its outline always
gently changing. These northern regions would appear to the southern observer as if they were constantly bathed in light. Could this be
the reason why many people thought of it as the abode of the gods,
the holy land? But it was only the distant observers who saw the light.
The peoples who were envied from afar, because it looked as if they
lived in radiant sunshine, in reality existed in deep gloom.

Some residual memories have remained of this shimmering light in
the far north. There is a reference in the Edda to the "light" and
"black" spirits that live beyond the world of man. Even Herodotus

has some strange tales to tell of the Hyperboreans, the "people beyond the north winds." What can be the origin of this curious name? And where did the northern storms come from in the days when these myths were rooted in reality? We can answer these questions now. The storms came from those huge shining white mountains of the gods and from the caves in the mountainsides. Beyond them, so it · was believed, lay the Elysian fields, inhabited by the mythical offspring of the giants and titans. These ideas slowly merged into the more ancient concept of Erebus, the dark land of forgetfulness. Clemens of Alexandria identified the country of the Hyperboreans with the classical Elysium, and Ptolemy called the Hyperborean Ocean the "Sea of the Dead." This was, of course, a long time after the dark mantle had dispersed. But could it not have been a subconscious folk-memory of the white glistening land of mists in the far north, the land that inspired Eduard Mörike's romantic soul to write the song of "Orplid"—"my country that radiates from afar"?

These gloomy mists have long since gone. But they still cover our ancient European past and shroud the origins of the white race in mystery. Risen from the Atlantic catastrophe, heirs to the civilization of the Atlantic Cro-Magnons, the white peoples of Europe have inherited Atlantis together with their red-skinned cousins across the Atlantic. They have forgotten it. They no longer have any folk memory. And yet the white race, the youngest branch of the species of man, its least stable yet at the same time its most powerful mutant, wears the crown and bears the scepter of Atlantis.

PART SIX

DAY ZERO

The Calendar of
the Mayas

WE HAVE NOW REACHED a vantage point from which we can survey the whole question of Atlantis.

We have established that the island of Atlantis did exist and that it perished within "a single dreadful day and a single dreadful night."

The event which destroyed Atlantis and which is associated with the deluge in Europe and Asia made an impact like no other event within human memory; or at any rate, not within our historical past. The crash of Asteroid A into the Atlantic brought a geological era to an end and ushered in the next, the geological present.

To arrive at the exact date of this momentous happening we have taken eight separate geological estimates ranging between 8000 and 20,000 years to calculate a mean date of 12,876 years ago, or about 10,900 B.C. We found that this date agreed very well with that obtained by de Geer from his counts of the half-yearly bands of Swedish varved clay. De Geer's date is accepted as the best modern value. If we work out the date from Plato's chronology we arrive at 9560 B.C., which is a very close approximation to de Geer's estimate. But even Plato's date must be regarded as an estimate, and not necessarily more reliable than de Geer's.

All geological and paleontological estimates are subject to this sort of difficulty and must to some extent be based on guesswork. Some, however, are founded on far less reliable evidence. We must, for instance, definitely reject as unacceptable the estimate based on the book of *Genesis* that gives the date of the deluge as 3308 B.C., according to the Gregorian calendar.

But there are still other possible sources of information and the first of them lies in the very Atlantis tradition itself. Plato's account is divided into two. In one of the dialogues, his maternal uncle Critias tells the members of the symposium what he had learned about Atlantis from Dropides and Solon. The account begins with the very quotation from which the year 9560 B.C. (Gregorian) has been calculated. But in the other dialogue the speaker, Critias, puts the story into the words of the Egyptian priest of Neith from whom Solon heard it. It is this priest who is speaking, and it is important to note that a more precise date is given in this part of the account than in the other. "According to our holy books the institution of our state has existed for 8000 years. Your fellow citizens were therefore born 9000 years ago . . ." Since it is the priest of Neith at Sais who speaks, the words "our state" refer to Egypt. But Egypt already existed when the war with Atlantis broke out, for the Atlantean sphere of influence was expressly described as extending "as far as Egypt and in Europe as far as Tyrrhenia." The critical time must be placed not 9000, but 8000 years before Solon's visit; that is, at 8560 B.C. (Gregorian). The Greeks only noticed the date as far as it concerned their own prehistory, which was 1000 years earlier. A careful examination of the text, however, will most certainly point to a date 1000 years later, the date of 8560 B.C. (Gregorian). This amended date is confirmed by a passage in Herodotus's Egyptian diary *Euterpe*.

In Chapter 143 Herodotus mentions a chronology that was related to him and the chronicler Hecataeus of Miletus by the priests of Amun at Thebes. The conversation took place near the colossal wooden coffins which held the mummies of the high priests. It was explained that this priestly office was hereditary in a certain family and passed from generation to generation. "They said that among these giants there was always a Piromis, the son of another Piromis, until they had shown him the 345 giants, always Piromis the son of Piromis, and led them neither to a god nor to a hero. . . . All of them, the priests explained, were of this kind: giants, never gods. But gods had ruled in Egypt before these men, although they did not associate with the mortals. . . ."

The "generation" by which son succeeded father was usually a span of about 20–25 years. On this count, 345 high priests would correspond to a period of between 7000 years and 8600 years, giving an average of 8000 years. According to the Gregorian calendar this would indicate a date of about 8500 B.C.

At any rate Plato and Herodotus agree that the critical period was 8000 years before their time and not 9000.

This difference of 1000 years is very important because it enables us to make use of other possibilities of dating that would not be relevant for the earlier date.

The country of the Mayas provides us with information that can be used to fix more precisely the revised date. This is not surprising, because this part of the world is not only situated in the immediate neighborhood of Atlantis, but came well within the cultural and political sphere of Atlantis. It was these red-skinned people of the Mesoamerican Maya region, closely related to the Atlanteans, who had more reason than any other people on Earth to record and remember this date. They were not only partners in the Altantean culture and civilization but also its natural heirs. Their country was very mountainous and therefore well protected against the tidal waves. It could not escape the global devastation, but it could offer some refuge from it, some oases where man's development could continue. Can we reasonably say that the chances of perpetuating the cultural achievements of the past were better in this region than in any other? We cannot prove this in the same way that we have proved the existence of Barrier Island X and its identity with Plato's Atlantis, but we can find some weighty reasons for belief.

If Atlantis had not existed there would be no way of explaining the origins of the Maya civilization.

Fortunately there is a document, the Maya calendar, whose accuracy and reliability leave nothing to be desired. Research into Maya documents was very long delayed. The religious fanaticism of the conquering Spaniards had, among other regrettable effects, that of obliterating the civilizations of Mesoamerica, whish were far superior to the Spanish. Their records and their history were destroyed. Barely anything that could be easily deciphered has been preserved.

C. W. Ceram in *Gods, Graves and Scholars* (1971) writes, "Hard upon the Spanish soldiers, high on their horses and swords in hand, followed the priests upon whose pyres the records and pictures that might have told us so much were incinerated. Don Juan de Zumárraga, first bishop of Mexico, destroyed every scrap of writing he could find in a gigantic auto-da-fé; the other bishops and priests followed his example; the soldiers, with no less zeal, demolished everything that was left. When Lord Kingsborough in 1848 completed his collection of what remained of the ancient Aztec records, not a single piece of Spanish provenance had been found. And of Mayan documents from preconquistador times exactly three manuscripts are left to us."

These three documents have remained undeciphered. One of them is the *Codex Troanus*. But oddly enough, it was not the three authentic codices which came to the aid of the research workers, but a small, yellowed, little-read manuscript dated 1566 and entitled *Relación de las cosas de Yucatán*. Its author was Diego de Landa, the second archbishop of Yucatán. He was a man of strong faith but also of an enquiring mind. It was a great stroke of luck that Charles Etienne Brasseur de Bourbourg acquired this key to deciphering the most important Maya documents, and that he knew how to make use of it. For this little book contained the symbols which the Mayas used to indicate their numbers, their days, and their months. This sign language was found in innumerable reliefs covering every temple and stair column and frieze. Until the discovery of the key, it had appeared to be nothing but a puzzling and unintelligible accumulation of bizarre human and animal faces carved in stone.

Then it was suddenly realized that these were not ornaments, but were the symbols for numbers, days, and months. These carvings represented astronomical data of the greatest importance.

Ceram writes,

"That everywhere in the Mayan art, in buildings that had been raised tier on tier in the jungle without the aid of draft animals or carts, in sculptures executed in stone with stone tools, there was not a single ornament or relief, animal frieze or sculptured figure, that was not directly related to some specific date. Every piece of Mayan construction was part of a great calendar in stone. There was no such thing as random arrangement; the Mayan aesthetic had a mathematical basis. Apparently meaningless repetitions and abrupt breaks in the conformation of the gruesome stone visages were, it appeared, occasioned by the need for expressing a certain number or some particular calendrical intercalation. . . . This calendrical correlation of Mayan art and architecture was unique."

There could be no doubt that this was a most astonishing discovery. How could it be explained? Were those who ordered these structures to be built monomaniacs, obsessed with an idée fixe that obliged them to have everything dated with the greatest possible precision?

There seems to be no other possible explanation. The Mayas do not appear to have erected their great sacred buildings for any such ephemeral reason as a victory, an epidemic, or similar memorial. Without exception, they erected their buildings only when the periodicity of their calendar demanded it. All the outward decoration of these structures consisted of the date of their erection. Every building was constructed to conform with the demands of the calendar; each was a dedication, as it were, to the lord of Time. So strong was this obsession that at the beginning of each of the most important calendar cycles, which spanned fifty-two years, they built a new perimeter, each larger than its predecessor, around the beautifully kept and well-preserved temple pyramids.

In 1925 excavations were carried out on the old serpent pyramid on the western outskirts of Mexico City, not far from the heart of this modern metropolis. This was not a simple temple pyramid, but consisted of core stone with eight superimposed "skins," each complete with its chronological ornaments. An examination of these revealed that a new skin was built around the former one every 52 years. This had continued for 364 years. Examples of this curious "onionskin" design have been found in other temple complexes that have been excavated since.

How can we understand the mentality of a people who could act in this way? It seems at first to be completely alien and incomprehensible. Indeed, we must not try to explain this mystery by any rational motive on the part of the Mayas. We must try to understand the mental attitudes of the royal and priestly builders. The Mayas were obsessed with their calendar to a unique and almost unbelievable degree. What could have caused such an obsession? Surely it can only have been due to a very strong and deep-seated fear of a purely transient existence.

Nowhere else have such primitive feelings had so powerful a creative effect on architectural design. It can surely be no accident that these feelings should dominate the civilization of the Mayas, who were apparently the only people who survived the Atlantic catastrophe in appreciable numbers. There must have been some real basis for these feelings, some specific cause for their obsession. The people who lived in this region must at some time have experienced a trauma so deep that it was ineradicably fixed in the collective memory. They must have experienced the moving of what they had believed to be immovable, the passing of what they had believed to be indestructible. They had experienced something like the end of the world, the extinction of the power and greatness of man. Only in some such manner could the fear of transience become such an obsession that it led to an overwhelming urge to try to prevent a repetition of the event that had caused it.

It is reasonable to conclude that it was their fear of sudden extinction that the Mayas were repeating in stone, over and over, generation after generation. And this fear must surely have had its roots in the most terrible catastrophe to befall mankind, a catastrophe that occurred at their own doorstep and wiped out the power and the glory of the world that had been before. We know from psychiatric practice that an individual who has suffered a great traumatic experience continues to react to it long after. The memory does not leave him; he is constantly having to reassert himself, to reassure himself. And so with a people. The Mayas continued to react. And their reaction expressed itself in the unique form of the finest and most ancient calendar in the world.

Recent research has shown just how good it is, and this is of vital importance. Through the Maya calendar, which goes back so far into the past, we have a record of observations of cycles that would otherwise have remained completely unknown. It is its great age that gives it the almost unbelievable accuracy that has astonished modern astronomers.

Professor H. Ludendorff, who was for many years head of the Astrophysical Observatory at Potsdam, studied the famous astronomical inscriptions in the Temple of the Sun at Palenque. The reliefs here were in particularly good condition and they probably date back to the first half of the fifth century A.D. The astronomical information they contain can therefore be checked without converting the Maya calendar into our present-day calendar. The inscription starts with an "earliest" date. This is 1,096,134 days before the date which concludes the main part of the inscription. This again is a "round" date. According to the Maya method of counting it is written as 9.10.10.0.0.

Now comes the surprise. A sidereal year contains 365.25636 days; 3001 sidereal years therefore contain the 1,096,134.3 days contained on the Palenque inscription with only a remainder of 0.3 days left over. Why did the Mayas choose this figure rather than the rounder value of precisely 3000 sidereal years? Ludendorff's theory is that this interval equals 2748 synodical revolutions of the planet Jupiter. The statistical probability that a given interval is both an integral multiple of the sidereal year and of the synodical revolution of some planet is so slight that the possibility of accident can be ruled out. The chances are 1:50,000.

In the Temple of the Cross another date was found in a prominent position. The interval between this date and the earliest date in the Temple of the Cross is 1,380,070 days. This again is close to the integral multiple of the sidereal year and the synodical revolution of a planet, in this case the planet Mars. The calculations here are: 3803 sidereal years equal 1,380,069.9 days; 1781 synodical Mars revolutions equal 1,380,066.0 days.

In this case there is a difference between the two values of almost 4 days, but Ludendorff stresses that there is great eccentricity in the orbit of the planet Mars, which makes it much more difficult to determine the syndical revolution of Mars than of Jupiter.

If we convert the Maya calendar into the Gregorian calendar we find that the round Maya date of 9.10.10.0.0. corresponds to February 5, 383. On this date, the sun was exactly halfway between two very bright fixed stars: Antares (alpha Scorpii) and Aldebaran (alpha Tauri). The Mayas were able to discover this without the aid of a telescope by observing the heliacal risings and settings. Ludendorff comes to the conclusion: "The Palenque inscriptions are in themselves evidence that the Mayas knew the sidereal year and the periods of revolution of the planets to a positively uncanny degree of accuracy. It is most unlikely that they had any precision measuring instruments and the observations they made must therefore have extended over extraordinarily long periods of time. This would be the only way to ensure such a high degree of accuracy in these astronomical data."

In Ludendorff's considered opinion, Maya astronomy can be traced back to this remote period of prehistory. Archaeological confirmation of his estimate is still lacking, because so far not enough tangible relics of this period have been found. Modern methods of measurements now enable us to date finds from many thousands of years ago, provided the objects are large enough. This can lead to much revision of earlier opinions, and it looks as if it will be the archaeologists and not the astronomers who will have to revise their estimate of the date.

It is extremely unlikely that Ludendorff's arguments will be refuted. The Mayas certainly did not have the equipment for measuring minute times and minute angles. Such equipment is essential if accurate astronomical information is to be found within the relatively short span of time of a few centuries. The accuracy of the Maya calendar cannot be explained except on the assumption that they carried out their observations over a very long period.

This is the opinion of some research workers, but others are still trying hard to find another explanation. Their aim is to find some plausible arithmetical method by which the Mayas could have calculated their earliest date backward. Presumably the astonishing accuracy of their calendar would therefore be due, not to long periods of observation, but to sheer luck. A revelation, perhaps? Or a dream? These attempts are bound to prove fruitless.

In contrast to them we have the astonishing accuracy of the Maya calendar and of Maya astronomy based on their earliest date. We have called this "Zero Day A," which initiated the epoch of the Atlantic catastrophe. According to Plato, Herodotus, and the Troano manuscript this must have happened in the ninth millennium, or about 8500 B. C.

The Zero Day A of the Maya era is June 5, 8498 B.C., according to the Gregorian calendar. This agrees extraordinarily well with other and less well authenticated dates.

If this date is correct we shall be able to determine the exact day on which Atlantis perished and even the approximate hour when the catastrophe began.

Can we be sure that the Mayas did count their time from the date of the Atlantic catastrophe that we have called Zero Day A?

The Romans counted their years *ab urbe condita*, that is, from the foundation of Rome, their capital and metropolis.

Christians count their years *post Christum natum*, that is, from the birth of the Christ. This count, which goes back to Dionysius the Areopagite, may be seven years out, but for our present purposes it is not the accuracy of the chronology that matters; it is the overwhelming importance of the event on which the chronology was based.

The Mohammedans count their years from the hegira, Mohammed's flight from Mecca to Medina. For them it is this particular world-shaking event that marks zero day.

If other cultures choose such monumental events for their earliest day, then there is every reason to suppose that the Mayas would have done the same. The crashing to the Earth of Asteroid A was most certainly a monumental event, ushering in a new era. On that day, the center of the primitive red-skinned civilization in the Atlantic was destroyed and unforgettable suffering inflicted upon the Maya peoples. Obsessed by fear of a periodic return of such a cataclysm, they were driven to erect buildings to conciliate the evil spirits, to make countless human sacrifices year after year, and to devote all their creative energies, indeed their whole lives, to this compulsive noting and recording the passage of time. The calendar was their god.

But the earliest date in the Maya calendar was also a world-shaking geological event; it brought the Earth from the Quaternary to the Quinternary Age.

And it introduced a new climatic era. During the Quaternary Age, with its much reduced obliquity of the ecliptic, the flora was largely independent of the motion of the sun. After the change, plants suddenly became noticeably dependent on the solar periodicity. This was a very great change. A people so obsessed with time, so highly gifted in astronomy, would certainly have noticed this, and this climatic change alone would have been enough for them to set their earliest day at the beginning of this new era.

If ever there was a day that shook the world, it was this day of horror. The Mayas had every reason to choose it as Zero Day A.

Let us spare a moment to consider the meaning of the term "Zero Day A." This term has been introduced by modern astronomers to distinguish the absolute (hence the initial A) Zero Day from another ordinary or historic Zero Day nearer to historical times. This is later than Zero Day A by 13 "long counts" of 144,000 days, which works out at 5127 years, 132 days. According to the Gregorian calendar this is October 15, 3373 B. C.

It should be mentioned that the striking preference of the Maya chronologists for the prime number 13 may have determined this. A ring of 13 long counts is a "baktun." Presumably this constituted an eon. If after the Spanish Conquest there had remained in the Maya country any native chronologist, and if he had been able to calculate in accordance with the very ancient tradition which was condemned by the conquerors as pagan, then he would have placed the next Zero Day in the year 1754.

The baktun periodicity was continued up to historical times. Twenty baktuns ended in 613 B.C. (Gregorian calendar). This was the last long count year B.C. Working back from this we find that there are 20 days on which a baktun began, of which Zero Day A is the last.

The astronomer Henseling has this to say about this unique day: "But—and this is the decisive factor—only one of the 21 beginnings of a long count (baktun Zero Days) of the Mayas between 613 B.C. and 8498 B.C. marked a natural event important enough to justify the beginning of even one of the three chronological elements. The only beginning of a long count which harmonized with the chronological system of the Mayas was the very first baktun Zero Day of them all, the beginning of June 8498 B.C. Gregorian calendar."

Here is the astronomical confirmation for the assumption that this first baktun Zero Day was indeed the true Zero Day A, the day on which the Maya calendar began.

The astronomical chronology of the Mayas had a fourfold root.

First, it was based on a continuous count of days from Zero Day A onward. In Henseling's opinion it is much to be admired in that "its invention and use postulates an extraordinary scientific maturity," a quality which "we have only been able to equal—without putting too fine a point on it—during the last three hundred years." This daily count produced the baktun periodicity. The choice of the Baktun number—144,000 days—is most ingenious. Not only is it divisible by a maximum number of integrals (14 out of the 20 first numbers), but it also constitutes a chronologically "handy unit" which is convenient to use.

Side by side with this admirable daily count ran the yearly count. The practical unit here was the civil round year, the "haab," which was divided into 18 cycles ("months") of 20 days each and brought up to the required number by 5 supplementary days. The Mayas, therefore, knew the exact number of days in the solar year thousands of years before the Egyptian, Mesopotamian, and ancient Eastern Mediterranean chronologists. They divided it differently from the Babylonians, who used another system of counting.

Four haab formed a group of four, which corresponds to the correction cycle of the very inaccurate Julian calendar; 4×13 haab constituted a calendar cycle of 52 years, which is the interval at which new perimeters were built around the temple mounds. The reason for the choice of a 52-year cycle is unknown.

Twenty-nine such calendar cycles produced the correction cycle proper of the Maya chronology for the solar year. Twenty calendar cycles of 1508 civil round years, or haab, were made to equal 1507 tropical solar years. This correction cycle of the Maya calendar was far superior to that of the ancient Egyptian Sothis calendar. The following table shows a comparison of four calendars. In the first column are listed the chronological systems. The second column gives their respective correction cycles in round years of 365 days each. The third column gives the number of days of the tropical solar years calculated from the systems, and in the fourth column is the residual error expressed in days accumulated within a million years. The residual error, in other words, is the difference from the true tropical solar year which, according to the most recent astronomical measurements, equals 365.242198 days.

TABLE OF CHRONOLOGIES

Chronological system	Correction cycle	Tropical number of days	Residual error
Julian	1461	365.250000	7802 (+)
Sothis	1520.33	365.240000	2198 (−)
Gregorian	1505.15	365.242500	302 (+)
Maya	1508	365.242129	69 (−)

It can easily be seen that the Maya calendar was far superior in accuracy, not only to its ancient equivalents, but it was nearly five times as accurate as the Gregorian calendar. The astronomically precise value of the correction cycle is 1507.03. If the Maya chronologists had chosen the nearest integral, 1507, instead of 1508, which they could easily have done, they would have achieved an even higher degree of accuracy and an even smaller residual error—no more than about 2 days. They would have paid for this, though, with the loss of divisibility: 1507 can be divided only into 11 × 137; but 1508 is divisible both by 4 and by the two numbers 13 and 29 which were important to Maya chronology. The ancient Maya chronologists thus chose for their correction cycle that numerical value which combined the closest possible approximation to the ideal value 1507.03 with the best possible divisibility. They could not have made a better choice for a useful long-term calendar. The very small residual error, 1 day in about 14,000 years, was in any case immaterial because their chronometric art included two further methods of correction.

The continuous day count, the baktun count, and the periodicity of the years and the calendar cycle were checked, first by a continuous count of 260-day periods. This period was called the "tzolkin" ("tonalamatl" in Aztec) and was based on the rhythm of the moon and of the eclipses and could be conveniently handled as the product of 13 × 20.

The second astronomical correction was based on the changes in the aspect of the planet Venus. Venus, because of its proximity to the sun, exhibits a change of phases like the moon, but the period is longer. It is about 2 hours less than 1.6 years. According to Svante Arrhenius, this was the reason why the Mayas introduced a negative correction by subtracting one day after every twelfth Venus period. The equation, 104 haab = 65 Venus periods = 146 tzolkin, made the correction simple and produced an astonishing degree of accuracy.

It is a fair assumption that this chronological system was perfectly established, and that the Maya astronomers could rely on it. According to Ludendorff and Henseling, they also had an amazingly detailed knowledge about the period of revolution of the giant planet Jupiter. This is about 12 years, and it would provide them with a further practical correction standard amenable to simple astronomical checks. It would, however, only be suitable for the Maya technique of astronomical observation if their periods of observation were long enough. It is more than likely that they had been accurately observing the stars long before Zero Day A. In order to count from this critical date at all they must have had at their disposal a vast amount of observed data accumulated over a very long period of time.

What then caused a critical and skeptical modern astronomer like Henseling to state that the Maya calendar could only have begun on the first baktun Zero Day? With this question we are approaching the crux of the matter.

The following summary of stellar positions and annual cycles within the last ten thousand years is based on very careful and precise checks by astronomers specializing in this field during the last few decades.

1. The tzolkin count began with the full moon of the winter solstice 8498 B.C. Gregorian calendar, because it was appropriate to it as a lunar and eclipse calendar;

2. The haab count began with the next Mayan New Year's Day at the spring equinox 8497 B.C. that is on the date required by theory;

3. This first day was also the beginning of the first new calendar round (4 × 13 haab) in which each day is allotted a quite specific double name to prevent any confusion of these details;

4. The continuous day count on which the baktun periodicity is based, began in the same way on the critical date, June 5, 8498 B.C. Gregorian calendar. This, as Henseling emphasizes, coincided with a conjunction of the three brightest celestial bodies, the sun, the moon, and Venus. We would say, at new moon and new Venus. This means that

5. The correction cycle of Venus also began on the same day. Even Henseling says, "It is impossible to regard this combination of facts as a coincidence."

But there is more to this initial date than Henseling could admit. For the modern astronomer must, of course, reject the idea that this initial Zero Day A had anything to do with the mythical Atlantis. That the Mayas could have had such a motive for choosing their first day is never even mentioned. The result, therefore, is an absence of any good reason why the Mayas selected this day and no other for their Zero Day A. Henseling inclines to the view that the triple conjunction of sun, moon, and Venus was the reason for choosing this particular day.

There is no doubt, however, that the Maya calendar does indeed go back to June 5, 8498 B.C. Gregorian calendar as its Zero Day. But this date is strikingly close to the date that has been calculated for the destruction of Atlantis. There is everything to suggest that Zero Day A is identical with the terrible day on which the great bang set off the catastrophe of the Atlantic. For all those who have followed so far, without bias and without fear or favor, the chain of evidence that has produced this result, the conclusion must be inescapable.

It was not the triple conjunction of sun, moon, and Venus; it was the onset of a new era, the start of the diluvial catastrophe and of the geological present that were the overwhelming reasons for choosing this truly zero day. But the prehistoric celestial constellation that Henseling discovered is indeed significant, though not in the way he supposed.

Figure 39 gives a diagrammatic representation of this constellation in the heliocentric scheme. Venus and Earth revolve in circular orbits around the sun. The moon, in a smaller circle, revolves around Earth. From a geocentric viewpoint, Venus and the moon are near the sun. Heliocentrically this corresponds to an Earth, moon, and Venus conjunction. This was the conjunction on the day the Earth captured Asteroid A. The eccentric elliptical orbit of the asteroid is entered in the diagram. As has been calculated, the asteroid approached from its perihelion, that is, from the direction of the sun past Venus. The effect of the triple conjunction was that the asteroid was influenced not only by Earth, but shortly before it had been influenced also by Venus and by the moon in such a way that its orbit was deflected even closer to the Earth's position.

Owing to their conjunction with the sun, which was inevitable according to the laws of celestial mechanics, Venus and the moon together brought about the fall of the asteroid into the Atlantic. It is most unlikely that this catastrophic crash into the Atlantic could have taken place without this help. The destruction of a world, the triggering of the greatest catastrophe in the history of mankind, was predestined in the orbits of the planets and of the asteroid. The course of

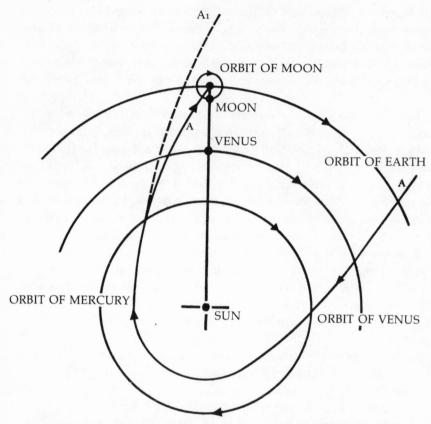

Fig. 39. The celestial constellation on June 5, 8498 B.C., 13.00 hrs dateline time (1:2000,000,000,000). A_1 undistorted orbit of Asteroid A; a true orbit of A because of deflection by Venus, Moon, and Earth.

events was determined by the inexorable clockwork of celestial mechanics.

This triple conjunction enables us to calculate the exact moment of impact even more accurately. If the two planets were involved, then the impact must have happened at sunset at the earliest and at the local hour of midnight at the latest. Most probably it happened at some intermediate time, about 20.00 hours local time at 75° west of Greenwich. On the date line 180° it was seven hours earlier; the impact would therefore have occurred at about 13.00 hours dateline time.

And so we can fix the moment of this earth-shattering event as accurately as we could possibly wish: at 13.00 hours dateline time on June 5, 8498 B.C. Gregorian calendar. On this day, the death throes of Atlantis began, and the crash that heralded the start of the present era made the whole Earth tremble.

Conclusion

THIS PRECISE DETERMINATION of the beginning of the Quinternary era provides us with a yardstick of the very first order. For the geologist it marks the transition from the fourth to the fifth geological age. To the paleontologist it gives a precise date for the hiatus between the two phases of advanced civilization of the Paleolithic and Neolithic Ages known as the Mesolithic Age. With the adjustment of the vital date from about 10,000 to 8498 B.C. Gregorian calendar, prehistory has doubly gained. First, it has gained a degree of accuracy that is particularly desirable in this context; second, it has gained a full thousand years of the period preceding the primitive civilizations of the Old World.

Why these civilizations should have grown up where and when they did has always been something of a puzzle. But we can now understand why this early flowering of civilizations on the banks of the Nile and Euphrates, on the Cyclades, and in the region of the megalithic structures all occurred at roughly the same period, around 4000 B.C. It was at this time that life began to reemerge from the ruins left by the deluge and the secondary aftereffects of the Atlantic catastrophe.

It is now possible to date objects going back about 30,000 years, provided they consist of organic material. This follows the discovery that all living organisms take up very minute quantities of a radioactive isotope of carbon, designated C^{14}, in their metabolic cycle. This isotope is produced in the highest reaches of the atmosphere by the cosmic radiation which is much more intense there, and added, more diffusely, to the envelope of the atmosphere. The take-up of such radioactive substances ceases with the death of the organism, which brings to an end the metabolism of the plant or animal concerned. The radioactive atoms taken up decay according to their half life and the decay radiation they emit decays at a defined rate. This activity can be measured, and conclusions drawn about the time that has passed since the death of the organism. The method is all the more valuable in that it lends itself to checking. The age of a giant redwood tree, for example, was determined radiologically at about 3000 years. The result was checked against the count of annual growth rings, and the difference was no more than 10 percent. Such checking has confirmed that the method is more accurate than any prehistoric or geological estimates. In view of the success of the radiological method, a cross-check has been carried out of an entire series of such estimates. Two of these checks are particularly relevant to our subject.

It has now been possible to determine with great accuracy the date when the inland ice sheet to the east and the west of the Atlantic advanced for the last time. In Two Creeks County in the state of Wisconsin, the last advance of the ice crushed a pine forest, snapped off the tree trunks, and left them with their tops pointing southward in the direction of the advance. Then the climate changed, the ice melted, and the disaster that had befallen the pine forest was revealed. The date when this happened had been estimated at 25,000 years ago. Professor Libby, with his C^{14} method, established that in fact it happened 11,000 years ago.

This date corresponds to about 9050 B.C. and indicates that the last glacial advance in North America occurred before the catastrophe.

A birch forest in Europe suffered a similar fate to that of the Wisconsin pine forest. Libby found a date of 10,800 years ago for this event, which again corresponds with the date of 9050 B.C.

The English lakes were hollowed out by glacier ice and subsequently filled with water from the melting glaciers. The measurement of pieces of peat and mud from this region produced an interval figure of 10,831 years. Glacier mud from Iceland gave 11,310 years. These values also agree with the American ones; the mean is a little over 11,000 years. The end of the Quaternary Age must have been later than this last glacial advance on both sides of the Atlantic. This conclusion is very different from those that had previously been reached by the experts. But it does confirm the date of the catastrophe, the year 8498 B.C.

Libby also measured postglacial relics. If his dating is correct, then they must go back to a date later than 8498 + 1950, or about 10,500 years.

In 1927, a strangely fluted arrowhead was found near Folsom in New Mexico, close to the remains of a buffalo. Later, other arrowheads of this type were found in various parts of the country, together with buffalo bones. These were relics of Folsom man, an early man of America. Libby measured some charred buffalo bones from a Folsom find in Texas. Their age came out at 9883 years, which again agrees.

Futher confirmation was soon to follow. In a cave that had collapsed many years ago, L. S. Cressman of the University of Oregon found a store of about 200 pairs of well-preserved sandals made of plant fibers. Their standard of craftsmanship was surprisingly high. Libby put their age at 9035 years. Charred bones of sloths and horses discovered along with handmade objects showed that as long ago as 9000 years people were living along the Straits of Magellan.

These were postglacial, postdiluvian people. They could settle on these stretches of land only after the climate had changed and the ice had gone. But in the warmer parts of Central America which escaped the ice, remains of antediluvian Ice Age man were found. Near Tepexpan in Mexico there is a bullfighting arena by the edge of what was formerly a marsh. Here, fossilized remains of an early man were found together with the bones of an extinct type of elephant. Helmut de Terra put the age of this layer at 11,000–12,000 years, and the samples of peat that he sent to Libby indicated an age of 11,300 years. Libby also tested charcoal found on a hearth in the cave near Lascaux in the Dordogne, below the famous Ice Age wall paintings. The test indicated 15,516 years.

The following table gives a summary of the respective ages of these finds, listing the oldest first:

Charcoal from Lascaux caves	15,516
Glacier mud (Iceland)	11,310
Peat from Tepexpan, Mexico	11,300
Last glacial advance (mean)	11,000 Quaternary
Pine forest, Two Creeks, Wisconsin	11,000
Birch forest, northern Europe	10,800
Peat, England	10,831
Buffalo bones, Folsom, Texas	9883
Sandals, Oregon	9035 Quinternary
Bones, Patagonia	9000

We can determine from this table the date of the catastrophe which ended the Quaternary Age and initiated the Quinternary Age. It must have been some time between the last glacial advance and the earliest established postglacial date, 11,000 years at the earliest and 9883 at the latest. The most likely date is halfway through this period, about 10,440 years ago within a spread of ± 560 years.

This gives the date of the catastrophe as 10,440–1950 = 8490 B.C. So the Libby tests also confirm the date that we have calculated: 8498 B.C. There cannot be much doubt that the starting date of the Maya calendar is identical with the catastrophic onset of the Quinternary Age.

But we must mention just one more way in which the American finds bear out our argument. According to the Libby test, Folsom man left a store of about 200 pairs of sandals of excellent craftsmanship in the caves of Oregon about 9000 years ago in the earliest postglacial age. Not only was he a good craftsman, but he had also established the principle of mass production. This means that long before the first postglacial settlements were built in Sumeria, mankind had reached a considerable level of civilization and cultural achievement in another part of the world. If this was a measure of attainment in the immediate postglacial period then that of Ice Age man who immediately preceded it can hardly have been lower. If we allow that a devastating global catastrophe intervened between the two periods, we should interpret the find of the sandals as indicating that those people who survived the catastrophe must have preserved the degree of civilization that is indicated by the find. If they could maintain their standard of civilization through such a cataclysm, it is probable that previous generations who lived before the disaster, and had been able to develop their civilization undisturbed, had attained an even higher level.

Our date for the Atlantic catastrophe has been established as soundly and as scientifically as any of the chronological landmarks during the later historical millennia; more soundly, in fact, than many of them. That the catastrophic end of the Quaternary Age and the Zero Day A of the Maya calendar came at one and the same time has been confirmed beyond all doubt. And we know that the Maya calender is genuine.

We have called these ancient records, retrieved from the walls of abandoned temples, to be our witness. And we have checked their evidence against that of the most accurate method of historical dating devised by modern man. Both witnesses, the old and the new, agree. They prove that Plato's account of the mythical isle is true. The statements that have been looked on with such skepticism are correct. Atlantis was the center of a highly sophisticated civilization, said Plato; it perished at a date 8000 years before Solon by earthquake, flood, and diluvial rains. And what the Bible and the lore of many nations says about the Flood is also true. We have proved it.

Otto Muck's Notes on
the Tradition of Atlantis

1. Plato (427–347 B.C.) was the scion of a noble Athenian family. In his younger years he wrote tragedies; Socrates introduced him to philosophy during the eight years he was his teacher. After Socrates's death, Plato first went to Euclid at Megara, later to Cyrene and Egypt, and finally to southern Italy and Sicily, where he studied the doctrine of the Pythagoreans. After an adventurous episode as a prisoner and slave he returned to Athens, where he founded the Academy some time after 387, and after several more journeys to Sicily, wholly devoted himself to the teaching of philosophy.

2. Timaeus of Locris in southern Italy, Pythagorean, explorer and astrologer, explains in the second part of the dialogue that bears his name, and that is not quoted here, the basic teachings of the Pythagorean cosmogony; as a follower of Socrates he is a historical figure, not invented by Plato.

3. Critias the Younger, great-grandson of Dropides, grandson of Critias the Elder, who passed Solon's account of Egypt on to his grandson, and maternal uncle of Plato. Famous conservative statesman, leading spirit of the "Thirty Tyrants"; also famous as a poet, orator, and philosopher, follower of Socrates. Fell, aged more than 90, in the Battle of Aegospotami (403).

4. Socrates (470–399 B.C.), Greek philosopher, was a compulsive teacher of his fellow citizens in the streets and market places of Athens. He has not left any written works. What we know of him and his doctrine is based on the writings of his pupils Xenophon and Plato. The principle of his doctrine, according to which the right action is based on judicious thought instead of objective orders such as custom, state, and religion, brought him into conflict with the Establishment. He was accused of godlessness and condemned to death by a cup of poison hemlock.

5. Bendis, Thracian goddess of the moon, therefore identified with Diana; an annual principal festival in honor of this goddess, the Bendidia, was held at Piraeus in the Bacchic fashion before the Panathenaea during the month of Thargelion. In view of the great religious importance of this goddess, equal in rank to the virgin Diana-Artemis, the account of Atlantis, offered the goddess "like a paean," gains special weight and credibility.

6. Hermocrates, son of Hermon, a Syracusan, famous general; according to Xenophon a pupil of Socrates; also a historical figure.

7. Solon (639–559 B.C.), of noble Attic descent, began as a merchant adventurer, conquered Salamis for the Athenians from the Megarans, gave Athens a new constitution which somewhat mitigated the difference between the

261

hereditary nobility and the common people; left Athens in 571 for Egypt, where he visited the priestly colleges at Heliopolis and Sais; traveled to Cyprus to King Philocyprus, who on Solon's advice moved his city of Aepia to a more favorable site and renamed it Soloi in his honor; in 563 he visited Croesus at Sardis and in 561 returned to Athens, where a year later Pisistratus established himself as the tyrant; Solon passed the last ten years of his life in retirement, a generally respected man. Unfortunately only fragments are preserved of his apparently numerous and famous poems. His note, verified by Plutarch about the account of Atlantis, begun but not complete, has been lost.

8. Phaëthon, son of Helios, could not control the sun chariot, caused a terrible conflagration on Earth; struck by Zeus's thunderbolt, he fell into the Eridanus river; the tears wept by his sisters were turned into amber; possibly a folk memory of a West Europoid people of the fall of the celestial body that unleashed the Atlantic catastrophe.

9. The venerable temple scribe—his name is said to have been Sonchis, his title Petan-Neith (heaven of Neith)—later refers with even greater emphasis to the texts containing the account of Atlantis; Crantor claims to have seen the same hieroglyphs at Sais about 300 years after Solon's journey.

10. Allusion to the diluvial catastrophe.

11. Strait of Gibraltar, during the Quaternary Age presumably only a very narrow entrance to the western basin of the Mediterranean, divided by an isthmus between North Africa, Sicily, and Italy.

12. The Bahamas and Antilles; this detail, which agrees with reality, vouches for the authenticity of the tradition.

13. The twin continent of North and South America; the concept of a continent in the far west totally contradicted the religious ideas of both the Egyptians and the Greeks; neither Solon nor Plato could have invented or guessed this detail.

14. The Atlantic; according to the classical concept the ocean was a river without end that flowed around the Earth's disk in the middle, which was centered on Olympus, the abode of the gods.

15. The great antiquity that was already traditionally accorded to them may be seen from the dating of these buildings in the mythical age of the gods.

16. The possible meaning of this sentence is that the extreme southeastern part of the island kingdom—to which the region of the exit of the western basin of the Mediterranean presumably also belonged—was a province under the jurisdiction of a governor (viceroy).

17. Of the colonies on the Atlantic islands and the fringe territories of the Old and the New World.

18. Presumably these were natural deposits of very rich mixed ores (copper, tin, arsenic, antimony, etc.), which also occurred in Cornwall; they were not metal alloys.

19. This detail, too, which agrees with paleozoological research, cannot have been an inspired correct invention of Plato's.

20. Presumably not the grape, but the banana (*Musa sapientium*).

21. Cereals.

22. The coconut palm.

23. Cleitho.

24. 300 ft = about 90 m.
25. 100 ft = about 30 m.
26. 50 stades = 30,000 ft = about 9 km.
27. 3 stades = 1800 ft = 540 m.
28. 2 stades = 1200 ft = 360 m.
29. 1 stade = 600 ft = 180 m.
30. 5 stades = 3000 ft = about 900 m.
31. 100 ft = about 30 m.
32. Statues of Aztec gods (Huitzilopochtli) or the giant statue of the Toltec god of healing (Quetzalcoatl) on the temple pyramid of Cholula come to mind; these or similar representations must have strongly contradicted the Greek ideal of a god and struck the Greeks as "barbaric."
33. Because this detail contradicted the Greek religion at Plato's time, the philosopher dissociated himself from it—as he also emphasized in advance the alien nature of the entire non-Greek account.
34. 1 stade = 600 ft = 180 m.
35. 50 stades = 30,000 ft = about 9 km.
36. 3000 stades = 1,800,000 ft = about 540 km.
37. 2000 stades = 1,200,000 ft = about 360 km.
38. 100 ft = about 30 m.
39. 1 stade = 600 ft = about 180 m.
40. 10,000 stades = 6,000,000 ft = about 1800 km.
41. An allotment: the inhabitants of a square of 100 sq. stades bordered by canals (about 3.3 sq.km = 330 ha).
42. 10 stades = 1.8 km.
43. Each ship therefore had a crew of 200; it must have been much larger than a Viking ship. It is noteworthy that the ancient Egyptians built ships of remarkable size; if the Atlanteans were a highly civilized seafaring nation they must have known how to build large ships for large crews.
44. "Without iron": it must be concluded that the Atlanteans also used iron at least for nonreligious purposes; if so, it must have been pure meteoric iron or pure magnetite. Extensive prehistoric slag heaps in India, for instance, are evidence of a very early use of iron.
45. This is the same motive as that of the biblical deluge: the miscegenation between the "sons of the god" and the "daughters of the Earth"; the origin of this parallelism is unknown.
46. "Punishment"; there can be no doubt that this means the deluge; the absence of the conclusion from which presumably further parallels to the Sumerian-biblical version could have been drawn is all the more regrettable.
47. The weakened protective function of the ozone layer, which resulted in the relatively powerful ultraviolet and radioactive irradiation during the last 1000–2000 years, is probably one of the explanations of the change of Quaternary to Holocene man in body shape, brain volume, and size.

The mutative changes of hereditary traits investigated and induced in animals by means of laboratory experiments today, operated in man for much longer than a thousand years after the catastrophe. Only mutative changes were able to survive; abrupt gene interference resulted in the extinction of previously extant human types and other creatures.

Illustration Credits

1. Plato. Vatican Museum. Photo Alinary.
2. Ptolemy's map of the world from *Cosmographia* by Sebastian Münster 1540.
3. Novus Orbis–the New World as the island of Atlantis from *Cosmographia* by Sebastian Münster 1540.

   The island of Atlantis according to Athanasius Kircher in *Mundus subterraneus* 1678.
4. Map of the island of Atlantis according to the modern Greek writer Kampanakis.

   Drawing of the island of Atlantis by Dr. Paul Schliemann 1912.
5. Reconstructions:

   Marduk shrine, Babylon. State Museum, Berlin. Copan, Honduras. Photo Irmgard Groth-Kimball
6. Temple of the Inscriptions, Palenque. Photo Irmgard Groth-Kimball, Mexico.

   Sun pyramid of Teotihuacan, Mexico. Photo Irmgard Groth-Kimball, Mexico.
7. Step pyramid of King Djoser near Sakkara. Photo Hirmer Verlag, Munich. Indian temple city.
8. Skulls and reconstructions of the Neanderthal, Aurignac, and Cro-Magnon types (the Neanderthal skull top right is from Monte Circeo; the head bottom left is a portrait of the Indian chief Sitting Bull.

   The reconstructions are drawings by Otto Muck.
9. Jade mask from Palenque. Photo Irmgard Groth-Kimball, Mexico
10. Young Basque from the Pyrenees. ATP Bilderdienst, Zurich.
11. Chart of the Atlantic, with depth indications.
12. Carolina Bay. Reproduction according to D. W. Johnson *The Origin of the Carolina Bay*. Columbia University Press. Photo British Museum.

    The Arizona Crater.
13. Volcanic landscape on the Azores, ATP Bilderdienst, Zurich.

    Negative photostat of a fathogram of the Midatlantic Ridge, taken October 1948.

    32°N.cf. November 1949 issue of *National Geographic Magazine*.
14. Loess terraces and terraced paddy fields in China. Photo Sueddeutscher Verlag, Munich.
15. Mastodon and Mammoth. Reconstructions. Drawings by Otto Muck.

16. Bison. Cave painting at Altamira, Spain.
Wild Horse. Cave painting at Cueva de los Casares, Provincia Guadalajara.
Prof. Herbert Kühn.
17. Mammoth Cave painting at Cabrerets, Pech-merle, Departement Lot,
France. From Herbert Kühn, *Felsbilder Europas* (Rock paintings of
Europe).
18. Astronomical relief from Palenque.
　　Photo Irmgard Groth-Kimball, Mexico.

INDEX

About the Author

OTTO HEINRICH MUCK was born in Vienna in 1892. After leaving school he became a Flying Officer during World War I. In 1921 he graduated as an engineer at the Munich College of Advanced Technology. He continued his studies reading Physics, Geophysics, and Early History. He published numerous articles on biological, geological, and cancer problems. He patented 2000 inventions used by leading industrial companies. In World War II he was the inventor of the U-boat schnorkel and a member of the Peenemünde Rocket Research Team. After the war he was credited for many inventions in the nutritional field, and received numerous patents while under contract to the Greek shipowner S. Niarchos for the development of methane tankers. Muck was scientific consultant to large industrial concerns and had wide-ranging artistic interests. Otto H. Muck died in 1956 as the result of an accident.